THE GOLDEN GRINDSTONE

THE
GOLDEN GRINDSTONE

One Man's Adventures in the Yukon

Recorded by Angus Graham

With an Introduction by Lawrence Millman

THE LYONS PRESS
Guilford, Connecticut
An Imprint of the Globe Pequot Press

To buy books in quantity for corporate use
or incentives, call **(800) 962–0973, ext. 4551,**
or e-mail **premiums@GlobePequot.com.**

The Lyons Press is an imprint of The Globe Pequot Press

10 9 8 7 6 5 4 3 2 1

Printed in the United States of America

ISBN-13: 978-1-59228-707-9
ISBN 10: 1-59228-707-7

Library of Congress Cataloging-in-Publication Data is available
on file.

CONTENTS

INTRODUCTION .... Page ix

OPENING SENTENCES 1

CHAP. I   THE GENERAL IDEA 3

       II   THE GEOGRAPHICAL PROBLEM 10

       III THE IMMIGRANT PLAN 18

       IV   EDMONTON 26

        V   ATHABASCA LANDING 36

       VI   THE ATHABASCA RIVER 44

      VII   GRAND RAPIDS 51

     VIII   THE SLAVE RIVER 59

       IX   GREAT SLAVE LAKE 66

        X   FORT SIMPSON 72

       XI   THE MACKENZIE RIVER 79

      XII   FORT McPHERSON 86

     XIII   THE ESKIMO 93

      XIV   FIRST TRAFFIC WITH THE INDIANS 103

       XV   THE PEEL RIVER 113

      XVI   THE UPPER PEEL RIVER AND
            THE VALLEY OF NOISES 121

     XVII   GOLD 130

    XVIII   THE WINTER CAMP 138

      XIX   PROSPECTING AND EXPLORATION 146

       XX   BEARS AND WOLVES 155

      XXI   THE WINTER NIGHT 164

     XXII   THE INDIANS' VISIT 173

XXIII DOGS 180

XXIV THE BROKEN KNEE 187

XXV THE LAST OF THE WHITE MEN 194

XXVI THE INDIAN CAMP 200

XXVII CARIBOU 210

XXVIII THE OLD LADY 221

XXIX FAMINE AND RIOT 229

XXX MITCHELL BECOMES AN INDIAN 236

XXXI AN INDIAN "VEILLÉE" .246

XXXII WOMEN 256

XXXIII THE CLOSEST SHAVE OF ALL 267

XXXIV THE SKIN BOATS 273

XXXV SUMMER HUNTING 281

XXXVI MITCHELL REMAINS AN INDIAN 288

XXXVII THE LAST OF THE INDIANS 298

LIST OF ILLUSTRATIONS

THE *AMISK* .... Page 38

OLD-FASHIONED FUR PRESS 75

ESKIMO PIPE 99

SHALE CLIFF IN THE PEEL RIVER CANYON 126

MITCHELL'S LOG CABIN AT WIND CITY 141

THE *COUREUR DE BOIS* 225

EMBROIDERY ON A LOUCHEUX MOCCASIN 262

MITCHELL'S WINTER MITTS 263

THE PEEL RIVER CANYON 279

MITCHELL'S SNOW-KNIFE 294

LIST OF MAPS

SKETCH MAP OF ROUTES TO THE
      YUKON GOLD FIELDS .... Page 11

DE SAINVILLE'S SURVEY OF THE PEEL RIVER 107

MAP OF THE PEEL RIVER VALLEY AND OF
      PART OF THE OGILVIE RANGE LYING
        TO THE SOUTH THEREOF 122

MITCHELL'S MAP OF THE WIND RIVER 149

INTRODUCTION:
INTO THE YUKON WILD

Frozen in time, and maybe just plain frozen as well, the figures still seem to be moving up the snow-covered, forty-five degree slope, a skein of antlike forms against a background of all-encompassing white. Some of them, bent low under their burdens, are slowed to an apparent crawl, while others seem to have a jauntiness in their step, as if they can already smell the gold.

Ask anyone for an image of the Klondike Gold Rush, and this scene of would-be miners ascending Alaska's Chilkoot Pass to the Yukon River basin is probably the first one they'll mention. They may even say that one of their ancestors was among the thousands who trekked the Chilkoot in 1897–98. Or they might have seen the scene in an old photograph or Hollywood movie. But what they may not know was that there were other, considerably less popular routes to the Klondike.

Some gold pilgrims started out at a muddy little hamlet in Alberta called Edmonton. From here, they would have their choice of several routes, each with its own hazards. For instance, one route meandered through "Dog-Eating Prairie," so named because eating one's dogs seemed to be the only way to survive it. Another boasted such uninviting features as "The Rapids of the Drowned" and "The Devil's Portage." Yet another, the Mackenzie River route, brought the aforesaid pilgrim nearly to the Arctic Ocean, then obliged him to paddle down a relatively unknown river such as the Rat or the Porcupine . . . and as if that wasn't enough, he would later need to find a mountain pass that might or might not deliver him to the Klondike.

Both those who reached the goldfields and those who didn't kept journals, often with increasingly terse entries; in one such journal, the last few lines were written with the writer's own blood, as—in a forlorn attempt to find sustenance—the fellow had already drunk the last of his ink. Desperate conditions require desperate measures. There's a famous scene in Charlie Chaplin's 1925 film *The Gold Rush* where Charlie, as The Lone Prospector, eats his boot, then the boot's laces, and then its nails, upon which he chews contentedly. This may be an exaggeration, but it's not much of one.

You may wonder why a person of apparently sound mind would be willing to endure such hardship, even court death, without knowing for sure whether he'd find any of the precious dust. Why, indeed? Because many of the gold-seekers relished the idea of adventure in the Great White North at least as much as they wanted to strike it rich. To quote Yukon bard Robert Service: "Yet it isn't the gold that I'm wanting, So much as just finding the gold." Service himself did not experience the Gold Rush, but he did experience the country where it took place, and he composed the poem in which those lines appear ("The Spell of the Yukon") as he was standing on the heights above Miles Canyon and gazing down on the majestic flow of the Yukon River.

Consider George M. Mitchell, an insurance broker in his early thirties and a resident of the not particularly exciting city of Toronto. Except for hunting or fishing forays into the local countryside, he pursued a more or less sedentary life. Inside this seemingly unexceptional man, however, there was another George Mitchell clambering to get out. The Klondike Gold Rush provided this second Mitchell with a much-needed spark, and clamber out he did. But rather than join the hordes on the Chilkoot Pass, he chose arguably the most obscure, arduous, and downright implausible route to the goldfields. It's as if he'd said to himself: "No one, not even me, would ever think of insuring a person so incautious as to try to reach the Klondike via the Peel River system and, specifically, the Wind River."

The surveyor William Ogilvie, for whom the Yukon's Ogilvie Mountains were named, had indicated to Mitchell that this route was practicable, although he, Ogilvie, had not investigated it himself. But what might be practicable for a man with Ogilvie's years of hard travel in the North might be an invitation to disaster for someone else. In fact, the Peel River region included some of the least explored country in North America . . . least explored, that is, by white outsiders. The region's inhabitants, the Tetlit Gwich'in, knew it perhaps as well as Mitchell knew Toronto, and if it hadn't been for their knowledge, Mitchell probably wouldn't have seen his stolid office at 36 Victoria Street in Toronto again.

After his return, Mitchell dined out on his Yukon adventures, retelling them, refining them, maybe even embellishing them a bit. He was a natural storyteller, but he wasn't a writer. In the early 1920s, he moved to Quebec City, where he met a peripatetic Scotsman named Angus Graham. Graham, a forester by trade, immediately sensed a book in Mitchell's tales. Thus the two men began meeting in Quebec's prestigious Garrison Club, with Mitchell talking a proverbial blue streak and his Scottish amanuensis scribbling away furiously.

Graham had only one previous book to his credit, a plodding tome about timber management written at the behest of the Quebec Forest Industries Association. But the meetings with Mitchell obviously inspired him, and the resulting book, *The Golden Grindstone*, is not only what's commonly called a page turner, but it's also one of the best books ever written about the Gold Rush. Graham later wrote novels, and as an amateur archaeologist, articles about various Scottish ruins, but none of his subsequent works can hold a candle to *The Golden Grindstone*. Even the book's throwaway lines stick in the mind, such as when Mitchell is describing the tribulations caused by a certain insect, and he says: "I have known a man [to] walk eighty miles to ask the priest to say special prayers against the mosquitoes."

The entire book seems to have stuck in James A. Michener's mind, because he used it as a model for his novel *Journey*. Like Mitchell, Michener's main character, an English adventurer named Lord Luton, attempts to reach the Klondike via the Peel River system; and like Mitchell, he suffers numerous setbacks along the way. But I dare say *The Golden Grindstone* is the far better book.

Actually, Graham's book has certain novel-like qualities itself. Consider its cast of characters. Here is Mitchell, alternately opinionated, blustery, egocentric, and beguiling, a performer whom Graham marshalls now to the center of the stage, now to the wings. Here are the gold-miners, a motley crew some of whom are immensely cultivated (one man gives lectures on astronomy at Mitchell's Wind River encampment) while others are brutes of the sort that enthralled Jack London. And here are the Gwich'in, with their arcane surgical procedures, their evil eyes, their obsession with tobacco, their hundred-year-old elders, and their subsistence culture.

To this reader, the book's most interesting feature is in fact its portrayal of the Gwich'in. Stuck for a winter in a *ni-vya-zeh*, the Gwich'in skin-covered lodge, Mitchell had an excellent opportunity to study his Athabascan-speaking hosts at close quarters; and the chapters of the book that describe his enforced overwintering have a genuine ethnographic value, certainly as much so as Cornelius Osgood's then contemporaneous monograph on the Gwich'in. But whereas Osgood regards his subjects as, well, subjects, Mitchell—in Graham's rendering—sees the Gwich'in as fellow human beings, albeit idiosyncratic ones. If they are not always sympathetically inclined toward their pale-skinned charge, it's because they still defer to the time-honored belief that the weak, regardless of their skin color, are at once a burden and a threat to the strong. Thus if you're moving camp in the dead of winter, and someone can't walk, you either abandon that person or dispose of him. Mitchell couldn't walk.

The hero of *The Golden Grindstone*, insofar as there is one, is Francis Tsik, who became chief of the Tetlit band in 1891 upon the death of his grandfather, Small Nipples (he'd acquired this curious name because his mother died in childbirth, and he tried to suckle her shrivelled breast). Chief Francis is that rare entity, a good leader, so it's not surprising that Mitchell made him promise to stay away from Dawson City, the Klondike's raucous epicenter and the downfall—via alcohol, prostitution, gambling, etc.—of many a native person. True to his word, Francis did remain in his backwoods home, but in 1903 a number of his constituents relocated to Dawson, where—for better or worse—they joined the twentieth century. As Francis now lived too far away to handle their affairs, they appointed a new chief, his nephew Julius. One imagines that Francis himself was none the worse for not having seen the bright lights of Dawson.

George Mitchell did not see those bright lights, either. Indeed, he never got closer to the goldfields than the Wind River country, whose distance from the Klondike would have been measured not by miles but by weeks of travel. And while his two best friends on the expedition, Cecil Merritt and Jack Patterson, returned to Toronto quite a bit richer than they'd set out, Mitchell's only keepsake from the trip was a stiff leg, which he had for the rest of his life. But he did discover something more valuable than any precious metal: a still-traditional group of people who did not need gold in order to be rich.

May I add that you will regard *The Golden Grindstone* as a worthy discovery, too?

Lawrence Millman
Cambridge, Massachusetts
July 2006

THE GOLDEN GRINDSTONE

OPENING SENTENCES

THE first of the Canadian Mitchells landed in the country on tiptoe and in the dark, with his claymore and the unexpired portion of the day's ration. Having come through the Battle of the Plains with honour, he found Quebec good—or at least better than contemporary Scotland —in spite of bombardment and famine, and so he established himself there, took up lands, and founded a dynasty. Mr. George M. Mitchell, whose adventures are recorded below, is his great-grandson.

Everyone in Quebec knows Mr. Mitchell, but a few lines are needed to tell outsiders what manner of man he is. You may think of him as he appears in St. Peter Street, the hatefully squalid riverside alley in which Quebec's " big business " is conducted, a short, thick-set, broad-shouldered figure, suggesting prodigies of strength, but trim and sedate in a dark-blue double-breasted suit and a speckless bowler hat that rebukes the old grey felts of his less careful colleagues —he stands looking up at the weather, the head of his cane held wide from his body in an attitude that recalls a portrait of Charles the Second, and estimates the chances for a big flight of snipe on the marshes at the week-end.

Or you may think of him on a summer afternoon at the Garrison Club, sitting with a guest at the small iron table under the old black walnut ; they have tea and toast, and Mr. Mitchell is lecturing the stranger for the good of his soul. It may be five thousand tons of beans, piled up on a rock in the Gulf of St. Lawrence with a nasty flaw in the insurance ; Mr. Mitchell knows what to do, who will take on the salvage, and how the insurance company may be made to take a charitable view.   Or it may be sugar—big forward purchases made and the bottom dropping out of Barbados.   Or the stranger may be simply a canner of fruit from Toronto who wishes to learn how he may sell his stuff to the French-Canadian wholesale trade.   In any of these cases he has come to the proper man.

But the picture which the reader of this book should chiefly try to form is that of Mr. Mitchell in his den.   It was his hospitable habit to receive his friends of an evening in a tiny sanctum withdrawn at the back of the hall—its walls hung with guns and rifles, pictures of dogs, Indians' knives and embroidered leatherwork, and the piece of a mammoth's tusk that he had found in the Valley of Noises. Here, if his hearers were interested, he would sometimes warm up to reminiscence, and it was in such evening conversations that he gave me the stories out of which this book is made.   While adding what seemed necessary for the general public I have otherwise followed my leader as faithfully as I knew how ; the responsibility for any faults in local knowledge is mine.

CHAPTER I

THE GENERAL IDEA

IN the winter of 1897 gold-fever, generated by the rich strikes made on the Klondike river in 1896, was epidemic in every country of the world, and the Bachelors Club in Toronto was one of the most active centres of infection. It was found that the symptoms appeared in their most acute form between the hours of six and seven in the evening, when the toils of the day were over and the infected subject had really nothing on his mind, even the problem of what to have for dinner being still comfortably remote. (An after-dinner phase was noted too, but this often gave way to treatment by wine, woman, or song.) This book is the case-history of a very acute attack contracted by its victims over their before-dinner scotches and soda.

On a certain evening a party of the sufferers were sitting in the smoking-room discussing the glorious prospects of a journey to the Yukon : some were already determined to go, some were in process of coming to a decision, and some were quite certainly not going but enjoyed talking big as if they were. The subject of immediate interest was a scare-story that had just come in about deaths by starvation and freezing on the Chilkoot Pass, and a big-mouthed person was arguing very forcibly that freezing to death was a matter of the merest carelessness—a fate well deserved by anyone who was fool enough not to take care of himself. Stories like that were not going to frighten *him* away from making a million dollars.

" But why should one go by the Chilkoot Pass anyway ? " somebody asked.

3

" How the Hell else are you going to get there ? " responded Big-Mouth churlishly.

" Well, you could go up the coast to wherever-it-is and then take a steamer up the Yukon to Dawson."

" You could, eh ? "

" Sure."

" The lower Yukon isn't navigable." Somebody else chipped in.

" Sure it's navigable. My dear fellow, the Yukon is about as big as the Mississippi, you've no idea . . ."

" It's all shoal water for the first four hundred miles. That's why the salmon go in there, because the seals can't get after them—isn't enough water to float a seal. And anyhow, there's only one steamer a year up the Alaska coast."

A less-imaginative person claimed audience, bringing down his empty tumbler on the table with an overarm sweep.

" You're all wet, both of you. Now you listen to me : I know something about this thing. The Chilkoot Pass is all right ; there's nothing to it just as a trip, as Ben says, but what can you do in a place that's lousy with people and nothing to eat ? The proper thing to do is to go on your own, keep out of the crowd, just take your dogs and your food and one fellow with you and sneak ashore somewhere in the Panhandle, and off."

" You're God-damn right, Jerry ; that's what I'm going to do, and I know just where I'm going to strike across country." This was a new speaker, who evidently had a red-hot plan. He made a circular gesture to capture the attention of all the party, and tapped impressively on the table with an inverted thumb-nail.

" Now look at me, you fellows," he went on, " I'm going to let you in on this, and don't you tell a soul—I give it to you to use yourselves if you want to. Have any of you ever heard of Telegraph Creek ? "

Naturally they hadn't.

" Well now, this is *right*. Years and years ago when Alaska still belonged to the Russians, some Yanks got the idea of building an overland telegraph line from San Francisco to Europe up the West Coast and through Alaska and Siberia, with the shortest possible stretch of submarine cable at the Behring Straits. I may be wrong about some details, but that's of no consequence. In any case, they formed a company and got a franchise from the Russians, and went to work cutting a right-of-way for their line through the woods, starting from this place Telegraph Creek and going away to Hell up into the North. Now the point is that that right-of-way must be there still, a clear road running plumb-straight from tide-water at the Creek over into the Yukon Valley, and probably not one person in ten thousand to-day knows a thing about it. I just happened to come across it in an old book in my dentist's waiting-room. So that's the way I'm going : on the first of March you'll see me hitting it up along that trail where probably no white man has passed for forty years. Boy, take these gentlemen's orders."

Mitchell had been keeping very quiet up till now, though his mind had become dangerously expansive during the lecture on Telegraph Creek. But when scotches and gins had been distributed he opened in a gentle tone.

" My dear Bob—you will forgive me for perhaps being a little difficult to persuade although I am drinking your scotch—but have you ever seen a road through the woods that has been left to itself for forty years ? "

" What d'you mean, left to itself ? "

" What I mean, Bob, is this : that if you cut out a right-of-way, or a road, or anything like that, and don't do anything more about it, the first thing you know all kinds of bushes begin to grow there, and little trees begin to poke up after a year or two, and before very long that road is just the most impassable place in the whole country. You can't edge your way through the alder sprouts in summer and your snow-shoes catch in them almost as badly in winter. I tell you I know the symptoms, from hunting among old logging roads."

" Oh, well, logging roads may be like that, but you can't tell me that a place like that's going to get all grown over. You go any damn way you like, but, as I said before, me for Telegraph Creek——" and he wandered out of the room, crestfallen and mumbling in protest.

" Poor Bob," said Mitchell regretfully, as he disappeared, " I'm sorry he got sore. But just the same, another little drink will not do us any harm, and I don't mind saying that my own idea is to go by the Mackenzie river."

" The Mackenzie ? " A blank and astonished company, quite unable to follow so revolutionary a suggestion.

" Yes, the Mackenzie. Go down the Mackenzie and then over the mountains westwards."

" But the Mackenzie runs into Hudson Bay. How will you get round the top ? "

" Hudson Bay ? "

" Joe, you're crazy ! "

" The Mackenzie, he said."

" What's Hudson Bay got to do with it ? " There was a chorus of disapprobation.

" Well, sure, Hudson Bay," repeated Joe, defensively but without conviction.

" But, my dear old boy, the Mackenzie *doesn't run* into Hudson Bay."

" Sure it does."

" No, it doesn't : not within a thousand miles " ; so Joe was finally extinguished.

" But, joking apart," said someone with a gin-ricky, " you're wrong about trying the Mackenzie. My old man went down the Mackenzie years ago for his summer vacation, and he ended up in Astoria, Oregon."

" Then I guess it was the Columbia, Mac, so I win again. But we'll see. Boy ! "

" Yes, sir."

" Go and give the secretary my compliments, please, and ask him if he will be so good as to lend us the copy of Spargo's Pocket Atlas of the World which I think he has in his office. Understand? Mr. Mitchell's compliments, and borrow the Pocket Atlas. And then take these gentlemen's orders."

" Very good, sir."

The atlas duly appeared, and was ransacked by the hopeful Mitchell while more drinks went round.

" Make your bets, gentlemen," he said ; " what odds am I offered on the mouth of the Mackenzie river? Hundred to one against Hudson Bay? Don't like that. Two to one on Astoria, Oregon? No? Five hundred to one on the Arctic Ocean? Oh, come, there's too much geography in this club all of a sudden—George can't bet at all. But seriously, there you are—see if I'm not right."

Spargo had made terrible sacrifices in shrinking to pocket size, but even a " Dominion of Canada " at eight hundred miles to the inch shows that the Slave and Mackenzie rivers run from south-east to north-west, or in a general sense gold-wards. And the Yukon was right beside them, less than an inch away—if one could hop over the Rockies somehow, as Mitchell had said.

" You figure you'd paddle down there in a canoe, eh? " asked the unimaginative Jerry, " and then do a bit of mountaineering? "

" No, Jerry, mountaineering is exactly what I don't intend to do, and that's one reason why I'm avoiding the Chilkoot Pass. You can get all the mountaineering you want there."

" Well, but what about the bloody mountains? "

" Jerry, if you weren't plain ignorant, you might have heard of the Hudson's Bay Company, and know that they've been getting furs down from that country for a hundred years past. And then, Jerry, if you had any ratiocinative power, you might figure that they don't go mountaineering with bales of beaver and kegs of powder and beads and all that, and that where they can carry pelts and wampum I can carry my little pick and gold pan. Finally, Jerry, if you weren't quite blind, you could see by this handsome little atlas that there are several large rivers running out of the Rocky Mountains both ways, into the Mackenzie on one side and into the Yukon on the other, which no doubt explains how the Hudson's Bay people avoid that mountaineering which seems to obsess you. As a matter of fact, I am quite confident that one can go by water nearly all the way."

The Mackenzie idea had now taken hold of the party ; intellectual breaths were recovered and began to issue in comment and advice. Mac had the map, and got in first.

" Well, sure," he said, " there's the Peace river right there, and Sir Alexander Mackenzie went up the Peace river when he discovered the Arctic Ocean."

" How the Hell could he do that, Mac ? "

" I don't know *how* the Hell he did it, or *why* the Hell he did it, but I know that over the Peace was where he went."

" Sure he did, but he can't have discovered the Arctic Regions."

" But I'm telling you he did discover——"

" But, Mac, look at the map ! The Peace doesn't go anywhere near——"

" I can't help that, Gordon, everybody knows——"

At last somebody got a word in edgeways.

" For God's sake, you fellows, dry up. Mackenzie went on *two* trips—*first* he went over by the Peace and *then* he went down the Mackenzie to the Arctic. Why else did he call himself Mackenzie ? And in any case the Peace has got no possible bearing on George's scheme."

" Mac's crazy, leave him alone," said Big-Mouth authoritatively, having possessed himself of the tiny Spargo. " Here's a fine great river, the Liar, no, I guess it's the

L, I, A, R, D, Liard—odd name that—anyhow, it runs just where George wants, and another river runs off the other way, right from its source, down into the Yukon. That's the place for you George, eh? Just a short portage, and away you go ! "

" Yes," answered Mitchell, " the Liard might be quite all right. And here's another one, much lower down, the —-what is it marked ?—the Peel. That might do too. And then I've heard that the Hudson's Bay people have a route from the Delta—somewhere down here—over to the Porcupine—there's the Porcupine—which brings one to the Yukon some distance *below* Dawson. That might turn out to be the best of all, but I don't know yet—I'm still working on the thing."

CHAPTER II

THE GEOGRAPHICAL PROBLEM

IN order that Mitchell's idea may be understood properly it is necessary to discuss the various routes which led to Dawson in a cooler atmosphere than that of the Bachelors Club. The sketch map on page 11 will help to make things clear.

Dawson is in the far-off north-western corner of Canada, on the Yukon river, and is the jumping-off place for the gold-field of the Klondike—this being the name of a tributary of the Yukon that joins the main river from the east at Dawson. The town is close to the boundary of Alaska, which belongs to the United States, and in fact the gold-field did its best to be in American territory, like so many other choice vineyards of the Canadian Naboth. Even to-day, with organized steamer services on the Yukon, a railway round the Chilkoot Pass, and aeroplanes for the paying, Dawson is a hard enough place to reach simply because it is so far away. It is, as a matter of fact, close on fourteen hundred miles from Vancouver, which is itself some twenty-two hundred miles from Toronto. But in 1898 there were numberless other troubles to be overcome besides mere mileage, and, as he had the invaluable faculty of recognizing trouble before he reached it, Mitchell set about his plans with an open and cautious mind.

There seemed, roughly speaking, to be three possible ways of going to Dawson. In the first place, one could start from a Pacific Coast port, such as Seattle or Vancouver, go all the way by sea to the mouth of the Yukon, and then

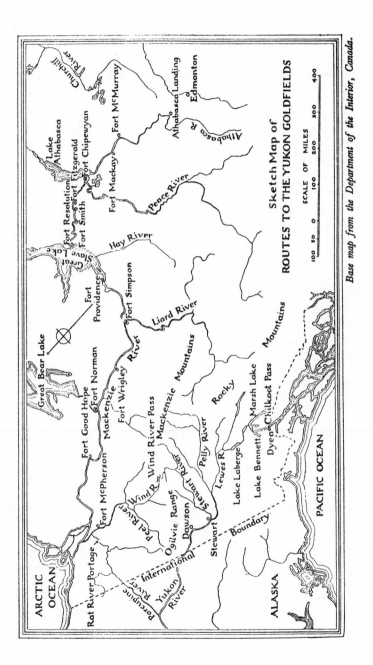

Sketch Map of
ROUTES TO THE YUKON GOLDFIELDS

SCALE OF MILES
100   50   0   100   200   300   400

Base map from the Department of the Interior, Canada.

up-river. In the second place, one could sail from the same port to Dyea on the Chilkoot Inlet, and continue northwards down the Whitehorse, Lewes, and Yukon rivers ; this meant crossing the coastal mountains by the Chilkoot Pass, which gave access from Dyea to Lake Bennett and the headwaters of the Whitehorse river. In the third place, one could leave civilization at Edmonton, on the eastern or inland side of the Rockies ; go down the Athabasca, Slave, and Mackenzie rivers to whatever point seemed good ; make one's way westwards to the Yukon over or through whatever mountains might lie in the way ; and complete the journey down the Yukon or, if one were already too far north by that time, return to Dawson up-stream.

The first of these alternatives Mitchell turned down after very summary consideration. Armchair geographers can easily forget how far away the mouth of the Yukon is, as maps of North America are very apt to cut Alaska out, or skew it up into the top left-hand corner where it escapes the reader's notice. But Mitchell soon realized that to get there from, say, Seattle, he would have to go first to Sitka, a matter of nine hundred and fifty miles up the coast ; then he would have to go westwards for twelve hundred miles across the Pacific to Unalaska in order to turn the end of the Aleutian Peninsula ; and then a further eight hundred miles northwards across the Behring Sea. That made the breadth of the Atlantic between Seattle and St. Michael's, the port at the mouth of the Yukon. From St. Michael's to Dawson by river is again sixteen hundred miles, and though this run is generally made by steamers in the open season, it was obvious that to row or pole a loaded scow for such a distance against the current and among endless bars and sand-banks would be an utterly hopeless task. So with something like forty-six hundred miles of actual distance to go, and difficult river navigation on top of that, Mitchell decided that this route, at any rate, was not for him.

Of the two remaining choices the armchair man would

probably have selected the first, that is to say the route which led over the Chilkoot Pass. He would have considered, no doubt, that the opening stage could be accomplished very easily by steamer, and the West Coast shipping companies were instant in persuasive propaganda. The difficulty of crossing the Pass must certainly have been exaggerated, seeing that the summit was only a couple of thousand feet up and the whole distance from Dyea to Lake Bennett was under thirty miles. And after Lake Bennett one had only to float down the river, which would again be simplicity itself.

Now it may well be said that to climb up two thousand feet, even when the going is steep and the weather arctic, is not necessarily an alarming performance, and it is also probably true that the Whitehorse Rapids, though a nasty place, need not be excessively dangerous to experienced canoemen. But Mitchell knew well enough that there was a great deal more than this to be said about the West Coast route. First there was the high cost, as the steamers charged exorbitant rates for passages up the coast. Then there was the difficulty of transport over the Pass, for Mitchell had been advised that a party of four or five men, such as his own would be, would require literally tons of equipment and supplies ; and, though the Pass might be a comparatively low one, the way up it was excessively steep, so that it was not at all clear how tons of impedimenta were to be moved over it, especially as no pack animals could be procured. Then again there would be thousands of other travellers, which would make the transport difficulty fifty times more embarrassing than it would have been to a party that was travelling by itself ; for instance, it was commonly said that the trail over the Pass was so jammed with people that newcomers sometimes had to wait at the bottom for days before they could edge themselves into the stream, and under conditions like these it would have been impossible to organize a pack-train even if the animals had been available. Nor would the quality of the other travellers have made matters easier, seeing that, besides the real miners, there were hordes of unfit and ill-equipped adventurers—city people, women, and misfits of every kind. The wildest stories were told about the strange types of people on the trail—how one man had brought a harmonium, another a crate of chickens, or another his cow ; and of the debris—cases of champagne, fine mink coats, and useless objects of every imaginable kind that their miserable and exhausted owners had jettisoned in the snow.

And supposing the Pass to be behind one the rivers still remained, and again Mitchell knew that he would not be on Easy Street when he reached Lake Bennett. He would first have to build his boat, and that meant finding the trees, cutting them down, and sawing them into planks, all on the top of a mountain in the northern winter, and with ten thousand other people fighting for timber and tackle and tools and the pick of the launching-places. Finally, his home-made and heavily loaded boat would certainly not run rapids like a canoe, so that the descent of the river might well turn out to be a thoroughly hazardous undertaking. It was common knowledge, indeed, that scores of boats had been lost in the Whitehorse Rapids. So the more he considered his chances the more determined Mitchell became to avoid the Chilkoot Pass and the upper Yukon.

But the Mackenzie river seemed to offer a much more favourable prospect. The boat journey would certainly be very long, as the distance by water to the head of the Mackenzie delta was something like two thousand miles ; but the rapids were far less formidable than those of the Whitehorse, and the waterway had been used by white men for more than a hundred years, so that a traveller need not rush into difficulties blindfold. Then there were posts of the Hudson's Bay Company at intervals all the way, where good guides could be hired or extra stores bought if they were needed. It might even be possible to buy a good river-boat on the spot, or at any rate to get expert help in building one. Even the distance seemed less if one forgot that it was two thirds the breadth of the Atlantic and remembered instead that Mackenzie, on his original voyage of discovery, went down from Fort Chipewyan to the Arctic Ocean in forty days, of which he spent nineteen in cruising round the Great Slave Lake.

At the same time, if he chose the Mackenzie route, Mitchell still had to make his westing, across the Rockies ; and it remained to consider whether the difficulties that he would meet with in that part of the journey would or would not be too serious. Reliable information seemed very hard to come by, for although there was plenty of talk about travel to the gold-fields, most of it was more or less wild and reflected the total ignorance of the talkers. There were some people, for instance, who contended that the Peace river provided a possible route to Klondike, though every map showed that the headwaters of the Peace were more than two hundred miles from those of the Yukon. The Liard was suggested too, and with some colour of likelihood seeing that one of its tributaries, the Finlayson, does actually rise in the neighbourhood of the Pelly, which again flows into the Lewes, a tributary of the Yukon, and that there is a practicable pass between them. But Mitchell found, on investigation, that though this route had been adopted by the Hudson's Bay Company immediately after the discovery of the pass for purposes of communication with the Yukon valley, it was abandoned again after two or three years' use because the navigation of the Liard was found to be altogether too dangerous.

The route which the Hudson's Bay Company developed in place of the Liard and Pelly rivers was a good deal longer but had proved much safer and was admitted to be quite a practicable one. It led down the Mackenzie to the Delta, thence up a short western tributary called the Rat, and so over a pass into the headwaters of the Porcupine. The

Porcupine is a very considerable river which runs into the Yukon, on its right bank, far below Dawson and in American territory ; and consequently a traveller bound for Dawson, after crossing the Rat portage, would still have a journey of seven or eight hundred miles before him, of which the second half would have to be made up-stream, against the current of the Yukon. Mitchell misdoubted this up-stream voyage on account of the current and the gravel-bars, but he felt none the less that the Mackenzie, Rat, and Porcupine rivers might still be preferable to the Chilkoot Pass. But the Mackenzie had another large tributary about which nobody talked at all. Mitchell's map showed him that this river, which was called the Peel, rose in the Rockies just south of the Arctic Circle, and it seemed as if its head-waters must be close to those of the Stewart, which runs down the other side of the mountains and joins the Yukon a hundred miles up-stream from Dawson City. Consequently, he argued, if there happened to be a pass through the mountains from the Peel to the Stewart, this route might well turn out to be the best of all.

The more he looked at his map the better he liked his idea. He would make his northing by the Mackenzie—all down-stream. He would avoid the long detour of the Rat and the Porcupine ; and he would have the current with him, not against him, when he got into the Yukon. There would be up-stream work on the Peel, but the distance would be rather less than from the mouth of the Porcupine to Dawson, and the navigation could hardly be worse. Everything depended on the existence of a suitable pass, and on that question there was absolutely no information to be had.

In the end the problem was solved by the purest chance : Mitchell, dining with some friends, ran into a man who had explored the northern Rockies some ten years earlier, and he obtained an answer to his question over the port. The explorer, William Ogilvie, not only confirmed what Mitchell had heard about the Chilkoot Pass, but assured him that the Peel river was a perfectly practicable route. There was an easy pass through the Rockies from the Peel to the Stewart—Ogilvie had not seen it himself but had heard of it from the Indians and had no doubt about its existence. The Peel, he understood, was a big river, and the current was probably stiffish, but the Indians navigated it freely, and he felt sure that a well-equipped party of experienced travellers should have no difficulty whatever in getting through.

CHAPTER III

THE IMMIGRANT TRAIN

AT the time of the Klondike rush Mitchell was still in his early thirties. He was established in business in Toronto, but finding insurance-broking far less interesting than fishing and hunting, he had always managed to spend a great deal of his time in the wilds, and he was, in his own words, " bush-wise, hardened, and fit, and with plenty of spring in his muscles ". He had killed every game animal and bird, from moose and caribou to snipe, and to solace his confinement in the office he belonged to a snug little fishing-club that owned a few miles of trout stream within easy reach of the city. By temperament he was always ready for what he called a " legitimate gamble ", and Ogilvie's story about the pass, hearsay though it was and ten years old, was quite good enough to resolve his remaining doubts about the Mackenzie route. It was also quite good enough for his two friends, Jack and Cecil, who were planning to join him in the enterprise ; and the three of them accordingly left Toronto at the end of December, 1897, and started out west.

Mitchell's first care was to establish relations with the Hudson's Bay Company, as it was desirable in the highest degree for a traveller in the North-West to carry the Company's blessing. The " Gentlemen Adventurers trading into Hudson's Bay " had been established at strategic points along those shores since 1670, and in the seventeen-seventies had begun to spread their trading posts all over the hinterland to meet the competition of certain Canadian

companies which were pushing up through the Great Lakes
and trying to deflect the stream of furs to their own establishments in Montreal. By 1821, when the Canadian interests were merged with the Hudson's Bay Company, the
traders were penetrating into the most distant corners of
the north-west country, and from that time until river
steamers and railways came in to simplify its problem the
Hudson's Bay Company worked a most elaborate system
of inland transport for the conveyance of its furs and trade-
goods. Convoys of boats, which were called " brigades ",
were organized at the various forts on the main rivers where
the furs from the tributary streams and neighbouring
territories were collected, and set off in spring, as soon as
the ice had gone out, either to deliver their cargoes on the
sea-board (or later at railhead) or, if the distance was
particularly long, to meet at some rendezvous other convoys
that had brought in supplies and trade goods. Thus the
Mackenzie river brigade, which had one of the longest
journeys, used to arrive at Great Slave Lake about the end
of June, bringing the produce of all the lower Mackenzie
district ; and from Great Slave Lake, in another three or
four weeks, it went up the Slave, Athabasca and Clearwater
rivers to Methy Portage, in what is now north-west Saskatchewan. Methy Portage is a carrying-place a few miles
broad which divides the waters which flow to the Arctic
Ocean from those which flow to Hudson Bay ; and here the
Mackenzie brigade met and exchanged cargoes with the
York Factory brigade, which had come in from Hudson
Bay with the year's supplies by way of the Nelson river,
Lake Winnipeg, and the Saskatchewan and Churchill rivers
and sundry communicating lakes. In this way the furs that
left the Mackenzie delta at the end of May could be got to
York Factory in good time for loading on board the ships,
which could not delay their sailing beyond the end of
September for fear of ice in the Straits. And besides its
water transport the company had a fleet of so-called Red

River carts, drawn by ponies, to cover the thousand miles of prairie between Edmonton and Winnipeg, to say nothing of a service of dog-sleighs for lighter work and the carrying of mail in winter. It is on record that eleven hundred men were employed on river work by the several fur companies at the end of the eighteenth century, and someone has left us a brave description of the Governor of the Hudson's Bay Company as he went through the wilderness in 1828—two great canoes, each with nine paddlers, bagpipes, a bugler, cases of sound red wine, and a *feu de joie* at every post. We may be confident that the Governor wore a white top-hat.

With this tradition behind them it was natural that, in any question concerning boats, canoes, sleighs, dogs, Indians, or transport and travel in general, the Company's men could be trusted to give the last word under all and any circumstances. At the same time, the Company and its factors enjoyed an immense prestige, and its forts served, like the monasteries of the Middle Ages, as islands of order and safety in a howling and dangerous world. Consequently Mitchell foresaw that good introductions to the factors would be of the greatest value to him, as enabling him to make use of their local experience and to call on them for help in other ways if need arose.

In pursuance of this aim he broke his westward journey at Winnipeg and called on Mr. Chipman, the Company's Chief Commissioner, at the head office there. Mr. Chipman knew nothing himself about the Peel river country except that some of the Company's finest skins, and especially moose hides, came out of it and that the local tribe of Indians, the Loucheux, had always had the good sense to keep it closed against all strangers, both red and white. But he fully approved of Mitchell's plans, provided that the Indians could be persuaded to let the party go through, and in particular he was sure that if Ogilvie had said that there was a pass from the Peel to the Stewart, a pass there would most certainly turn out to be.

Mr. Chipman was also delighted to give Mitchell facilities for dealing with the personnel of the forts, and provided him with a circular letter of credit that saved him from having to carry cash. Ordinary miners usually carried cash, which was a great inconvenience, though many of them had nothing to carry at all and " for the love of God," said Mitchell, " how they ever got through I don't know." Mr. Chipman also arranged for Mitchell to buy his heavy stores and equipment at the Company's depôt at Edmonton ; this was a real boon, as the Company was well known to supply nothing but the best of any kind of goods, whether to white man or Indian, and also because it saved the very heavy cost of freight over a thousand miles of railway.

When this business had been put through Mitchell and his friends wasted no time in Winnipeg, which was suffering most unpleasantly from a land boom and rush of its own. All sorts of people were pouring through to take up home-steads in the prairies ; Doukhobors had begun to appear, and other peculiar-looking specimens from central Europe, besides the ordinary run of English and Canadians from the older provinces. There were many Americans too, migrating northwards from exhausted land in the Dakotas. For Winnipeg the Yukon rush was a matter of no interest at all, and those who went on it were generally regarded as crazy. So, as prices were sky-high and the place ex-tremely primitive, the party scraped the mud of Portage Avenue from off its boots as soon as might be and got into a westbound train. (A chestnut is told about this mud, how that a straw hat, floating on its surface, was thought to be the last emerging trace of a farmer and load of hay, engulfed beneath.)

It had occurred to them that they had better begin to get some idea of the kind of people that they would meet on the river and at the mines, so they travelled west from Winnipeg in an immigrant car. The Canadian Pacific Railway was a less perfect organization at that time than it is to-day—the trains went more slowly and less certainly, and the accommodation, or at least that provided for immigrants, left something to be desired. Mitchell was very vehement in his description of the old wooden car, with its rows of upper and lower bunks, its smoking oily lamp, and a coal stove at the end where the passengers did their own cooking as the spirit moved them. Somebody was always cooking, and some party was always playing cards, all day and all night. The travellers seem to have been drawn from all classes in all the countries of the world : " a fine lot of boys taking them all together, without allowing for their moral and physical disabilities ". Mitchell enumerated good sound farmers' lads from Ontario and the Maritime Provinces ; broken-down members of the liberal professions, including even priests ; gun-men and card-sharks ; the ex-mayor of an important Ontario city ; wanderers and optimists from every part of America, both north and south ; experienced miners from Idaho and the Australian gold-fields ; and a good sprinkling of French-Canadians of the pioneer class. He summed them up as` " the boys that are always looking for the land behind the mountains ".

" The first night," he said, " was pretty well devoted to regulating and holding down the excess liquor that a great many of our chums had been given by their friends as a send-off, and this entailed a bit of rough work—bloody noses and so on, but no real fighting. Things settled down gradually so that I could get a bit of sleep. Next morning there was an early dash for the water tap and cooking stove, and I learned a lot about cooking that day that I had never learned before—how to make flap-jacks, for instance, and the real proper way to fry eggs with bacon. Every few hours the train stopped at some place which is a city now but was only a few houses and a water-tank then, and a few more fellows would get in. When any new bunch got into the car they looked at us like strange dogs coming into a kennel, to see how good we were to fight, and we looked at them to see how good they were to fight, and each bunch settled down into its own quarters after a bit of pushing and dared not tread on anybody's toes or take half an inch of seat more than they should get. By about the second day the top-dog was on top and the under-dog was underneath, and we kept those relative positions."

The snow was deep on the prairie and the train was stopped several times by drifts. Sometimes they stopped near a farm, where there might be fresh bread for sale, and on one glorious occasion Mitchell and Jack slipped out on their snow-shoes before anyone else had noticed that there was a house beside the line, and by the time the rest of the crowd arrived had bought everything on the place that was edible—pigs, eggs, game, butter and a great batch of brand-new loaves—at ten times what the Scots farmer's wife thought they were worth. " When our friends from the train arrived," he said, " the market was bare. But we didn't make hogs of ourselves—we divided it all up squarely at a profit of about three hundred per cent."

Regina and Calgary, when they reached them, were just as primitive as Winnipeg had been, though Regina had this claim to fame—that it was the headquarters of the Royal North-West Mounted Police. Here again Mitchell had introductions to present, to some of the members of this very distinguished corps, so the party took a few days' holiday from the immigrant car and recollected itself in the hospitable atmosphere of the officers' mess.

It was on the last lap of the railway journey, between Calgary and Edmonton, that Mitchell got his first sight of real wild life, as it was supposed to be lived in the West. The train had stopped at an extremely wayside station and had stayed stopped for an extraordinarily long time ; nothing was happening, and there was nobody to be seen— it was as if the railway system had just died in its sleep. At last Mitchell grew tired of waiting, and got out of the car to enjoy the sunshine and brisk zero air outside. As he stamped about the platform he noticed a siding beyond the station with a construction train standing in it, and presently the broad-brimmed hat, red coat, and exquisite breeches of a policeman approached him from that direction. The policeman proved to be a cheery and very young Englishman, whom he had lately met at Regina ; they hailed one another, and the policeman at once enquired if Mitchell would like to have some fun.

" Sure," said Mitchell.

" You may get hurt," the policeman objected in an encouraging tone.

" That's all right," replied Mitchell, who liked that sort of thing in those days, and does not, perhaps, dislike it very actively now.

The policeman explained that there was a construction gang of Italian navvies in the siding, that a construction paymaster had come up in a pay-car with money for monthly wages, and that the navvies were threatening to rush the pay-car and sack it. A very large sum was involved, as there were hundreds of Italians in the gang and they got pretty high wages. And he would be very much obliged if Mitchell would come and help him maintain order as his deputy.

Mitchell accepted the offer greedily, so the policeman swore him in as a special constable on the spot. Then he asked,

" Are you armed ? "

" Yes," replied Mitchell.

" Give me your gun."

Mitchell gave him his revolver—" gun " means " revolver " in the West—and the policeman took it and gave it back to him saying,

" Now you are officially armed. Let's go."

When they reached the siding they found the pay-car empty, as the terrified paymaster had sent the men away on the pretext of getting their dinners, but really because he dared not face the music. A pay-bench was arranged at one end of the car, and the paymaster was shivering behind it.

" Have you got some chalk ? " the policeman asked as they entered.

" Yes."

The policeman took the chalk and drew a broad white line, like the back line of a tennis court, right across the floor of the car three yards in front of the pay-bench. Then he and Mitchell took up positions behind the bench and the paymaster called the men back. The first man came in peaceably and was paid. Then another one or two came singly, and then two together, and all these were allowed to come up to the bench. Then several came in together and began to surge forward with a threatening air ; the paymaster thought that they were going to rush and gave himself up for lost.

" Halt ! " commanded the policeman. But the Italians didn't halt.

" Go back to the door," the policeman called, but they still came on, jabbering and waving their arms. Then " prrrt " went the policeman's revolver as he sprayed a row of bullets all along the chalk line. The Italians shrank back, and he told them that any man who crossed the line would get a bullet, signalling to Mitchell to fire if any of them did. But their blood-pressure was already greatly reduced ; there was no more difficulty about getting them up to the pay-bench one by one, and the pay-out was completed in peace.

CHAPTER IV

EDMONTON

EDMONTON is the natural jumping-off place for the Mackenzie river basin and had been a fur trading post ever since 1795, when the Hudson's Bay Company and the North-West Fur Company both established forts there. The town commanded two routes to Winnipeg, one overland across the prairies and the other down the North Saskatchewan river, which was easily navigable by steamers and by the so-called York boats. At the same time the distance from Edmonton to Athabasca Landing was no more than ninety-eight miles of easy trail over prairie and low rolling hills ; and from Athabasca Landing the Athabasca river communicated directly with the Slave river and Great Slave Lake, and so with the Mackenzie river and the Arctic Ocean.

In 1898 the town was very small and rustic, consisting simply of one main street with a few rudimentary cross streets, all laid out on the flat prairie. There was one hotel, one bank, a large outfitting and hardware store, and three small churches, with houses for about five hundred people ; but many of the inhabitants, being retired Hudson's Bay factors, had built themselves comfortable and pleasant-looking houses, and these gave the place an air of maturity and well-being that is not found in crude little prairie hamlets. There was also Fort Edmonton, a great hexagonal stone building with bastions for artillery and two embattled gateways ; here the Hudson's Bay Company had its trading post, stores of provisions, equipment, and material of all kinds, and workshops where boats, sleighs, carts, harness, and so forth were made and repaired for the Company's inland voyages and transport operations in general. The railway did not yet reach the town itself, but came to an end on the southern bank of the river.

Into this pleasant little backwater the gold-rush had burst like a tropical storm. Every building was crammed with people, and hundreds were camping out all round the town in rags of tents and bivouacs, many of them having no proper equipment and no idea of how to look after themselves. The temperature, meanwhile, was everywhere down to forty below zero Fahrenheit. All the strange misfits from the immigrant car were among the crowds, with Chinese and Japanese as well come in from the West. The more responsible types were the experts and trained miners from the older gold-fields, and the Russians in particular were a fine lot of men, though they were hated by the Anglo-Saxons for their cruel and ruthless ways. There were some syndicates of Englishmen, too, which attracted a good deal of attention, as the members were rich and had brought out servants and luxurious supplies, and elaborate kits of all the most useless things that the London outfitters could devise.

Some of this mixed gang were moderately level-headed, but Mitchell's account suggests that many were simply mad with the thought of gold. Only a minority had organized plans for their journey, and by far the greater number of those who passed through Edmonton were heading for Peace River Landing with the idea of going up the Peace and over the mountains from the watershed. They refused to recognize that the Peace does not give on to the Yukon basin at all, and that they would be left confronted with hundreds of miles of unexplored mountain country, in spite of the advice in this sense that the Hudson's Bay men offered them ; they had simply made up their minds that they could go anywhere, and go they would. Mitchell does not believe that more than one or two of these people ever arrived at Dawson.

Another Bedlamite symptom was the general disregard for the value of money. Five-dollar bills were taken to light cigars, and one-dollar bills were used for a still humbler purpose. Some of the Englishmen idly left fifty cases of their champagne outside in the zero weather, so that most of it froze and was ruined ; they auctioned off the lot in the middle of the main street for twenty-five or thirty cents a case, and if a bottle or two turned out good the successful bidders knocked off the heads and drank the contents on the spot, topping them off with whisky. Revolvers went off quite frequently ; the nights were never quiet, what with poker, singing, and devilment of all sorts ; and the hundreds of ponies that had been driven up over the American border made the confusion still worse with their continual stampedes.

But the Mounted Police were always in and out, and while they left cheerful chaos alone they quickly interfered to prevent serious disorder. They had a remarkable appreciation of the point at which civil commotion should be considered to have begun. One day Mitchell had taken his washing to an enterprising Chinaman, who had started some kind of a laundry near the hotel, when some rough-necks came in, well lit with liquor, and demanded their clean clothes. The Chinaman asked for the usual tallies of torn paper in order to identify their parcels, and at that the rough-necks opened fire with their forty-fives so that the air was thick with bullets. Mitchell dropped under the counter, but by the time the smoke had cleared up and he was showing a cautious eyebrow, the police were in the shack and were actively quelling the riot. The rough-necks were truly penitent at once—they had meant no harm and pointed out that they had only been shooting patterns along the roof.

Edmonton's social tone in gold-rush times can be read very clearly between the lines of Mitchell's history of a friend of his called Beadle. (I will quote Mitchell himself.) " Beadle was an independent fur trader from Slave Lake, who always used to drive down to Edmonton with his dog team once a year for business and—recreation. (And, mind you, that's going on for eight hundred miles, along the river to Edmonton.) He was a very capable man—must have been, to get away with what he did ; in fact, I don't know why the Hudson's Bay people put up with him at all, as he was infringing their trading rights and making an excellent thing out of it. I suppose nobody felt quite like shooting him out and out, and nothing except shooting would have had any effect on him.

" But whatever he was in the North he was a fair terror when he got to Edmonton, at least for the first few days. There was always one day when he entertained the town— that was his treat—and that was how I first met him. I happened to walk into the hotel one day, and there he was at the bar, standing drinks to everybody. He saw me come in and called out,

" ' Hullo, tenderfoot, come and have a drink.'

" I looked at him pretty coolly across the room and called back,

" ' All right, Sourbelly, don't mind if I do,' and went up to him at the bar. He slid the bottle over to me and I poured out an equal drink to his (four fingers of scotch) and took it down neat, just like that, and he did the same.

" Then I said, ' Now you have one on me,' and we had the same over again, four fingers of scotch without water.

" After that I said to him, ' Well, now I'm through. I'm very glad to have met you, Mr. Beadle, and I'll wish you a very good evening.'

" Beadle didn't like that : he looked at me rather ugly and began,

" ' Oh, you're a quitter, are you, a quitter, eh ? ' and that kind of stuff.

" I wasn't going to have any of that, but I didn't want a row, so I just said plainly and firmly,

" ' No, Mr. Beadle, I'm not a quitter. I've had a drink on you and you've had a drink on me, and so we're square. It's fine for you to have some more because you're free, but I've got to work to-morrow and I know my limit. So I'll say many thanks again, and good night.'

" So then Beadle clapped me on the back and said,

" ' Tenderfoot, you're all right. And now if you want anything to go round town in, there's my dog-team and my Indian—I shall be drinking for a fortnight and shan't need them—so they're at your service.'

" Beadle had a beautiful team of pure black huskies, beautifully matched and splendidly turned out. Each had the tail of a silver fox set upright on his saddle with the tip curling forwards over his head. I had to go down to the Fort every day, so the team came in very handy, and the Indian had it waiting for me at the hotel door every day at nine o'clock. I was driving down the main street one morning in fine style, lying down in the sleigh under the robes, when suddenly a cat crossed right under the leader's nose. You should have seen those dogs go ! The Indian grabbed at the thong that trailed on the ground behind the sleigh, but missed it, and the team got away down a side-street and up a lane and over a paling into somebody's yard—I thought I was a dead man and just cowered down in the sleigh waiting to have my brains dashed out—and then out again and back into the main street, and killed the cat right opposite the Imperial Bank ! There were a thousand people looking on by the time it was all over. Luckily Beadle wasn't there or he would have murdered his Indian : it is a terrible disgrace to have a team of dogs run away, and the man should have been on the job and caught the thong.

" The day before Beadle went back north he sent for the hotel-keeper and told him that he wanted to marry the cook and take her back with him. So the hotel-keeper called her out of the kitchen and put it up to her, and at first she said she was willing. But later on we heard a terrible uproar in the kitchen, and it turned out that the cook had changed her mind and wouldn't go unless the kitchen-maid went too, as she had to have another white person with her ; but the kitchen-maid said that she wouldn't go unless she could be married to the Indian dog-runner. So at last, after a lot of trouble, they fixed it up that way and all four were married next morning. I saw them going away as happy as larks—Beadle and the Indian and the two white girls."

For the greater part of March Mitchell and his friends were busy at Edmonton assembling and packing their stores. They intended to add two experienced miners to the party, and so laid in three years' provisions for five men. They were not rationing themselves on the champagne scale and took only what was strictly necessary— flour, cabin-biscuits, oatmeal, tea, sugar, salt pork, salt beef, dried prunes, molasses, salt, pepper, baking-powder, tobacco, and some bacon, rice, tinned milk, and dried potatoes as occasional luxuries. Then there were the household stores—cooking-pots, tinware, knives, forks and spoons ; matches, candles and paraffin oil ; a collapsible sheet-iron stove and stove-pipe ; tenting and ropes, blankets, ammunition, spare boots and clothes ; cheese-cloth to make mosquito nets ; and a ready-made glass window against the day when they should build a house. Liquor they knew was not allowed to go down the river, so they only took a case or two of whisky, and some brandy that would be let through as medical stores. And on top of all was the mining equipment and tools—picks and shovels, both long and short ; a selection of crow-bars for breaking and moving rock ; rock-drills for blasting ; axe-heads and mallet-heads ; wedges and special chilled chisels ; saws of all kinds for felling, cross-cutting and ripping out planks ; a very full carpenter's outfit with screws, nails, wire and rivets ; a brazing furnace with its bellows ; gunpowder, dynamite and fuses ; and several prospectors' outfits of picks and gold-pans. There were fully ten tons in all.

March was as hard as iron in 1898, and the sleigh-road to Athabasca Landing was still good at the end of the month in spite of the heavy traffic that had been going over it for many weeks past. The distance could be covered in three days under favourable conditions, and there were depôt camps at certain places along the road where teamsters could pass the night if they arrived at a convenient hour and there was still room for another man or two to squeeze himself inside. Mitchell and his party divided their goods into three parts, each of which made a load for a large sleigh ; the sleighs were driven by regular teamsters, and one member of the party accompanied each.

Mitchell himself travelled with an old Scotsman called Storey, who drove a good pair of heavy Clydesdales. It was most bitterly cold, and Mitchell was fortunate in possessing an outfit of caribou calf-skin clothes, that had been made for him by an old Cree woman, the wife of a pensioned-off buffalo hunter, with whom he had made friends in the fort at Edmonton. She had made him a short coat with a hood, two pairs of breeches, and a blanket ; they were very durable but light and warm, and as the coat and breeches fastened with tags instead of buttons, they would fit nicely over any quantity of other clothes that might be worn underneath.

As Mitchell and Storey went forward they heard an awful uproar of dogs proceeding from a whirl of grey bodies and flying snow, and Mitchell supposed that some madman was killing his dog-team. But Storey assured him that it was only some driver who was stopping a dog-fight, and when they approached they found Sergeant

Andersen of the Mounted Police in the middle of the mellay, preserving the life of the under dog with difficulty, by means of an axe-handle. Mitchell heard afterwards that he was just starting on a particularly dangerous mission, to arrest a *wisteneau* in an Indian camp. This is the story of the affair, as Mitchell told it.

" Perhaps you don't know, my dear Graham, that Indian witch-doctors aren't always very nice boys. One of the little habits that they sometimes take to is eating new-born babies ; a witch-doctor who does this is called a *wisteneau*, and the Indians regard him with the utmost reverence and fear. It takes them a very long time to see through his villainy, and when they do God knows what happens to the *wisteneau*. That is the kind of thing that white men may as well not ask—anyhow, he disappears. But until that moment comes they keep the *wisteneau* like the apple of their eye, and would never by any chance let him be taken.

" So what Andersen did was this. He made his camp about a mile from the Indians' camp and waited for bad weather. After several days a blizzard came on, and then, when the wind and snow were at their worst, he drove his dog-team slap-bang into the middle of the Indians' camp, burst into the *wisteneau's* teepee, handcuffed the *wisteneau* and threw him on the sleigh, and then drove off before a bloody Indian knew that he was there. They chased him for several miles, but he got away and took the *wisteneau* into Edmonton, where he was tried and hanged."

" But, Mr. Mitchell, how could the sergeant tell which teepee the *wisteneau* was in ? "

" Oh, they keep a *wisteneau* in a particular kind of teepee. He's kept by himself, so it's a one-man teepee, small, and has dried bladders and skunks' tails, and that kind of thing, hanging outside. It's easy enough to tell a *wisteneau's* teepee."

The first night Mitchell and Storey slept out-of-doors, rolled up in their blankets by the road-side. Mitchell woke up in the night dreaming of an earthquake—heavy things were thumping beside him and there were queer swishings and janglings in the darkness. He woke Storey, who said it was the horses, frightened by the extreme cold : it seemed that horses were accustomed to pass nights in the open on this journey, covered with heavy buffalo-skins but unable to lie down, and that when the cold was very severe they liked to draw close in to the men for moral support. The second night they passed at a wayside depôt that was crowded to the doors with rioting teamsters and miners. One enterprising man, who complained of having a cold, picked up the lantern, removed the chimney and wick, and drank a good draught of the paraffin straight out of the glass container. Whether on account of the verdigris that he sucked off the rim of the container, or because lamp-oil and gin mix badly, he shortly keeled over and passed completely out, and was only revived by a jorum of mustard and hot water that Mitchell succeeded in forcing down his throat.

As they went on next day a strange teamster came running towards them along the road, and asked Mitchell if he would be good enough to drive his team for a little while, as his hands were very cold and he would like to get them warm. Mitchell protested that he had no experience at all in managing heavy sleighs, but eventually consented to take charge of the team, which was waiting a short distance ahead of them. He had hardly gone half a mile when, on reaching the top of a little crest, he found that he was confronted with an absolute abyss—the road turned sharply to the left and dived down a breakneck slope into a very deep ravine. He was already over the crest and moving downhill before he realized what had happened, and the only expedient seemed to be to lash the horses and keep them away from the sleigh which was quickly gathering momentum just at their heels. He took the corner somehow and by pure luck reached the bottom without mishap ; then, when he looked back, he saw a cheering and uproarious gallery looking on from the crest of the hill. It had all been a practical joke, as that kind of thing is understood in the great North-West. So the tenderfoot repaid himself by walking back slowly up the hill, and asking politely if he could be of service by taking any more of the sleighs down the ravine.

CHAPTER V

ATHABASCA LANDING

" IT was early morning when we pulled up past the top of the Twottenow Hills—that means a hole between two mountains—and saw Athabasca Landing lying at our feet. It was a glorious scene with the sun breaking through the winter clouds and striking low on the settlement and the white sweep of the river. Storey pointed out the chief factor's house on my right—that was Mr. Woods, to whom I had a letter of introduction from Mr. Chipman—and on my left the English chapel, the R.C. mission, the police barracks, and the Hudson's Bay post with its offices, fur stores, warehouses, and a large shipbuilding yard. That yard was where they built the Hudson's Bay scows and York boats, and where I had to get busy soon.

" We dashed down the hill and rounded up in front of the Hudson's Bay post with a grand-stand finish. I told Storey to get the horses put into the barn while I went into the post to present my letter. The first man I saw was a grizzled old sourdough dealing out rations to some squaws and children. I asked him where I could find Mr. Woods, and said I wanted to give him a letter.

" ' Give it to me,' said the man.

" ' Not on your life,' I said, ' this is for Mr. Woods himself.'

" ' All right,' he said, ' sit down there,' and he went on with his job doling out a little molasses, a few beans, a little pork, some tea, tobacco, and so on. These squaws I found intensely interesting—sitting all the time patiently until their names were called and accepting everything with a curtsey and a ' thank you '.

" When the old bird got through his job he told me to come inside.

" ' Now,' he said, ' what about that letter ? '

" ' I'll give it to Mr. Woods when I see him,' I answered.

" ' I am Woods.'

" Then we shook hands and he asked me to come up to his house to breakfast."

As soon as Mitchell had established himself at Athabasca Landing, and before his partners had arrived with the balance of the stores, he set about procuring a vessel for the river voyage. Canoes were out of the question for so large a load as his party had to transport, and so the choice lay between a scow and a York boat. Scows are like overgrown punts, flat-bottomed and with square ends, and are good for heavy cargoes especially in shallow water. But they are very heavy for portaging, can only be sailed with the wind dead astern, and present great resistance to an adverse current. York boats (so called after York Factory on Hudson Bay) are boat-shaped and were developed by the Company as an improvement on the scow for their sailing qualities and convenience in unloading and portaging, but their capacity is less than that of the scow. Woods favoured the scow for Mitchell's purpose, seeing that his load was a heavy one and that light draft would be of more importance to him than power of manœuvre ; so Mitchell took his advice and arranged for the scow to be built in the Company's yard.

The plans were for a craft thirty-three feet long and twelve feet wide, drawing eighteen inches of water when fully loaded. The bow and stern were square and sloping like a punt, there was a short deck forward and aft, and three rowing benches suitably spaced amidships. There are usually six rowers in a scow, but Mitchell's party of five would give only four rowers and a steersman. The rowing would be done with eighteen-foot sweeps, working between thole-pins, the rowers rising from and falling back upon their seats with the stroke ; and the steering with a thirty-foot sweep set on an iron pin. The timbers were specially heavy and strong, and were whip-sawed in the yard out of logs cut in the woods near by.

THE *AMISK*.

The next question was to complete the strength of the party by engaging two men with experience in the mining of free gold, that is to say of gold that occurs as nuggets or dust in beds of gravel and sand. Mitchell may be quoted on this in full.

" I was cooking in my tent one afternoon when a big ugly-looking Scotsman came in and asked me if I needed a good expert free-gold miner. I said I did, and asked him his name.

" ' James Craigie, of Edinburgh.'

" ' All right, Craigie, but you have been a long time away from Edinburgh : where have you been ? '

" ' Chicago.'

" ' A damn bad place.'

" ' Well, yes.'

" After a long conversation with him I found that he was all he said, an experienced free-gold miner who understood building sluices and rockers and cradles, and could handle quicksilver. He was a tall spare man with red hair, bad teeth and a broken nose ; I sized him up as a damn good blackguard and as one that would be true to his salt.

" Then he asked me if I wanted a second man : I did. He said he knew of a Welsh miner who could work into a hill or underground, and shore up any tunnel we required. Strong as a bull and wicked as Hell ; had to be handled with a club. I said, all right, I would take him on. I did so, and he turned out to be all that Craigie said of him, except that he was a bit more of a blackguard than I thought he was. Both Craigie and this man Smith proved infinitely useful : Craigie in particular made many suggestions about the scow that were of the greatest value. He made us attach a couple of good steel rods lengthways along the bottom, to save the timbers from damage through striking rocks and stony bottom in rapids ; and later on built us a couple of pumps for pumping out the bilges and keeping her dry inside."

Before the gold-rush Athabasca Landing had been a tiny settlement of forty or fifty white people, with a transient population of a couple of hundred Indians. When Mitchell was there at least a thousand strangers had descended on the place from all parts of the world, and were camped round about performing all the same wild antics as had been going on in Edmonton. Again his own account cannot be bettered.

" The days at Athabasca Landing were brilliant, extremely cold, and full of activity. The nights were equally brilliant but vastly more lurid. Between the night and the day I don't think I ever got more than three hours' sleep : we were on for poker, fan-tan, or any legitimate gamble, but the decent class of miners absolutely tabooed any rotten monkey-business. There were mysterious little camps out in the bush where very decent fellows were lured by free rum and high gambling, or very attractive dancing : if these places went too far we simply went and cleaned them up and ran the ladies and gentlemen concerned back to where they came from.

" There was one large tent which was very, very cheerful and active, but in passing by one night I heard the shrieks of a woman in trouble. The flap of the tent was securely tied, so I slit the canvas with my knife and jumped in. To my disgust there was a very handsome young girl tied up to the tent-pole by her hands, stripped to the waist and getting an awful licking with dog-whips. I immediately jumped out of the tent again, fired four or five shots and yelled ' Murder ', which brought all the miners on to the scene and my particular old friend Sergeant McGillicuddy of the Mounted Police. He went into the tent through the cut and there was a damned good free-for-all. When the mess was cleaned up we found that this was a rotten bunch of snipe from the Chicago sewers. The poor girl had a damned good heart, whatever her morals may have been, and had put up all the money for the outfit, and the men were now trying to make it so hot for her that she would go home. However, next day we had a miners' meeting, took eighty per cent of their outfit and gave it to the girl, and let her pick up another gang to go north with her. (Incidentally these gentlemen weren't pleased and I had quite considerable trouble with them later on, but it didn't culminate.)"

This story prompted me to ask what a miners' meeting was like, and this is what I was told.

" Miners' meetings were very short and simple. What happened was something like this. Some fellow would come along and report Mr. So-and-so for something that was outside the pale of the law. Then a certain number of miners would gather together and summon the accused before the bar—which was really a plank, sometimes with a bottle of whisky on it that had been taken off the unfortunate chap. Then a chairman would be elected to conduct the proceedings ; and he would open the meeting, saying,

" ' Gentlemen, this meeting is officially open. John Doe is accused of '—whatever it was. ' Who is the accuser ? '

" ' I am,' says Richard Roe.

" ' Who is for the defence ? ' Nobody chirps.

" ' John Doe, have you anything to say ? '

" John Doe has a Hell of a lot to say, and says it in no measured terms. He gets a fair hearing. Then,

" ' Witnesses for the prosecution.' We hear them if there are any.

" ' Witnesses for the defence.' Still nobody.

" ' John Doe, you are condemned to leave this burg pronto, which means immediately, or now. If you are found here after this noon other measures will be taken.'

" If he was found it was a case of ' shoot him up '. We would chase him up the hill towards Edmonton—start him running and shoot him up as he ran."

" Wasn't there a good deal of shooting, Mr. Mitchell, one way and another ? " I ventured to enquire.

" Well, yes, there was some shooting. We all had guns. I always carried three guns myself : one long-barrelled thing, mainly for show, strapped to my leg like you see in the Wild West movies ; a forty-five in my belt, in case a heavy bullet was wanted ; and an automatic in my armpit—that was what I depended on for real quick business. But it never came to anything very much : there were heaps of disputes over cards and ladies and dog-teams, but as a rule these were nipped in the bud before any blood was shed. There was no fellow really killed at Athabasca Landing."

But Mitchell did not spend the whole of his time at the Landing in an odour of blood and thunder. In the first place he enjoyed much kind hospitality from the factor and Mrs. Woods ; in fact, they invited him to stay at their house, but he excused himself, thinking it better to stick to his tent. Mrs. Woods, it may be said, was the daughter of one of the greatest missionaries who ever went into the north country ; he had kept the peace between Blackfeet and Crees in time of war by the force of his personal influence, and when, at the last, he was found dead on the prairie and no cause could be assigned for his death, both Crees and Blackfeet firmly made up their minds that he had been taken straight up to Heaven.

Then he had humbler friends.

" There was one very charming chap there who I heard say could bake. I went over to buy a couple of loaves of bread, which he sold me at a fairly good robber's price like everything else at the Landing. Then he invited me into his tent back of his bakeshop. In the tent he drew a curtain and we went into another tent that was got up like a regular Englishman's den : books on a shelf, a picture of his old home, tobacco jar with his college colours, and a mandolin hanging on the wall. He was an Oxford or Cambridge man, and really white—I don't know which to give the credit for him.

" Then there was Peachey Pruden. Peachey was a little French half-breed who had a little hutch hidden away about two miles down the river—he was a trader. I often used to visit him, as he was a good pal and lots of fun. He had a magnificent pair of moose which he had taken young and trained to harness : I had many a joy-ride with him, or by myself, behind those moose. But one day Peachey came tearing up to the police station crying out that one of his moose had been shot dead and that he had just missed catching the fellow that did it. Sergeant McGillicuddy and as many of us as had any clothes on started in pursuit ; but I think this man is running still, as we never got him."

CHAPTER VI

THE ATHABASCA RIVER

THE Athabasca river drops about a thousand feet in the two hundred-odd miles of its course between Athabasca Landing and Fort McMurray. As a consequence of this there is a good deal of white water to be passed and, in the last sixty or seventy miles above Fort McMurray, where much of the total fall occurs, there is a series of formidable rapids. The modern railway turns these rapids, as it has its river terminus at Waterways, opposite Fort McMurray, and the old canoe route that led over Methy Portage into the Clearwater river likewise avoided them, as the Clearwater also joins the Athabasca at Fort McMurray. But Mitchell's party had to pass the rapids, and they decided that they had better engage a local guide to take them through.

Mitchell accordingly applied to the factor in the hope of securing Saviard, the Company's chief guide. Saviard was a half-breed, a tall dignified Indian as far as his looks went but very much a Frenchman in his speech and ways. He was by far the best guide on the river, but his price was commensurably high, and Mitchell's party could not afford the twelve hundred dollars that he asked for the trip to Fort McMurray. But Woods knew of another good half-breed guide, Scots this time, called Philip Atkinson, and produced him for inspection. He proved to be six-foot-two and as strong as an ox, with a cheerful boyish manner and an appearance of Scots stability ; and as his price, was no more than a hundred and fifty dollars, Mitchell engaged him gladly.

When the time for final preparations came Atkinson at once became valuable, as he could give expert advice on how to load the scow. The proper arrangement of the cargo was naturally of great importance, both for the stability of the scow herself and for the protection of the perishable stores. Underneath the forward deck was considered to be the driest place, and here they stowed whatever had to be kept dry, and mounted the cooking-stove permanently on a foundation of boiler-plate. More cargo was stowed between the rowing benches, and under the after deck the heavy implements that might be allowed to get wet, in case she should sometimes ship a sea in rapids or storms. It was only after they had run their first rapid that they realized that they had made no arrangement for disposing of water that came inboard, even in heavy rain ; so on Atkinson's advice they put in strakes from end to end, restowing the cargo on garboards well clear of the bottom. It was then that Craigie distinguished himself by building the suction pumps to keep these bilges dry. They called the scow the *Amisk*, which means " beaver " in the Cree language.

At last, on the first of May, everything was ready for the start ; the ice had gone out with the spring freshet, and the whole flotilla of boats was to leave the Landing in the afternoon. Mitchell's party was all on board and waiting, but there was no sign of Atkinson ; and as they couldn't start without their guide, Mitchell went up to the Fort to see if Woods knew what had become of him. This is his account of what followed.

" I walked in at the gate of the Fort and looked about, but there wasn't a soul to be seen. Then I noticed that all the doors were shut and some of the windows had the shutters up, and at the same time I heard a Hell of a row coming from somewhere at the back. So I went up to Woods' office and knocked at the door. Woods pulled me inside and said in a sort of a stage-whisper,

" ' Don't you know your man Atkinson's on the tear ? '

" ' No,' I said, ' I don't know anything about it. But, look here, I'm all ready to start, and I came up here just on purpose to look for Atkinson. Where is he, and what's wrong ? '

" Well, it seemed that Master Atkinson had got hold of some liquor, and was raging drunk and raising Hell in the guides' quarters, and that everybody was afraid to show their noses outside, much less go near him. So we went round to the back to see what we could do with him. And there he was in the guides' quarters, dressed in his best caribou skin breeches and a short blue jacket, with a little feathered bonnet riding on the side of his head, and a broad red sash round his middle with two bottles of rum stuck in it like a pirate's pistols. He was standing with his legs apart and his arms stretched—another bottle of rum in either hand—crazy and singing at the top of his voice. He was a glorious figure of a man, a real giant.

" I walked right up to him and said, ' Philip, you're coming right down to the boat with me now, and you're going to hand over that rum for me to keep for you.' Either some habit of obedience or just sheer surprise calmed him, and he handed over his bottles and followed me down to the river without a word.

" When I had got him safe on board I said, ' Now, Philip, I'm very angry with you for getting drunk and going crazy. I see you can't be trusted with money, so this is what I'm going to do. I'm going to give Mr. Woods a hundred and thirty dollars, and he'll look after your wife and family while you're away and you'll get the balance from him when you come back, but for yourself you'll only get twenty dollars on this trip.'

" I had tipped Woods off, while we were walking down from the Fort, as to what I wanted him to say, so he chimed in then and interceded on Philip's behalf, saying he was sure Philip was sorry he'd got full and asking me to make

it twenty-five dollars instead of twenty. So I told Philip
that, as Mr. Woods had spoken for him and I had a very
high opinion of Mr. Woods, I would give him twenty-five
dollars when we reached Fort McMurray and return him
the rest of his rum. So he was quite content, knowing that
his wife and children would not starve while he was away
and feeling that Woods had really obtained very handsome
terms for him by timely intercession. I never had any more
trouble with Philip after that."

" But, Mr. Mitchell," I said, " weren't you taking quite
a chance when you tackled Philip like that? I mean,
I've always heard that a tight Indian is just about the most
dangerous creature on earth ; and to take his liquor away
from him like that must have been pretty risky."

" Taking liquor away from Indians? No, it isn't commonly done. In fact, that's the only time I think I ever
saw it done."

The Atkinson affair having been tided over, Woods
returned to the Fort and fired a gun, and at the signal all
the boats shoved out into the river together with a tremendous confusion of shouts and whooping, and a fusillade
of shots. They swirled along with the current, and though
there were no rapids in the first part of the journey, navigation was made difficult by the great cakes of ice and roots
and trunks of trees that were being brought down by the
spring freshet. The banks were of clay and sand, or sometimes tar-sand, without rocks or boulders, and the flood
water as it ate into them brought down solid sections of the
low cliffs with the pines and poplars that were growing on
their crests. " The trees went down upright in their ranks,"
said Mitchell, " like soldiers standing at attention."

A current of this strength made it unnecessary to row
except in the rapids, so they kept four-hour watches through
the day and tied up to the bank at night to sleep. The days
were still short, so they had breakfast before starting in the
morning, and ran all day without making any stop at noon ;

but the stove was kept going all the time with a pot of hot beans on it, so that anyone could get his lunch when he happened to feel hungry. Mitchell was most particular about feeding well, or as well as their rations allowed. They took the cooking in weekly shifts, and the man who was cook for the time being cooked properly, even baking bread. An ordinary meal would be beans with pork or bacon, bannock or cabin biscuits, a jug of tea, and porridge in the morning. They took some eggs from the Landing, and as they met Indians from time to time they were able to buy fish, moose-meat, partridge, and ptarmigan, for which they paid with a few cupfuls of flour, or some bacon, or a little tea. The cold at night was intense, and there was constant heavy rain, or sometimes sleet or snow, so that they were nearly always wet. They had left their tents behind but had sleeping-bags of heavy brown canvas lined with duffle, and inside these again were blankets— the prospective sleeper rolled himself in the blankets and then got into the bag feet foremost, pulling the flap over his head. But as they were always wet themselves when they turned into their bags, the blankets and linings soon became permanently damp, and the bags had to be slit up to allow them to be dried.

In rapids everyone had to row all the time, as the boat must move faster than the current to keep steerage way. Mitchell was learning to steer, so Atkinson kept him up on the after deck, where he himself was managing the long steering sweep and shouting instructions in a mixture of French and Cree. When a boulder appeared ahead— they looked black and oily, like porpoises—Atkinson would steer straight towards it, and then, when the bow was nearly upon it, he would swing the sweep and the scow would pass safely to the side. To try to slip past a rock is a fatal mistake, as the boat is drawn towards it by suction and smashed ; but if the steersman goes straight at the rock and catches the division of the water upon it he is carried clear. All eddies and boilings are treated in this same way, as any disturbance of the water may mean a boulder that is barely submerged.

Atkinson was a splendid boatman and a tower of strength as well. Once the *Amisk* went on to a gravel bar and stuck fast ; the whole party went overboard and tried to hand her off, but she remained firmly set. Then Atkinson suddenly shouted " *gardez-vous* ", bent down under the stern and raised the whole after part of the boat on his shoulders. The current did the rest, and she nosed herself gently over the bar. Other parties, that had no guides, often asked for Atkinson to come and pilot them through difficult places, and Mitchell always let him go, both for the sake of neighbourliness and to give Atkinson the chance of earning five or ten dollars for himself. Many of the other parties had Indian helpers who were, or soon became, Atkinson's friends, and whenever boats tied up near one another in the evening the Indians and half-breeds used to spend most of the night at a gambling game to which they were madly devoted. The game is a glorified form of hunt-the-slipper, played with beavers' teeth that are passed from hand to hand under a blanket ; the object is to guess who has got the teeth, and a player who guesses wrong pays a forfeit. The stakes may be money, knives, clothes, wives, or anything that comes handy, and the game is accompanied by the thumping of drums or copper kettles, which keeps up the excitement of the players and makes the night impossible for everyone else who is within earshot. Atkinson was so good, or so lucky, at this game that Mitchell became quite embarrassed by the amount of gear that he brought back to the scow every morning ; and it was certain that he had all the cash as well. But a couple of nights before they reached Fort McMurray he came to Mitchell in despair —he had lost all his winnings, his twenty-five dollars of cash, the balance of his credit with Mr. Woods, and the very clothes that he had on ; and unless Mr. Mitchell would help him he would have to walk all the way home starving and a beggar. Mitchell grub-staked him twenty-five dollars to avert this dreadful calamity ; but before they finally parted his luck had turned, and he was happy and rich once more.

It was during the descent of the Athabasca river that Mitchell first saw a real northern trapper's hunting cabin. They had just suffered some accident, and on pulling into a convenient bay for repairs they came on the little log house standing just above the water. The strangers were surprised to see that its roof was decorated with the skulls of several bears, wolves, and beavers, one of the beaver skulls being ornamented with paint as a peace-offering to the spirit of the dead beaver. It seems that all the hunters in the North, both red and white, preserved the skulls of animals in this way as a tribute to their spirits : and it was usual for the Indians who had killed a bear to dance solemnly round the body and apologize to the bear for having taken its life. Mitchell quoted me the kind of ceremonial song that used to be sung by his own Indians up in the North, and it was something like this :

"We apologize for depriving you of your life—you who are the real owner of the forests and woods and rivers, which God gave you to be your own place to live in. We are compelled to take your spirit from you in order that we may live—for our own immediate food and also to take your skin to sell so that we may support our wives and children."

But honours of this kind were paid only to animals that were considered noble, while wolverines and coyotes, whose habits were all evil and destructive, were treated with ignominy and contempt, as being the spirits of degraded white men, or of the devil.

CHAPTER VII

GRAND RAPIDS

THE worst rapids on the Athabasca river are the so-called Grand Rapids, where the river falls sixty feet in about half a mile. The speed of the current increases very much just before the rapids begin, and it is advisable to go ashore after rounding the last bend above the rapids to study the state of the water and the position of any boats that there may be ahead. The rapids are divided into two channels by a small island that lies in the middle of the river : the left-hand channel is a raging torrent in which no boat can live, and the right-hand channel, though passable, is so rough that boats have to be unloaded and taken down empty.

The practice accordingly is to land at the upper end of the island and unload the cargo, and then convey it to the other end over a narrow-gauge tramway that the Hudson's Bay Company has built for the purpose. The cargo must then be piled at the lower end and a guard mounted over it to prevent other travellers from helping themselves. Then a long rope is attached to the end of the boat, and she is shoved out into the current and carefully roped down the rapid with nobody on board. She is thrown about like a cork and sometimes turns somersaults, but is unlikely to be lost out and out. Then she is swung inshore by the rope at the lower end of the island, the cargo is restowed, and the party proceeds as quickly as it possibly can. Mitchell remarked that no courtesies were wasted on that island.

There were no regular police north of the Landing in
1898, and so a special patrol had to be sent down ahead of
the flotilla to prevent the miners from taking liquor into
the North-West Territories. Sergeant Andersen, when he
returned from the arrest of the *wisteneau*, had passed the
Amisk in a fast canoe a few hours after she had started. As
each boat was unloaded at the upper point of the island
he examined her cargo and had all the liquor destroyed ;
Mitchell had to empty a keg of whisky overboard, but the
sergeant, knowing that his was a reliable party and not
simply a gang of roughs, allowed him to keep some brandy
to use as medicine and one case of whisky to break their fall
into a drinkless state.

The constable having his hands full Andersen asked
Mitchell if he would come over and help him to go
through the cargo of a boat which was manned by Chicago
toughs.

" You may get hurt," he said ; " they're a dangerous
bunch."

" That's all right with me," said Mitchell.

" You understand that you're acting officially as my
deputy ? "

" Sure."

" Are you armed ? "

" Oh, God, yes," said Mitchell, remembering the affair
of the rebellious Italian navvies. " I've heard all this stuff
before. Let's go ! "

The Chicago men received them fairly affably—called
the sergeant " colonel " and asked them if they would
have a drink. Andersen refused pretty curtly, telling them
to " cut all that out " and to get the covers off the cargo
as he had come to inspect the boat for liquor. At that
they hemmed and hawed, protesting that they had just
packed up, and had got no liquor, in fact they had got
practically nothing of any kind. But Andersen wanted to
see their cargo none the less, and finally ordered Mitchell to

rip the covers off himself. At first he found only pork, beans, bacon and ordinary equipment, but down at the bottom there were four nice kegs of American rye.

"Mitchell, break up those kegs," said Andersen, so Mitchell took up an axe, stove in a keg, and spilled the rye. A howl went up from the owners, and he was immediately covered by six revolvers.

"Now then, boys, hands up—hands up, everybody," said the sergeant, waving his own revolver from side to side so as to cover everybody by turns. For a moment nobody moved, and then the toughs, gradually overawed by his uniform and his air of authority, began to put their hands up one by one. Then Mitchell stove in and split the rest of the kegs.

While they were on the island, waiting for their turn to use the tramway, Mitchell observed Jack beckoning to him and grinning as if he knew of a joke in preparation. Mitchell went over to him and Jack pointed to a dirty old half-breed, who was sitting on the ground near by, whittling at a stick.

"Who do you see there?" he asked.

Mitchell didn't hesitate a moment—it was the face of a greatly revered statesman of the last generation, that used to gleam in oleograph from the wall of every parlour in Ontario.

"Well," he replied, "it's Sir James B. Macalister. Who else?"

They approached the old fellow and tried to get into conversation. He was surly at first, and rebuffed their offer of tobacco ; but Mitchell had a master-key in the flask of brandy that the police had allowed him to keep for medicinal use. After they had warmed his heart with a *petit coup* they asked him his name.

"James B. Macalister," was the astonishing reply. Mitchell collected his wits first and tried to argue.

"But how can that be, when he never came west of

Winnipeg ? " The old man's answer was given with bitter
scorn.

" It's hard," he said, " to tell where an old crow flies."
Rough water extended for two or three miles below Grand
Rapids, but after this was passed they had twenty miles
of easy navigation. Then came Burnt Rapids, where the
stream opened out to a breadth of three hundred yards,
and became shallow and full of boulders. Atkinson, knowing the place well, kept the scow close to the western bank,
where the deepest channel lay. Below Burnt Rapids there
was again a reach of smooth water, followed by Boiler
Rapids, Drowned Rapids, Middle Rapids, and Long Rapids,
all in a stretch of less than ten miles. These were all
shallow and bouldery, and in Boiler Rapids the navigable
channel was very crooked, so that the scow required most
careful handling. Below these again came Crooked Rapids,
caused by a ledge of limestone that projected across the
stream from the eastern bank, and Stony Rapids, where
the water was shallow and ran over a bed of solid rock.

All these rapids were passed safely, thanks to Philip
Atkinson's excellent navigation, and nothing of interest
happened until they reached Cascade Rapids, the last of the
series. Cascade Rapids is quite different from the others
as the whole river drops bodily over a limestone step which
stretches right across in the shape of a horse-shoe. (The
river is getting on for two miles broad at this point.) The
height of the drop varies from six feet to twelve feet according
to the state of the water, and it is impossible to see the fall
as one comes down towards it ; but the Hudson's Bay
Company has put up conspicuous warning marks on the
right bank above the fall and has also fixed large iron rings
into the rock to which boats can be tied for the purpose of
unloading cargo. Boats have to be roped down the fall
empty and the cargo portaged and reloaded below the fall,
just as is done at Grand Rapids. When Mitchell went down
the drop at Cascade Rapids was about ten feet, but having

a good guide they navigated almost to the brink of the fall
and tied up to the lowest of the iron rings, and so were
able to reduce the length of their portage to a hundred yards.
" There were two jokes about Cascade Rapids," Mitchell
said. " Just after us there came a long, narrow, badly-
made scow—all Yankees on board, and their captain was a
know-it-all—and they concluded that they would run her
over fully loaded. I can see it as if it was to-day—the fore
part of the scow sticking out over the water ; then she broke
her back and the rear part came down on the top of the
fore part, and they lost nearly all the cargo and two men's
lives.

" But the best joke of all was this. About half a mile
above the main fall there is another rapid of the same sort
with a drop of only four or five feet. Two big Swede boys
were going down in a boat by themselves, and when they
came to the small fall they heard the noise of the water,
unloaded, portaged, and went ahead thinking that they were
O.K. Then they came to the real Cascade and were swept
clean over. They lost their boat and the whole of their
outfit, but by good luck and good swimming they managed
to reach a little rocky island ; but as this was right in
the middle of the white water nobody could reach them,
and it began to look as if they would starve or be drowned
after all.

" Then Jack proposed that he and I should go out to
them in a canoe with a long line, so that we could get let
down into easier water on the line after taking them on
board. The miners thought we were crazy, and said that
they wouldn't allow anyone to risk his life ; but Jack was
a good canoeman, and I was willing to try, so we made it
clear that we were going willy-nilly. But first of all we had
to get hold of a canoe, and as there was an American party
that had four we figured that we could borrow one of these.
But do you think they would lend ? Not on your life !
They guessed they were their canoes, and they'd paid

for them and they wanted them, ' and so, Mister, if you want a canoe, we guess you'll have to go somewhere else——' and all that sort of business, while the poor boys on the rock were going down on their knees and holding up their hands towards us, thinking that we were going to leave them out there. At last I offered to buy the God-damn canoe, but the miners were gathering round and beginning to be ugly, and the Yankees thought they were being intimidated and stiffened up still more, and there was no doing anything with them.

" At last the miners, who had been for stopping us by force half an hour before, just rushed the Yanks and took away one of their canoes at the point of the gun. They gave us a great send-off, offering us drinks of brandy and firing their guns into the air. We got out to the rock and made the Swedes lie down in the bottom of the canoe and threatened to kill them if they moved—the canoe could only just carry them, and they were nearly crazy with fright. Then the miners let us down on the line till we got into an eddy, and so we got back to the shore.

" After the miners had finished giving us a reception one of the Americans asked for the canoe back. This started a wild riot among the crowd, and the nearest man biffed the American in the face and told him that the canoe now belonged to me and Jack, a present from all the miners. They damn nearly took another one as well."

Below the foot of the rapids the Athabasca river changes very much for the better, as the fall from Fort McMurray to Lake Athabasca is only a hundred feet and this is spread over a hundred and fifty miles. The miners accordingly had no more white water to pass, as the current flowed evenly at a rate of three miles an hour ; their troubles arose rather from shallows and mud-banks, on which the *Amisk* was constantly running aground. There were also frequent storms with very heavy rain and sleet.

As they approached Lake Athabasca Mitchell found that

they were beginning to meet Indians of a different type from those that they had seen farther south. All the Indians in this part of the country are Crees of one sort or another, but the Athabasca bands no doubt led a much more varied life than the prairie Crees, with fishing, wild-fowling, moose-hunting on the lakes and rivers and caribou-hunting on the uplands, and this may have given them a larger outlook on the world. The party depended a good deal for fresh food on trade with the Indians whom they met along the river banks, as they had no time to spend on fishing for themselves except on Sundays—they always tied up for Sundays—and their hunting expeditions were never very fruitful. Occasionally they managed to stalk a bear that was feeding by the water's edge, but moose and caribou always got away unhurt.

But before it actually got out into Lake Athabasca the flotilla had another spell of difficult navigation, as the river has formed a delta at its mouth which is no better than a maze of small channels twisting about among flat sands. For the best part of a week the *Amisk* had to be rowed or poled along the muddy backwaters, running aground in shallows and fetching up miserably in *culs-de-sac*, and it was not until the first of June—a month from Athabasca Landing—that she reached the open lake.

It is a peculiarity of Lake Athabasca that it is both filled and emptied at its south-west end : only the extreme tip of the lake separates the mouth of the Athabasca, its principal affluent, from the intake of the Slave, while the main body of water stretches into the north-east for a hundred and fifty miles. Mitchell, of course, was concerned to enter the Slave, and Fort Chipewyan, which stands on the right bank of the Slave just at the intake, was his immediate objective. But although the length of the open-water crossing seems insignificant on a small map, when he entered the lake the opposite shore was not in sight and he accordingly had to set a course to west-north-west by compass. The result was fairly successful, as he arrived at a point only about ten miles to the east of the Fort.

However, by the time they reached the land night was already coming on, and he therefore decided to tie up where he was until the morning, although the shore was rocky and exposed. Several other boats had followed the *Amisk's* lead across the lake and had tied up near her, and at three o'clock in the morning Mitchell was suddenly aroused by shouting and uproar. An alarm had been raised that ice was coming down from Fond du Lac, and a wall of white did certainly appear through the darkness along the eastern horizon. The sea was high and rising, and the lee shore looked nastier every moment, so Mitchell upped anchor and ran for it, setting his crew to the sweeps to claw the scow off reefs and points. The white line proved to be a squall, and they scudded along before it shipping heavy seas and in great danger of swamping. They were short-handed as Jack, who had gone ashore in the evening to look for Fort Chipewyan from a hill-top, had not come back ; and to add to their difficulties one man lost his nerve at a critical moment, and refused to row until Mitchell clipped some slivers out of his oar with bullets. But they got into shelter at last and the storm died down at sunrise ; and then, rounding a last point, they raised the glorious sight of the shining white buildings of Fort Chipewyan.

CHAPTER VIII

THE SLAVE RIVER

MITCHELL'S first care on arriving at Fort Chipewyan was to organize a party to go in search of his lost man. There were a number of local Indians and half-breeds employed about the Fort, and he was just preparing to set out with them when Jack strolled calmly up the trail—he had been benighted on his reconnaissance and had realized that the boats had been forced out from the lee shore by the storm. So the *Amisk* pushed off without any further delay and began her journey down the Slave, towards Great Slave Lake.

The Slave river consists of two reaches of comparatively easy water divided by a stretch of most violent and dangerous rapids. The upper reach, between Fort Chipewyan and Fort Fitzgerald, is a hundred miles long, and in this distance the water drops forty-five feet. Between Fort Smith and Great Slave Lake, in the lower reach, the water again falls forty-five feet, this time in just over three hundred miles. But in the middle, between Fort Fitzgerald and Fort Smith, come the rapids, the drop being a hundred and twenty-five feet in only sixteen miles.

Mitchell had made careful enquiries about the rapids from the Hudson's Bay people, and had been told to keep a sharp look-out for the landing-place on the left bank, above Pelican Rapids, where he would have to discharge his cargo. From that point the cargo would go down to Fort Smith by road, while the scow could be run empty, with the help of a pilot, as far as the so-called Mountain Portage. There

she would have to be taken ashore herself and hauled overland round an impassable rapid ; the portage did not
really cross a mountain, but only climbed sharply up a
sandy hill and down a steep descent to quiet water on
the other side—a distance of about three hundred yards
in all.

The mark of the landing-place was a small two-storied
cabin that was not easy to see from the river, but they
managed to pick it out and ran the *Amisk* in towards it
through swift water. Mitchell went on with the story in
this way.

" No sooner had our nose touched the bank than we were
miraculously surrounded by a much excited bunch of Indians
and half-breeds, each one claiming to be the only man
who could contract with us to take the stuff over to Fort
Smith in Red River carts and to pilot the empty boat down
to the Mountain Portage, where we had to take her ashore.
The joke about these Indians was that a damn little villain
with a pilot's peaked cap and long greasy hair proved
beyond doubt that he was the only qualified man. He
wanted fifty dollars ; all right. But then he wanted his
brother-in-law for bowman, at ten dollars, and four of his
relatives as oarsmen at five dollars each. At that I got mad
and started in to talk to him, but all the other Indians
seemed to be on his side and it began to look like the makings
of a damn good fight when there quietly surged in a tall
sandy-haired Scot. The Indians evaporated at once, and
the new man asked us what the trouble was, and said that
' it was just like that rascal Beaulieu '. He produced a pilot
for us called Pierre Écureuil, who was really a buffalo-
hunter—there was a small herd of woodland buffalo still
existing somewhere west of Fort Smith, and they were the
only truly wild buffalo left in North America at that time.
Écureuil was quite content to take us down with our own
crew for twenty dollars, and he turned out to be a thorough
gentleman of an Indian. He was chief of his tribe, and was

tremendously proud of a large silver Queen Victoria's medal that had been given him as his insignia. (He showed it to me afterwards at Fort Smith.) The Hudson's Bay man also took charge of our cargo and gave me an itemized receipt for it, guaranteeing to deliver it at Fort Smith. There was no fuss or trouble about anything.

" Then we went down to the head of the Pelican Rapids. Now I'm sure you didn't know, my dear Angus, that there were such things as pelicans up there in the North ; but you're wrong, because they breed on an island in this rapid where no man nor animal can get at them. It was marvellous to see the great mass of white pelicans, rising and falling in their flight, as we came past. Écureuil told us about two traders who had been on their way down in a canoe some years before—one of them went on ahead along the shore to survey the rapids after arranging with his pal to fire two shots if the rapids were passable ; but he disturbed the pelicans, and as they rose he forgot his arrangement and fired, his pal heard the shots and immediately started, and was lost in the rapids. The man who fired the shots was never heard of again.

" We went down the rapids with Pierre Écureuil at the sweep and me beside him, and Smith on the front platform with a pole. As we were shooting one very narrow swift place I saw a horizontal tree hanging over the water and shouted to Smith to lie down. But instead of flopping down like a sensible man he turned round and asked ' Why ? ', and was immediately knocked overboard by the tree striking his back-side. (He was known ever afterwards as ' Why-Smith '.) But when he had been salved he claimed that he had lost a *valuable heirloom* of an old silver watch that can't have been worth more than two dollars and a half : but he made such a howl about it later among the camps that a deputation came to me representing that we should replace the loss. The miners had held a meeting and had assessed the value of the watch at twenty-five dollars, so it came out pretty expensive by the time he was pacified. But it was better to pay than to appear to use men badly."

They pulled into a bay at the foot of the portage in the evening, and began to prepare for hauling the scow up the ascent. Their block and tackle looked rather weak for the job, but there was a smart young French half-breed hanging about who said (untruly) that he was brother-in-law to the factor at the Fort and assured Mitchell that he could get them the use of heavier tackle. He offered to take Mitchell up to the Fort to make the arrangements, and they started off, the half-breed setting the pace at a slow trot. Presently the trot got faster, and a little while later he began to run ; and when they got near the Fort he broke into a sprint and dashed up to the gate as fast as he could. But Mitchell had tumbled to the half-breed's idea, which was to get into the Fort first and then brag that he had beaten the white man, and so he had kept pace with him all the way and managed to beat him on the sprint at the last moment.

Fort Smith was a substantial log post, with a big parade-ground in front of the main building, log cabins for visitors and bettermost Indians, and space for a large number of teepees. As Mitchell came in at the gate he was amazed to see a squaw, wearing pink silk corsets outside her other clothes and a pair of high-heeled shoes, strolling about the parade-ground. It appeared that she lived in one of the huts, and was a more or less acknowledged institution— the priest said that she always showed her mettle in this way when strangers arrived. Mitchell was kindly received by the Company's people, and secured the loan of a heavy block and tackle for the next day. He spent the night in one of the cabins after having successfully resisted a warm invitation (not from the pink corsets) to spend it elsewhere.

Early the next morning Mitchell started back towards the landing-place, shepherding six Indian boys who carried the block and tackle. As he ran down towards the foot of the portage he saw that a regular ring had been formed for a fight, and on pushing his way into the crowd was alarmed to find Jack stripped to the waist and preparing to take on an immense Swede from one of the other boats. Jack was a good boxer and in splendid condition, but Mitchell saw at once that he would be eaten up, as the other man was six-foot-two, had hands like hams, and might have weighed sixteen stone. His long drooping moustaches and golden beard that shone in the sunshine made him a perfect type of the traditional Viking raider.

So Mitchell jumped into the ring and asked what the trouble was. The Swede answered quietly and firmly that Jack had got the *Amisk* ready to be hauled up the portage, whereas it was his own boat that had the right of way and should go first—Jack would not admit this and so they were going to fight it out. But Mitchell most fortunately happened to remember that just before he had started for the Fort the previous evening the Swede's boat had come up to the landing, and that they had thrown him their painter and snubbed his boat up behind the *Amisk*. The Swede, when he was reminded of this, quite willingly acknowledged that he had made a mistake and shook hands on it with Jack. So the fight was off, by rather a narrow margin.

" But the Swede had a Chicago rat in his crew," Mitchell continued, " the meanest son of a B. that ever was seen— narrow face, squinty eyes, two long exposed yellow teeth, and signs of sin and corruption all over him. This bastard stood well behind the Swede and called me all the names in the calendar. I asked him to get out into the middle and fight : he didn't want to a bit, but the crowd were hot and wanted a fight, so they stripped us both and we went to it.

" The fight went on so long that I really can't describe it, but I know I had a whisper from one of my own side to watch for kicking, biting, and eye-gouging, so I did a lot of foot-work and kept away while he was all for a clinch. The last thing I know was that my two partners were holding me and saying that the fight had been over for ten minutes, but the other man was dead to the world. I had one eye closed and one lip split, an ear bitten, and my chest scratched all over as if I had been in a fight with a cat or something. After I had washed down and recovered a bit the whole gang carried me round cheering, including the other man's own party. I guess he wasn't popular anywhere, and it was a public benefit to put him out of action for a bit. But neither Jack nor anyone else on the river would have had any chance at all against that Swede."

After that interlude they hauled the scow over the portage and got her down safely to Fort Smith, where they tied her up to wait for the arrival of the cargo.

" Now, Graham, you mustn't run away with the idea that life on the river was all a sort of long happy adventure. I had one very unpleasant experience at Fort Smith, which I must tell you about next.

" I was walking back over the portage to look for the carts that were bringing up our goods when I met an old man who looked like a professor. (Are you a Mason? No : you're not.) Well, as he passed me he gave the masonic signal of great distress ; I answered, and he said he was in great distress and danger, so we slipped into the bush for an explanation. It seemed that he had grub-staked a party and they were all blackguards. They used to beat him and ill-treat him in every way, domineering over him and giving him no food—and now he was afraid that they would shoot him. He was a tall, grey-haired and rather frail man with blue eyes—an American, but a gentlemanly American, a very English American, like a professor. I offered him the protection of our party, took him down to Fort Smith, and called a miners' meeting and put it to the crowd to call out the members of his two boats' crews. The men of course began ' what the Hell ' (this and that) and I accused them squarely of ill-treating the old gentleman, demanded the miners' protection for him, and suggested that he should take his share and separate from his party.

But it turned out that he had provided everything for the whole outfit, in fact it was just another case like that of the poor girl at Athabasca Landing. So the miners arranged that he should pick four volunteers and take one of his boats and whatever supplies he wanted, and this was done and everything ended well. There was never any lack of volunteers, because by no means all the boats were happy and many of the parties were fighting among themselves."

CHAPTER IX

GREAT SLAVE LAKE

AFTER he left Fort Smith Mitchell appears to have been free from " happy adventures " for some little time. The voyage down the lower part of the Slave, to Great Slave Lake, was achieved without serious incident ; though Jack shot a wolf at Salt river which turned out to be a miserable Indian dog, and it was necessary to hold a dark and hasty funeral before the owner should arrive to claim five hundred dollars damages. The stream meanders slowly through flat alluvial country, in some places making detours of ten or fifteen miles between points that may be half a mile apart or less.

The weather was now improving, as June was well begun, though the ice had not long gone out and the ground was still frozen at a few inches depth. Warm days and sunshine made life in the boats much easier, but brought the new and frightful scourge of mosquitoes. It seems to be a law of nature that the farther one goes towards the north the more numerous and more virulent are the mosquitoes that one encounters. Nothing that has yet been printed does justice to the northern mosquitoes, and the subject is one at which the mind boggles and the nib runs into the paper. But something of their quality may be suggested by the simile of a pyramid that stands upon its point. At the point is the single mosquito that zings round a bedroom in the South of France—and the occupant says next morning that she could not sleep until they had killed that creature. Next comes, perhaps, a picnic among the Fens, at which the children are bitten and their parent makes her displeasure known. A zone of more serious trouble begins, for an approximate guess, on the upper Penobscot, where rich men find that it is really impossible to fish unless they have special gnat-proof gloves and nets fastened over their hats. Norway and Newfoundland are worse again, and it is generally from this part of the pyramid that the hair-raising stories and letters to *The Times* originate. But beyond the places which travellers pay to visit there are the North Woods proper, into which we are paid to go ; and here I have known a man walk eighty miles to ask the priest to say special prayers against the mosquitoes. Beyond all others, at the pyramid's towering base, come the mosquitoes of the Barren Lands of which Mitchell could only say " the horror of it, Graham ! Put that in the book and tell them —— the horror of the mosquitoes ! "

Actually Mitchell and his partners suffered a good deal less from the mosquitoes than the rest of the miners on the river, as he had foreseen this trouble and brought a good stock of cheese-cloth with his stores from Edmonton. Each man made himself a kind of enclosure like a gardener's " cold frame ", with boards on edge for the sides and a cheese-cloth top, and slept in peace while the rest of the miners stifled with blankets over their heads or stamped about raving in the darkness.

The passage out of the Slave river into Great Slave Lake was difficult, as the river has formed a delta and there were the usual muddy channels and accumulations of driftwood to be negotiated. In some places the mud had been laid down several feet deep on the top of old beds of driftwood. After taking many wrong courses and wandering up a lagoon that led into a lake, the *Amisk* finally reached the mouth of the river in the middle of a howling storm. Great Slave Lake is more than two hundred and fifty miles long and has an arm a hundred miles long running out of its centre at right angles ; consequently there is nearly as much water in it as there is land in Scotland. The course from the mouth of the Slave to the intake of the Mackenzie lay right across the middle of the broadest part, well out of sight of land ; and as the distance was about a hundred miles the boats could not well leave shelter until the weather improved. Mitchell had brought a fishing-net, and spent his time catching whitefish, and the land-locked salmon that is called *inconnu* in the North.

Since his exploits in the Rapids and at Fort Smith Mitchell had begun to be something of a marked man. It was known, too, that he planned to go up the Peel, and a rumour had got about that he had some very special information from the Government about rich deposits of gold to be found in that region. So for one reason and another it had become the habit of a number of other parties to follow the *Amisk's* lead rather closely, and Mitchell consequently picked up a great many friends among the miners in general.

It was during the wait at the mouth of the Slave that he first met McQuaide, to whom he became particularly attached. McQuaide was much the most experienced of all the miners who went up the Peel, and he was also a constant help and support to Mitchell later on, when scurvy and other troubles came upon them during the winter night. His career had been exceedingly chequered. He had run away from his home, a manse in the north of Scotland, at a very early age, and gone out to the American prairies. At eighteen he was serving in the American army and took part in a battle with the Indians in which he had been almost the only white survivor. McQuaide was very badly wounded, but saved himself by shamming dead while the Indians scalped the corpses which lay on and around him ; he supposed that the Indians were so drunk with bloodshed that they simply missed him over, and could not account for his own survival in any other way. His body was covered with scars from the Indian wars, and he had one bullet in his chest, another under his collar-bone, and a flint arrow-head in his shoulder. The arrow-head could easily have been taken out, as it was only just under the skin, but he preferred to keep it, saying that it was his mascot. When Mitchell knew him he was a man of sixty, slightly stooped by the stress of life, with a long narrow face, thick grey hair, and steady intelligent eyes. Like all real miners he dressed in the most ordinary way possible, and without the slightest suggestion of the traditional Wild West.

Mitchell's comments on the history of this man McQuaide and of two other professional miners, the Geck brothers, who were also his friends, threw a brilliant light on life as it had been lived in the older West.

" McQuaide once cleaned up a hundred thousand dollars in a year, and he spent those hundred thousand dollars in two weeks. He went down into a town in Oregon and bought the theatre and two hotels, and chartered every horse and rig in town ; and for that time everybody was drinking and riding round and enjoying himself—all on McQuaide. And the Gecks did very much the same thing in Idaho. On two or three occasions they would buy a town, stay as long as the money lasted, and then clear out. I don't know of any honest-to-God prospector, no matter how much money he made, who died in civilization. There were some mean narrow scutts who retired and built churches and hospitals, and their souls are to-day rotting in Hell. The whole idea of free-gold mining is to make it quick and spend it quick, and then go back to the old game."

The most improbable of all Mitchell's northern friends was an English girl, whom he calls " Miss Bellows " for purposes of narrative. There was no explanation for Miss Bellows, but she was evidently in exactly her right place on a gold-rush. Mitchell described her as a great strapping creature, six feet high and built like a man, but with a fresh English complexion and always cheerful and smiling. She could pull a sweep or do any heavy work as well as a man, and everybody adored her. " And if any man tried to make advances to her," said Mitchell, " she laid him out cold. Oh yes ; often did it."

" I never could make out how Miss Bellows came to be where she was, and of course on the river one never made any enquiries about a person's history or private affairs. She used to speak about her home in England, and riding across country and shooting with her brothers : I think there are some virile women in the same way as there are some effeminate men, and that she was one who couldn't stand for a woman's life at all and just had to be doing men's work. It was an odd thing too how that girl seemed to disappear. I don't know if she was drowned in the great storm which struck us later on, or was lost somewhere on shore, but we never saw her again after we passed Fort Norman, and I never could hear what happened to her at all."

On the third day of their detention at the mouth of the Slave it occurred to Mitchell that the Hudson's Bay Company's steamer, which had passed them on her way downstream from Fort Smith, was probably still at Fort Resolution, and that the captain might be induced to give the boats a tow across the lake when he sailed. The distance to Fort Resolution was only about eight miles, so he set out on foot along the shore ; but all of a sudden he found his way cut off by a wide still lagoon, that was far too deep to wade and showed no signs of shoaling in either direction. Mitchell was consequently reduced to swimming across, and for his clothes and gun he made a little raft of driftwood, which he towed behind him by his teeth. By this means he succeeded in reaching the Fort, where he found the steamer almost ready to sail. The captain, being already behind his time, was impatient to get on, and he began by saying roundly that he'd be God-damned if he'd wait for anybody. But Mitchell was persuasive, and arranged to send off two swift canoes immediately to bring on the boats ; and at this the captain finally agreed to put off sailing until early the next day. To make the tow easy the captain had the thirty or forty boats of the flotilla attached with bridles to a long hawser, one behind the other, and gave strict orders that boats which got into trouble were to cut themselves loose immediately. In this way they made a safe and easy run, calling at Hay River Mission and then on towards the intake of the Mackenzie. They were quite out of sight of land for a day and a half.

But towards the end of the second day in tow things livened up with a rush. They were passing between Big Island and the southern shore of the discharge, but the channel was so broad that nobody realized how soon they would be in the Mackenzie. Then suddenly they felt the current, and felt it strong. The captain, who had their money safely in his pocket and was taking no risks with his steamer, immediately cut loose the tow, and everyone was left to fend for himself with the boats still attached to the hawser and the current becoming swifter every moment. They were right in the rapids before they knew it, and Mitchell can give no coherent account of how they ever got down. He only says of rapids in general, that " if you're a boatman you're a boatman, but if you're not you're drowned ".

CHAPTER X

FORT SIMPSON

GREAT SLAVE LAKE discharges itself by two channels, one passing to the south and the other to the north of Big Island. Below the island the Mackenzie river proper, formed of the united channels, is ten miles broad and has an easy current ; but it narrows steadily in the succeeding twenty miles until, at Fort Providence, it is not more than half a mile across and the current again runs strongly. Mitchell put in at Fort Providence to enquire about the navigation of the river, but left again when he had obtained his information. He planned to give his party a rest when they reached Fort Simpson, a hundred and fifty miles down-stream.

They left Fort Providence with a good east wind astern and, keeping to the northern bank, ran down with a brisk current until the Mackenzie widened out to form Mills Lake. There they had a tiresome spell at the sweeps in the dead water, but after they had passed the lake they had a swift current again which held all the way down to Fort Simpson. It was by this time the middle of June, and in that high latitude—Fort Providence is well to the north of the sixty-first parallel—the sun was above the horizon for nineteen hours out of the twenty-four. Mitchell had adapted his routine to the lengthening daylight by starting early and camping late, and tying up at midday for a rest and a meal on shore. But as the river grew wider and the nights became shorter and finally gave way to the midnight sun, they abandoned the shore altogether and worked and slept in shifts, doing all their cooking on board. The Hudson's Bay people taught them to make a kind of sea anchor out of two tin pails lowered into the water over the bows—as the scow drifted with the stream the pails held the current and kept her in deep water, so that all hands could sleep at once without danger of running aground.

Towards the evening of the third day out from Fort Providence they swung round a bend and saw the wide mouth of the Liard breaking the western bank. Fort Simpson stood on an island beyond the opening, at the angle formed by the banks of the two rivers at their junction. Mitchell noticed with surprise, as they crossed over to the landing, that the water of the Liard, which was muddy and discoloured, swept down the left bank of the main waterway below the confluence as a separate stream, and did not mingle with the clearer water of the Mackenzie proper until the river banks drew in to a narrow passage some miles below.

Fort Simpson was the most important of the Hudson's Bay Company's posts in the Mackenzie basin. It was a strong and well-fortified place, as there were no police in the North-West in those days and the owners of valuable property took no chances of being raided by thieves. When Mitchell climbed the steps cut in the clay cliff above the landing he found before him a massive palisade enclosing the Fort buildings and parade-ground. The wall was built of stout spruce logs fifteen feet high and a foot in diameter, with their tops sharpened to points ; all round the inside ran a firing-platform, with loopholes for musketry defence, while at the corners there were bastions, mounting guns, with magazines on ground level underneath. The gate was very heavy and strong, being made of round timbers reinforced with stout beams on the inner side.

In the centre of the parade-ground, directly in face of the gate, stood an enormous flagstaff with four guns disposed about its base. As in all the Company's establishments, it flew the Union Jack and the Company's own flag—red, with the initials " H.B.C. " in white. There is a well-known story about this flag, how that an American, nettled by such a reminder that the wilderness was British, enquired what " H.B.C. " meant, anyway. They answered him, " Here before Christ."

The buildings of the Fort lay on three sides of the enclosure, fronting on the parade-ground. On the right were Chief Factor Camsell's house and quarters for the Company's officers, who formed a kind of general staff and were available to replace casualties at outlying posts. This main block of buildings was flanked on each side by a garden, with the Indian trading-room and the fur-store lying beyond and an ice-house in rear. Beside the fur-store Mitchell found an old-fashioned wooden press, that was used for reducing the fur-bales to a convenient size for transport. It was a heavy lumbering thing and was worked with a roller and levers like the Inquisitors' rack—a long beam was laid across the top of the fur-bale, and as the roller turned the beam was drawn downwards by ropes, so that the bale was pressed tightly together. Each bale weighed ninety pounds, and two of them were considered to make a fair load for a man on a portage.

On the left of the parade-ground, facing the dwelling-house, were an equipment shop, a warehouse and a provision store, while the third side of the enclosure was taken up with the factor's office, a depôt, the petty officers' quarters, a carpenter's shop, and cabins for the Company's Indian servants and Indian guests. (Ordinary passing Indians were made to camp outside the enclosure, but famous hunters and fur-takers were entertained inside the Fort as a special mark of honour.) The powder magazine lay at a safe distance behind. In front of the factor's office was a sundial with a leaden face that had been made out of the lead-foil lining of old tea-chests. Sundials, like Union Jacks, were part of the regular equipment of the Company's posts, and the correct setting for the dial at each post had been carefully worked out by a skilled person at the head office. The enclosure itself was flanked to north and south by a cultivated field, beyond which again lay on the one side the Anglican church, cemetery, and mission house, and on the other a byre for the milch-cows, bull and working oxen and an enclo-

OLD-FASHIONED FUR PRESS.

sure for calves. The Roman Catholic church and mission-ary's house stood by the bank of the river to the south of the palisade.

Mitchell was made free of the officers' mess and was astonished to find how successfully a high latitude could be kept from interfering with domestic life. The chief factor's house was English down to the copper heaters under the breakfast bacon and eggs ; the wine was French, and very sound indeed ; and the officers' quarters were comfortable and pleasantly furnished—they included a large library and even a billiard-room. As it had always been the Company's practice to send out current authors in their first editions for factors' winter reading, one may suppose that at the end of a hundred years or more the Fort libraries must have merited the attention of a serious book-thief. One of them may even have preserved, in manuscript, a record of the remarks made by the boatmen and portageurs who worked the billiard-table over from Hudson Bay. The whole place was in fact a monument to what is called the " adaptability " of the Englishman abroad—the faculty of faking the externals of his old life so skilfully that the need for any personal adaptation may be comfortably ignored.

The gardens and farm gave Mitchell a further surprise. The two plots by the factor's house were already full of early flowers, and there was a fine kitchen-garden too, outside the enclosure, where all the ordinary vegetables were beginning to come up as serenely as if they had been in southern Ontario. It seems, in fact, that the long daylight of the northern summer allows the plants to work, as it were, double tides, so that they may finish their growth before they are caught by the early autumn frosts. A cabbage, for instance, that is set out on the twentieth of May in the Province of Quebec may be expected to mature by about the fifth of August : in the southernmost part of the Province, on latitude forty-five, the sun would be up for twelve hundred hours during the time between those two dates— that is to say, it would be " up " in the Nautical Almanac, although not necessarily shining. The Nautical Almanac stops short at latitude sixty, while Fort Simpson lies still farther north on sixty-two, but it shows that on the sixtieth parallel, say at Fort Smith, a cabbage that is set out as late as the fifteenth of June would obtain the same twelve hundred hours of theoretical sunlight by the twenty-first of August. And in the Arctic Circle itself two months of the midnight sun would give more than fourteen hundred hours of continuous daylight.

Living as they did in the wilds, the Hudson's Bay people could naturally do themselves well in the matter of game and fish, and wherever Mitchell went he found fine fresh whitefish on the table, and *inconnu*, and wild-fowl of the spring migration. Whitefish was one of the staple foods in the North, and vast quantities of it were caught in Great Slave Lake and dried at Fort Resolution to supply to the other posts. Chipewyan in the same way supplied the bulk of the caribou and moose meat, and the dried breasts of geese and swans which Mitchell had seen stacked up in thousands in the store-sheds. Starvation and avoidable rigours were quite foreign to the chief factor's scheme of existence.

The chief factor himself was a great power in the far North-West. He was a small man with a tremendous presence—delicate features, grey hair, a drooping moustache, and penetrating eyes. He wore a monocle without a string. Personal authority and the Company's long-standing prestige were a factor's only support in dealing with the Indians when the Civil Power was a thousand miles away in the South ; but it was essential for the purposes of the fur-trade—apart from any question of public order—that the Indians should be peaceful and contented, and should not be distracted from their hunting by wars and turmoil. The Company had always left the Indians pretty much to themselves, allowing them to live their own lives as Indians and, in particular, to keep their religion ; it had only interfered in wars and major villainies, such as the massacre of successful hunting parties and the theft of their furs. Mitchell, who knows the story from the Indians' side, believes that things went well under the Company's régime, and that subject to certain allowances for primitive ways the Indians of the West and North were honest and self-respecting men until civilization spread over the Prairies and swallowed them.

Camsell, at any rate, managed his Indians by the Company's traditional method with complete success. The Indians respected and loved him, appreciating his cool dry manner—by which Americans, on the other hand, were sometimes roused to fury. In times of trouble he would walk into an Indian council, say that he had heard that " his children " were sick in their minds, and invite them to tell him what was wrong. If anyone tried to be rude Camsell would make a sign to his own followers and a couple of them would shoulder the offender out ; after that the rest of the council would probably be very affable, Camsell would forgive the insult, and the rude person would be allowed to come in again. Then, after hours of talk and a great deal of tobacco and tea, the trouble would gradually be smoothed away. And if " bad Indians " committed any outrageous crime Camsell was perfectly fearless in taking more drastic measures.

CHAPTER XI

THE MACKENZIE RIVER

THE *Amisk* seemed the least bit cramped and a thought squalid when they returned to her after their two days of holiday among the amenities of Fort Simpson. The weather had turned very hot, the sweeps seemed extraordinarily heavy, and the mosquitoes were appallingly bad. Nevertheless, the current was greatly in their favour, especially in the hundred miles below Fort Wrigley, where the channel was narrowed to about half a mile by high hills that stretched along either bank. Below this reach the river again became broad and some islands appeared in the channel, but the current kept up a speed of at least four miles an hour and, with the daylight continually lengthening, the *Amisk* was able to make Fort Norman in just five days. She arrived on the twenty-fifth of June.

It was on one of these days, when they were near the inflow of the Nahanni river, that they first got a sight of high snow-covered mountains on the western horizon. Not far from Fort Norman they passed a great column of smoke rising from the eastern bank : they wondered if it could possibly be a volcano, as there seemed to be no forest in the neighbourhood that could support a fire of such a size, but when they reached Fort Norman they were told that it was a seam of coal burning in the ground. This seam must have been burning for more than a hundred years, as Mackenzie noted the same smoke when he made his first voyage of discovery in 1789 ; actually there is a good deal of lignite coal here and there in the North-

West, and later on Mitchell found outcrops burning in more than one place in the valley of the Peel.

Fort Norman stands in the southern angle of the Mackenzie and Great Bear rivers, at their confluence, with a big flat-topped mountain rising sheer up from the water's edge in front of it, across the Great Bear. The clerk in charge was " young " Gaudet,[1] son of " old " Gaudet, who was chief trader at Fort Good Hope, and he welcomed Mitchell as an old friend, as he had met him on board the steamer which towed the *Amisk* and the rest of the miners' flotilla across Great Slave Lake. He also urged him to stay a few days at Fort Norman, pointing out that the ice from Great Bear Lake had not yet come down into the Mackenzie and that the local Indians expected it from hour to hour. It would obviously have been fatal for a small boat to become involved in the outrush of the ice from the mouth of the Great Bear river, so Mitchell accepted the invitation and agreed to wait for the break-up.

Mitchell had only one adventure, a mild one but odd in its way, while he was staying at Fort Norman. He related it as follows.

" Gaudet was showing me round his establishment one day and took me to see his store of winter firewood, which was piled near the visitors' quarters. He was very proud of the way in which the wood had been split and stacked, and you may imagine that a year's supply for the Fort was no mean quantity. As we were walking along the stack I was suddenly surprised by seeing a girl dash round the corner of one of the visitors' cabins and scuttle away behind the wood-pile. It was the same little American kid that we had rescued at Athabasca Landing when her gang were beating her up : she looked scared out of her wits, and I tell you she was in a hurry ! And then after her

---

[1] Among French-Canadians the final " t " of such names as Gaudet, Bourget, Fiset, or Turcot is pronounced as if the spelling were " Gaudette ", etc.

came the big English girl Miss Bellows, with her face all
flushed purple and looking like thunder. She couldn't turn
corners as quick as the kid, and dodging round the cabin
and the cord-wood made her madder than ever. I don't
know what the trouble was, but as she went past I heard
her say, ' I wish you would stop still long enough to let
me kick your bottom ! ' "

After two days Mitchell got tired of waiting for the ice
and took his chance. The ice did not actually come out
until some days later, when they were well away down-
stream ; they saw it floating past them broken up into
small floes that could do no harm. They did encounter
the gravest danger, however, in the course of this run from
Fort Norman to Fort Good Hope, as they were struck by
a most terrible storm, which was remembered long afterwards as the principal event of that year. Mitchell's own
account is better than any paraphrase.

" On the afternoon of the day we left Fort Norman we
were keeping along the right bank, using the sweeps—and
sweating at it. The air was pestilent : there were waves
of heat beating over the water, and then suddenly a cold
current, and a peculiar dead feeling all over everything.
There were also certain strange murmurings up in the
trees. It was clear that there was a Hell of a storm brewing
up—in fact, it was a day when you might expect a damn
good earthquake.

" I told the gang that we were in for a storm, but they
said I had the belly-ache. However, towards the evening
I saw the mouth of a creek about fifty yards ahead, and
told the boys ' pull port, back starboard ' to swing her in.
Whether through stubbornness or through lack of energy,
due to the heat, I don't know, but they missed the creek
by ten yards and I swung her nose into the bank and told
them to row back the ten yards up-stream. And then
occurred the only mutiny of the whole trip—they said they
would see me in Hell before they'd row another bloody

stroke. I saw there was trouble coming, so I told them flat and then that if they wouldn't row I'd resign the captaincy and leave the boat at Fort Good Hope, taking out my share. Then they decided to row, but it was one Hell of a pull against the sweeping current and we took more than half an hour to make the ten yards back to the mouth of the creek.

" When we got inside we held on up the creek for a quarter of a mile, and camped on shore. I can tell you that was a very unpleasant night—the man who was cooking left no plate or cup for me, nobody spoke to me or looked my way, and there was very little talk, and what there was was lurid, as everybody was on edge. Then about midnight the storm broke. Spruces and pines waved in the wind like grass, the thunder and lightning were appalling, and the rain came down in a deluge. The boys had enough sense left to jump to it and cover up our goods, and after that there was nothing to be done but sit still and wait for it to pass. We were stormbound by that creek for three days.

" One fellow thought he'd go for a hunting-trip while we were waiting and came back with a bear-cub under each arm. But when he was two hundred yards from the boat he dropped the cubs and ran—he found that old Mrs. Bear was right on his heels. But she changed her mind and ended by spanking the cubs before she removed them. Even that didn't cheer the gang up.

" When I thought the storm was over I gave the word to push her off, which was carried out very nastily. But when we got back into the main river we found that half a mile of bank just wasn't there—it had been washed clean out, five hundred feet back into the land. The boys looked at it, and then they pulled in the sweeps and each and every one never said a damn word but came aft to where I was steering and shook hands. Craigie said afterwards, ' I always thought you were fey, and now I know you must be.' "

The rainfall had been so heavy that the Mackenzie, although it is three or four miles broad in that part, had risen five feet, and the scow had great difficulty in avoiding the washed-out trees and debris of all sorts that was floating down. The Sans Sault Rapid, however, when they reached it, was all the easier to negotiate on account of the high water. Before reaching Fort Good Hope they passed the Ramparts, where the river narrows to about three hundred yards, and flows for several miles between sheer limestone cliffs. The air was thick with swallows, which were nesting in the precipices.

Two miles below the Ramparts there is a wide bay on the eastern bank, and the buildings of Fort Good Hope spread out along the bay without any surrounding fortifications. The *Amisk* arrived in a deluge of warm rain, with the mosquitoes raging, and Mitchell jumped ashore intent on rigging his mosquito-proof frame. While he was thus engaged he heard an educated voice enquiring, in rather carefully precise English, whether Mr. George Mitchell had arrived. It was the chief trader, " old " Gaudet, who had just got a letter from Winnipeg commending Mitchell to his hospitality ; he had come down to meet the boat and invite the three principals of the party to dinner.

Old Mr. Gaudet made a very remarkable figure, especially on the border of the Arctic Circle. He was a French-Canadian of the finest and oldest type ; tall, of an extremely distinguished appearance, and dressed in what had been the height of the Montreal fashion in 1850. His coat was of fine black broadcloth, paling a little towards green—full-skirted, high in the collar, and sloping about the shoulders. His neck was set fast in a high white stock reinforced with a black cravat ; his very tall hat was made of beaver ; and his trousers were strapped under his boots. He carried a green umbrella that was wide enough to shelter three men. He had served the Hudson's Bay Company at one or another of the far northern posts for forty-seven years, and, in accordance with the French-Canadian tradition, had raised a family of thirteen sons and daughters. The Gaudets were indeed a quiverful of arrows in the hands of the Company, as all the seven sons were being raised to its service and three of them were already in responsible positions at the time of Mitchell's visit.

The old man was credited with at least one feat of extraordinary strength and courage. He had gone out to get firewood with a sleigh and a team of five very heavy massive dogs, cross-bred between mastiffs and great Danes. He was chopping at a little distance from the team when he heard the noise of a terrific dog-fight, and dashing back to the trail he found such a tumbling confusion of snarling snapping dogs that at first he could hardly make out what was going on. Then he suddenly realized that in the middle of the turmoil there were two huge wolves—each of them had got one dog down, and the other three dogs were trying to get home on the wolves. Gaudet was so tall and strong that he could reach out over the scuffle and fight downwards into it, swinging his axe at the wolves and keeping the edge turned from the dogs as they whirled about. He killed the wolves and saved two of his team, but it was only done at the direst risk to himself; for dogs, when they are fighting, do not distinguish persons, and if he had slipped and fallen dogs or wolves indifferently would have torn him to pieces.

Fort Good Hope was a much less ambitious place than Fort Simpson. It consisted simply of the chief trader's dwelling-house, withdrawn a little from the river-bank, a store and trading-shop by the landing, some cabins for Indian servants, a church, and two plots of cultivated ground. But Mitchell was astounded to find how Gaudet, in spite of a lifetime of exile, had managed to put the stamp of French Canada on every part of the settlement. Just as Camsell at Fort Simpson had made himself something like an English country house, so Gaudet had turned Fort Good

Hope into an old-fashioned *manoir*—as it might have been on the shores of Lac St. Pierre. His house was low and wide, with a bell-cast roof hanging over a roomy veranda. The furniture was fine old heavy stuff, made in Quebec in days before the tradition of French craftsmanship had quite died out. The dinner, which was served with great ceremony, carried out the same idea ; there was *soupe aux pois, perdrix aux choux,* and *graisse de rôt* on the side. All round the house were flower-beds in a blaze of bloom, and at the back a large garden of flourishing vegetables. (The celery of Fort Good Hope is said to be the best in the world.)

But it was the church which struck Mitchell as being especially typical of a French-Canadian settlement. Where the Englishman had thought of cellar, library, and billiard-room the *Canadien* had built himself a church—very much in the spirit of the seventeenth-century pioneers. The whole of the building had been done by the Fort's own personnel, and everything that the church contained had been made by hand on the spot except the windows, the bells, the pictures, and the altar furnishings and communion plate. Even the timbers were spiked together with home-made wooden pins. Mitchell's respect for the people of Fort Good Hope increased with every hour of his stay, and he sailed for Fort McPherson on the third day with very great regret.

CHAPTER XII

FORT McPHERSON

AFTER his account of Fort Good Hope there is a gap in Mitchell's narrative. He has nothing to tell of the last lap down the Mackenzie to the head of the Delta, nor of the passage through the channels into the Peel. Probably nothing happened, and the Delta is best forgotten as it seems to have been a dreary place of mud-banks and depressing flat islands, with stunted spruce trees growing on soil that still showed solid ice wherever the outer face of a bank had been freshly washed away. When he begins to speak again it is in bitter and forcible words, for his subject is the " tracking " of the *Amisk* up-stream against the current of the Peel. So far, of course, their progress had been down-stream, but with their entry into the Peel they began the second part of their journey, and the rest of their navigation was all against the stream until the day when fresh ice drove them into winter quarters. Tracking was constantly required, as the currents of the Peel and the Wind rivers were often too violent for rowing or poling, so that it became a kind of background to their lives.

Tracking is simply towing in its crudest form. Towing, as one sees it in England, is done by a horse, and the very word suggests a well-kept towpath, where soldiers and nursemaids walk out on summer evenings, while the waterway is a calm and orderly canal obstructed by nothing but the floats of patient fishermen. But tracking differs from towing in all these essential features. In the first

place there is no horse ; tracking is necessarily done by
the crew of the boat. In the second place there is no towpath, and the men have to find their way as best they can
—along the shingle, if there happens to be a convenient
beach ; through the woods or over cliffs if the banks are
steep ; or from rock to rock, and often deep in the water.
In the third place the stream is invariably swift and rough,
and may be so much obstructed by rocks and sand-bars
that the craft will require the nicest manœuvring by the
steersman.

"Tracking," said Mitchell, "is the damnedest hard
labour at all times, and when you first try it it's Hell. You
pull your guts out—you think you're getting killed. We
had our first dose of it going up from the Delta to Fort
McPherson, and I tell you the boys were sorry for themselves !

"Our tracking line was a hundred and fifty feet long and
about as thick as your middle finger. It was the kind of
line that is made specially for the Hudson's Bay Company
in the North of Ireland—pure flax, and quite unbreakable.
You attach the line to the bow of the boat with a bridle,
on the side away from the shore, extend it to its full length,
and space the crew out along it as desired. Each man has
a canvas sling which he attaches to the line with a knot
that can be undone, and he slips his head and one arm
through this and pulls with the sling over his shoulder.
The sling must always be loose, so that you can duck out
of it quick, because if the steersman makes the slightest
mistake the boat may take charge and sweep the whole
bloody crew off the cliff into the river. And if she does
take charge like that she may go down a couple of miles
before she can be stopped and brought up in some eddy
or bay. You have to make your way wherever there
happens to be footing along the bank, and if there is thick
bush you send the two best axemen ahead to clear a path.
And when you are going in the water you mustn't go deeper

than the crotch, for then the water begins to float your
weight and you lose all power for pulling. After you've
got the boys all out along the line and stepping her along
nicely, perhaps the channel switches over to the opposite
bank ; and then you have to get them across the river and
start all over again. No, I can tell you we miners found
tracking the last damn thing on God's earth."

They arrived at Fort McPherson on the twelfth of July :
Mitchell expected to stop there for some little time as he
had to collect information about the unknown country
ahead and engage a guide who could bring him to Ogilvie's
pass. A first view showed them the Fort buildings, heavy,
solid, and bleak, standing about seventy feet above the
river on its right bank, at the top of a raw bluff of
sandy clay. Between the bluff and the river lay a great
beach of sand, two hundred yards or more in breadth.
There was no palisade about the Fort, which consisted
simply of the dwelling-house of the officer in charge, the
Indian trading-room, and stores for provisions and fur
built on three sides of a square that fronted on the river ;
while in the background there were the usual cabins for
the Company's servants and a few nondescript shacks
probably put up by Indians who had had to winter at
the Fort for one reason or another. To the south of the
Fort stood the house of a former missionary bishop, in
which his widow still lived, and the new log building of
the Anglican mission, the summer station of the missionary
from Herschel Island in the Beaufort Sea. The country
round about was flat and very bare, covered with coarse
grass and a few summer flowers. Some scrubby spruce
appeared here and there in the distance, but there was
no large timber to be seen, as trees cannot grow to any size
in that country except in the sheltered valleys.

Fort McPherson, or Peel's River House, was founded in
1840 for the purpose of trade with the Loucheux Indians,
who inhabit the valleys of the Peel and of its tributaries

the Good Hope, the Bonnet Plume, the Wind, the Hart,
and the Blackstone. It was the report of Sir John Franklin,
who discovered the Peel in 1826, that first drew the attention of the Hudson's Bay Company to the wealth of the
Peel river country in fur-bearing animals, and in 1898
this was still the Company's richest territory. The Eskimo
who lived along the shores of the Beaufort Sea also came
up to Fort McPherson to trade, as Aklavik, the modern
post on the lower part of the Delta, had not yet come into
existence. The clerk in charge, John Firth, was an Orkney-
man, who had come out to the Company's service as a
boy and had risen from dog-runner to factor through sheer
excellence, honesty, and force of character. He looked
like a man of granite—square, broad, and powerful—and
there was a formidable quietness about him which had a
compelling effect on the Eskimo and Indians. They felt
that his cool grey-blue eyes were looking right into their
thoughts, and minded their manners accordingly.

Once, it was said, there had been an Eskimo chief who
omitted to mind his manners. Firth was discussing with
him some matter connected with the Eskimo trading and
the chief, who was a notorious bully, showed himself so
obnoxious and domineering and so full of impossible
demands that at last Firth had to order him publicly out
of the house. Half an hour later there came a knock on
the door. Firth unlatched the door and was opening it
warily when the Eskimo chief, who was outside, drove at
him with a long heavy snow-knife. Firth was just in time
to slam the door to as the blow fell, and the point of the
knife sank four inches into the planking ; then he quickly
whisked the door open again, and this brought the Eskimo
into the house headlong, on his face. Then Firth grabbed
him, ran him to the edge of the bluff, and kicked him
over.

This heroic interchange had the happiest possible result.
Firth expected very bad trouble and marshalled his men,

and soon the whole band of Eskimo was seen to be climbing up the bluffs, as if to attack the Fort. But as they came on the chief laid down his weapons as a sign of peace, Firth went alone to meet him, and everything blew over in a hurricane of complimentary eloquence. Firth, it appeared, was the strongest man in the North ; the chief now loved him like a brother, and had given the Eskimo instructions to go up and trade.

From the moment of his arrival Mitchell began to come into contact with the Loucheux, as the whole tribe, six or seven hundred in number, was camped round about the Fort. His first impression of them was quite unfavourable. Their teepees, in the first place, looked very ragged and mean, as they had given up the old-fashioned teepee covers of caribou hide and were using odd pieces of sacking, old sail-cloth, or what not. The people themselves also made a disappointing appearance. The regular summer clothing of the Loucheux was of the lightest possible caribou skin tanned brown, the men wearing a short coat and trousers and the women a blouse and short skirt, some-times with gaiters. But for some reason best known to themselves they invariably discarded their Indian clothes at a certain stage of their annual journey down the Peel, and appeared at Fort McPherson in most battered and nondescript European garments which they kept carefully cached for this purpose from year to year. At the same time they assumed a humble and penitent appearance, either because they considered this to be the proper demeanour of Christians (they were all Christian at the Fort and wished to stand in well with the missionary), or because they hoped that an air of dejection and poverty would help them to get good prices for their furs. The Indians in this way did themselves much less than justice in the eyes of a casual observer, and it was not until Mitchell saw some of them wrestling with the Eskimo, in matches which Firth organized as a safety-valve to old-standing enmity, that he began to realize the beauty of their figures. They were not tall men, averaging perhaps five-foot-nine, but they were very straight and upstanding, with broad shoulders, narrow hips, and delicate hands and feet. In the wrestling each man held by a sash that was wound tightly round his opponent's middle, and never shifted his grip ; and though the Eskimo were in general much bigger men, most of them measuring six feet or over, the Indians were so much quicker and more agile that they won four matches out of five.

Actually, on the strength of the very close knowledge which he obtained of them later, Mitchell holds firmly that the Loucheux were far superior to the other Indian tribes, as they had always lived an isolated life in the Peel river country and had retained the savage and ancient virtues.

" I want you, Graham, to lay great stress on the purity of my Indians' race. They had lived in their valley from time immemorial. They never went out of it, and they never allowed anyone to come in. They made no bones about shooting a Stick Indian from the Dawson side of the mountains, or a Red River Indian, if they found them in the valley, and they had fought terrible wars with the Eskimo before the Hudson's Bay Company came and made peace. And the Company helped them to keep white men out—they didn't want to see such a valuable hunting territory spoiled any more than the Indians. So you may take it that when I went up there they were still a virgin tribe. They told the truth, and despised a ' fork-tonged man '. They respected caches—that is one of the most important of Indian laws. They kept to the hunting-grounds that the chief allotted them. They married one wife and stuck to her, though the wives did not always stick to them. They traded honestly. Of course, they weren't kind to intruders, as I've told you, or to prisoners of war, and they punished the girls very heavily if they took up with white men down at the Fort. But they overlooked lapses from virtue inside their own community—which were as a matter of fact confined to a given set of 'bad girls'—and the girls in question generally married quite satisfactorily in the end.

"I grant you that their Christianity didn't amount to very much except at the Fort. There were a few, of course, who were really and truly Christians, in the bush or out of it, but the majority pretty well cached their Christianity with their European clothes, until they wanted it again next summer. But I maintain that even as pagans they lived a fine orderly life, with only minor disturbances and friction that the chief could easily iron out, whereas the Eskimo, who were pagans too at that time—pagans to a man, didn't even pretend to be Christians—as far as I could see were just so dirty and—well, I think we'll have to say that comparisons are odious and leave it at that. You've got to be extremely careful what you put in a book!"

CHAPTER XIII

THE ESKIMO

"DURRTY and disagree'ble ; a fule, a thief, and a liar," were the famous words in which a certain Scotsman summed up the character of his dead wife, and, with the attribution of base cunning in place of folly, they would serve very well to express the Indians' appreciation of the Eskimo.

The enmity of the two races was solidly rooted in the past. Hearne's Indian escort, in 1771, joyfully massacred an Eskimo band near the mouth of the Coppermine river ; Mackenzie, in 1793, was warned by the Hares that the Eskimo would certainly murder him if he went down to the Arctic Ocean ; and Richardson writes of Loucheux (who had guns) killing Eskimo (who had none) in 1847. The same thing went on in the East, where the Nascopies got guns from the white men while the Eskimo still depended on bows and arrows, and drove the Eskimo out of the Gulf of St. Lawrence for good and all. But by 1898 the Lower Mackenzie had long been pacified by the Hudson's Bay Company, and everyone was careful to avoid raising bad blood by any mention of bygone troubles. But there was no love lost on either side, as plenty of the older people were survivors of actual atrocities.

One of his old Indian friends told Mitchell about a massacre in which the whole of his own family had been killed. He was a little boy at the time, and was fishing at the mouth of the Rat river with a band of fifteen or twenty Indians. As they were working quietly at their

93

nets a flotilla of *kayaks* swept down upon them, and all
except the boy were killed before they could reach for
their weapons. The boy saved himself by plunging into
the reeds and lying with his nose barely above the surface
of the water—"just like a musk-rat"—until the Eskimo
had gone away.

"But"—I quote Mitchell's account—"a better joke on
the Eskimo happened like this. There was a small party
of Indians camped, and some of the boys in ranging around
saw the Eskimo creeping up through the grass and scrubby
bushes. They warned their people, but the head Indian
immediately sized up the situation and gave instructions
for everyone to go on with whatever he was doing, either
work or play, just as if they suspected nothing. He knew,
you see, that there was a deep narrow crevasse in the
earth between the camp and where the Eskimo were crawling, which would defend his people if the Eskimo made
a rush ; and he figured that with such a luscious killing
in front of them they would rush right in without firing
their arrows first.

"And he was right. They rushed, and they never
arrived. They were into the crevasse before they knew it.
And any that balked were quickly overtaken by the Indian
runners and killed." And he added, "But, oh, didn't
Firth give Hell to anyone who talked of those doings—
Indian or Eskimo ! "

I have made this digression into history because Mitchell's
account of the Eskimo stands in urgent need of explanation.
For while all other travellers, both clerical and lay, unite
in a chorus of praise, Mitchell appears as a most damaging
witness on the side of the Devil.

"You can't print it, my dear fellow," he said himself.
"The Eskimo are white-haired boys nowadays, and you
can't possibly put what I say about them into a book.
They won't like it at Ottawa, and the missionaries will
eat you alive. Then there's the Archbishop of Rupert's

Land ; he lived with them for thirty years and knows
more about them than any man ; and he sticks up for
them through thick and thin. I don't think we can get
away with it."

I will therefore ask the apologists of the Eskimo to remember the ancient tradition of alternate massacres that
Mitchell has faithfully absorbed from his Indian friends.
And if they have read, in the foregoing pages, his stric-
tures on certain prospectors from God's Own Country (and
particularly from the city of Chicago), they will have
realized that he is intolerant of all bad neighbours. He
has also urged me to point out that all these things happened long ago, when the Eskimo were still, as he put it,
" an utterly lawless and ignorant people—none of them
Christians, and never even seen a policeman " ; and it is
charitable, too, to suppose that the chief, who was really
and truly unprintable, may have happened to be an ex-
ceptionally nasty fellow.

" That Eskimo encampment on the sands was really a
wonderful sight. The whole tribe from Herschel Island
and the north coast had come up to do their trade, and
there must have been three or four hundred of them altogether. They came up in three different kinds of boats—
the women's boats, what they call *umiak*, which are big
clumsy things for heavy loads ; another kind of skin boat
that is long and narrow and has a high pointed bow and
stern ; and the *kayaks*. There were flotillas of *kayaks*,
and the men and boys seemed to be out in them all the
time. (The damnedest cockleshells to manage, Graham :
I got a ducking in a *kayak* more than once !)

" The first thing that surprised you about the Eskimo
was the size of them. We here in the East have heard of
the Labrador Eskimo as being little stumpy people, but
these were great big devils, six feet high and weighing
two hundred pounds and up. Even the girls were going
on six feet. Then it was strange to see them going round

in thick furs all the time. You know it's mighty hot in the Arctic in summer, and as I told you the Indians have thin clothes of caribou skin for summer, and only wear furs in winter. But there were the Eskimo all in the most beautiful furs in spite of the broiling sun. The men and women dressed very much alike, in a coat with a hood, trousers, and long boots. The men's coats reached half-way down to the knee, and the women's coats were rather longer, with peaks hanging down front and back. The clothes were exquisitely made, all of seal skin inlaid with different-coloured furs in most elaborate patterns. The boots were rawhide seal skin, made like moccasins but knee-length.

" One thing they were very particular about and that was the wolverine fur for lining their hoods. In cold weather, as you know, the breath forms great icicles on any fur round the face, moustache and so on, but icicles don't form on wolverine fur and so it's the only thing for lining parkas. The wolverine doesn't go down to the coast, so they have to get these skins from the Indians, and they'll give a fine rifle and several hundred rounds of ammunition for a wolverine skin. I sometimes wondered how it was that some of the Indians had got new and expensive American rifles, and that was the explanation : American whalers would give an Eskimo a rifle and four or five hundred rounds on the understanding that he would hunt fresh bear meat and walrus for their ship only, and the same Eskimo would no doubt make the same agreement with several ships, and so have several rifles and a lot of ammunition to spare.

" As you know, the Eskimo live in igloos in winter, made of snow blocks carved to fit, but in summer they put up any old shelters of canvas or skin. The sands were just covered with them ; the damnedest-looking nondescript kind of places, but they all had long low entrance passages that you had to crawl along to get inside, just like the winter houses. I don't know what they did this for, but I suppose it was so that they could spear intruders easily while they were in an awkward position.

"I went into their houses pretty often when I was bargaining with them for the things I wanted to buy, but I can tell you I always got out again as quick as ever I could. The atmosphere inside was quite fearful. It was hot weather to start with, but they kept their lamp going just the same—a big stone basin of seal oil, with a wick. There was no opening for air, and the only light came from the lamp. Then they had their food stored in there, and it was all fish and seal meat that they had brought up with them from the coast, so you can imagine that it was getting, well, fully mature. I don't believe they ever ate their meat and blubber till it was rotten, and the fish had gone so far that they used to make a hole in the skin and suck them, like oranges. As for filth on the floor, well, for the book you can say ' domestic hygiene was not practised ' (and that's a thing no Indian would dream of doing). And you might perhaps add ' surplus clothing was discarded within doors '—actually they were all stark-naked, the sons of guns ! And the places were crammed full too —seething sweating masses of humanity ! Yet in a way they were amiable happy-looking sort of devils, and generous to a degree. They'd offer you anything they possessed— high fish, rotten blubber, anything. It was their custom to share out everything equally to all."

I asked a question here about the women, and how they got on in this kind of palæolithic society.

"The women were very stoical," Mitchell answered. "They never cried out whatever was done to them. I once saw two Eskimo bargaining over some duffles that one of them had just bought in the store—the other offered his wife for the duffles and a rifle, but that didn't seem to be quite enough. Then another girl came out of the tent, and as soon as the first man saw her he quickly agreed to trade the duffles and the rifle and all his purchases for the two girls, and off they went with him on the spot. So you see divorce among the Eskimo was a very easy affair indeed. It simply consisted of an Eskimo seeing something he wanted and bringing out a wife to swap for it—or if that wasn't enough, two wives. I really believe some of the women rather enjoyed the transfer : they probably got no worse beating in one place than another, and the food was always shared out equally through the whole gang anyhow, so they wouldn't starve any worse with one man than with another. And they looked as if they hoped the change might be interesting.

" They were just as dishonest as they were dirty and immoral. Terrible thieves ! Where our scow was pulled up on the sands it was unfortunately close to their camp and two or three hundred yards from the base of the cliffs, and we could never leave her without someone on guard and damn well wide awake too. If you nodded off for a few minutes, the next thing would be a bullet head and black beady eyes peering over the gunwale, and they would slip quietly in and steal anything before you knew. They were extremely clever at moving quietly in spite of their heavy fur clothes. Sometimes rather too many used to come around together, but a shot in the air or in the sand used to drive them away.

" The Indians were so very different in that way. If an Indian wanted something he would ask for it, humbly, and yet with dignity, and you'd be glad to give it him—a little tea, or tobacco, or something like that. The boys always said I should end by giving our whole stock away to the Indians, but I tell you they had reason to be glad of it before all was said and done. However, that part of the story's still to come. There was another very curious difference between the Indians and the Eskimo—and didn't the Indians despise the Eskimo for it ! You know how you and I, or Indians, or anyone else I ever met, when we

sleep round a fire, put our feet towards the fire and keep
our heads on the outside of the circle—wrap them up in
a blanket or something. Well, the Eskimo do just the very
opposite—put their heads close up to their blubber lamp
and their feet outside. The Indians can't get over that
at all.

"Another great difference is the way they smoke. The
Indians call the Eskimo 'smoke-eaters' because they say
the smoke never comes out again. The Eskimo pipe is
like a Chinese opium pipe, with a little flat platform for
the tobacco instead of a bowl. I bought one of these
pipes from a dirty old sinner and brought it out with me,

ESKIMO PIPE.

though I never smoked it, you may be sure ! The stem
was made of two pieces of wood grooved and fitted together
lengthwise, so that the grooves formed a tube, and was all
bound round with copper wire. The little flat bowl was
made of brass from an old cartridge, and the old boy kept
his pipe-cleaner, 'a thin spike of ivory, ready tied on to
the pipe. The Eskimo prepares his pipe with great ceremony ; he takes some strong black prick tobacco, pulverizes
it, and puts it in his pipe mixed up with caribou hair—a
most abominable contraption. He only takes enough for
about three full draws, and I don't know what he manages
to do with the smoke, for he certainly never seems to emit
any. The Indians of course get the very best briar pipes
from the Hudson's Bay Company, and smoke strong prick

tobacco or sometimes plug. Men, women and children all smoke pipes.

" But I will say that the Eskimo do beautiful handwork, both men and women. The patterns of inlaid fur on their clothing were marvellous ; and their raw sealskin boots were beautifully sewn and absolutely watertight. All that was the women's work. And the men too were extraordinarily skilful the way they made all their hunting equipment with very poor tools, and, what was most cunning of all, little toy models of boats and sleighs to sell round the Fort. I bought a perfect model of a hunter's *kayak*, all complete with double paddle and a set of spears on a rack just as they have them. One of the spears even had a loose head attached to the haft by a long line, and another had a bladder to let the hunter follow up a wounded seal or walrus when it was under the water.

" Then I got a whole array of their fish-hooks and a fishing-line made of very fine strips of whale-bone. The hooks were extraordinary things—just a nail or some sort of spike, without a barb, driven through the wide end of a flat piece of bone so as to point upwards. They were very cunningly made and weighted so as to hang the right way in the water, but having no barbs they often let the fish get off. Firth had been urging the Eskimo to make barbs for years, but they never would do it.

" But the most wonderful things of all that the Eskimo make are the snow-knives. (I didn't get my snow-knife then ; I'll tell you about that later on.) They make them out of any old bit of steel or an old gun-barrel—shape them, hollow out the blood-rib, and retemper them, and they'll take an edge like a razor. They are really intended for cutting out blocks of snow to build the winter houses with, but in summer they carry them naked in their hands, like a kind of swagger-cane. Only a man who has killed a bear is allowed to carry a snow-knife like this—and it's only when he's killed his bear that he's allowed to wear *tutoks*, that's to say two large ivory buttons fitted through holes in the cheek by the corners of the mouth.

" Oh, I can tell you a good joke about *tutoks*. One day I was walking on the sands with a big tall Scots miner called McInnes when three Eskimo came along. As they came abreast of us the tallest of them stepped in front of McInnes, pulled out his right *tutok*, and stuck his tongue out at him through the hole. This was meant to be an insult—and so it was, a damned insult. McInnes looked at him quietly for a second or two and then put his fingers in his mouth, pulled out his upper plate of false teeth, and held them in front of the Eskimo's face. The Eskimo just turned and fled, thinking that McInnes was bewitched.

" I saw a terrible murder on those sands one day, Angus. I and a couple of other miners had walked a few miles north from the Fort along the river, and we were watching some broods of young ducks in the driftwood near the cliff when we saw an Eskimo walking by himself. We supposed he was going to his nets. Then we saw three other Eskimo were following him, and when they overtook him they halted him, apparently for a parley. Suddenly while they were parleying an Eskimo on each side seized his arms and wrenched them backwards very quickly, so that his shoulders must have been dislocated. Then the third man took his snow-knife, ripped the other one's seal-skin shirt open down the front, and began to scratch his belly from the midriff downwards with the point—first gently and then with increasing force, until he actually disembowelled the poor wretch. Then they took several articles from him, dragged the carcase up towards the cliffs and covered it lightly with brushwood and sand.

" We were of course very much paralysed by all this. One of us was damned fool enough to want to rush into the fray, but the others most wisely restrained him, pointing out damned clearly that if we mixed up in it the Eskimo would accuse us of the murder and bring lots of evidence to prove it, too.   They were quite right ; I know we could have done no good.   I had a talk with the Eskimo inter-preter afterwards, and he told me for the love of God not to say a word.   He knew all about it : one of the Eskimo who had held the wretched man's arms told him.   He told him that the murderer had said, ' You've a louse on you, biting you ; I'll dig him out—dig him out—dig him out——' all the time he was cutting into him.

" The interpreter said this kind of thing often happened in a family feud, but if anyone began to investigate there was blank ignorance everywhere.   Firth, too, said that Eskimo often disappeared, and old Indians also sometimes, but he never got any change out of making enquiries—some plausible story was always told.   And of course when things like that go on the missionary is the very last man of all to hear of them.   In fact, my dear boy, you can't believe what the secrecy of the savage is.   It's like in Ireland, where they do some *terrible* murders, but the parish priest never knows, can never tell you a thing. . . ."

CHAPTER XIV

FIRST TRAFFIC WITH THE INDIANS

ON his arrival at Fort McPherson Mitchell had lost no time in opening his problem to Firth and asking for his help. Firth heard him through with attention and courtesy, but in a silence so sepulchral that Mitchell, used as he was to uncommunicative Scotsmen, felt a whisper of suspicion that he had something at the back of his mind. Direct questions about the Peel river country and the mountains fell totally flat from the first. "I couldna say," delivered with the blankest neutrality of expression, was Firth's usual formula for reply, with "Mebbe" as a slightly less discouraging variant. However, he undertook readily to look round among the Indians who came in to trade for someone who could guide Mitchell's party to the Pass, and admitted, cautiously enough, "There's them that kens it." Mitchell was left with the impression that one of this mysterious fraternity could probably be found, but Firth would promise no more than that he would do his best.

Mitchell was thus committed to making some stay at Fort McPherson, and, as he has a natural flair for what is primitive, he made the best of his opportunities for getting to know something about the Indians. This was, of course, the busy season for trade among both Indians and Eskimo, and Mitchell used to pass hours in the trading-room watching their proceedings. From what he has told me I gather that Indian trading must have been one of the darkest mysteries of commerce, its obscurity arising from the fact that the Indians—at least in those days—did not understand the nature of dollars and cents. No money passed in any transaction, and money could not be used as the standard of value in barter ; but as some kind of standard was essential for computing prices the Company and the Indians had long ago adopted the beaver skin as their unit of currency. But it was just at this point that the economic difficulties began. The expression " one skin " was very far from meaning the actual pelt of any individual beaver, but related to the so-called " made-beaver ", the ideal or imaginary skin of an adult beaver in prime condition, the value of which was known to both the parties. To the Company the value of " one skin " was fifty cents, and to price the trade goods in " skins " was simple enough ; but as the market prices of furs varied from one year to the next the system led to this highly anomalous result—that skins themselves had to be priced in terms of " skins." To make the system work it was necessary for the parties to agree how many " skins " should be paid for a skin of each quality, and this question was always arranged by the chief and the Company's trader at a conference held before the trading began. Once this scale had been fixed the prices that each Indian would receive followed more or less automatically upon the grading of his furs except in so far as the Indian could establish some kind of claim to particularly favourable treatment.

Mitchell was soon in the market himself, bargaining for models and toys from the Eskimo and for moccasins and bead-work from the Loucheux : he found that bacon, tea, rice, nails, and such-like from the *Amisk's* cargo had a high value in trade, while a barrel of plain boiled sweets, which Cecil had bought as an afterthought at Fort Chipewyan, was worth more than its weight in gold, as neither Eskimo nor Indians ever came by sweet things in the ordinary course. Paraffin candles, too, were much in demand by the Eskimo, as food and not as illuminants, but with an Arctic winter ahead candles were far too valuable to be squandered in trade.

One day when Mitchell was on guard duty on board the *Amisk* two Indians came down across the sands to speak to him. One was a man called Andrew Bonnet Plume, who could speak English and was sometimes called upon when an interpreter was needed, and the other was a young man, of thirty years or less, called Francis, whom Mitchell had not seen before. (The Indians all had English or Scots names as well as Indian ones, as they were all christened by the missionary at Fort McPherson.)

This young man Mitchell says roundly was the handsomest Indian he ever saw in the North. " He was tall and erect, with a high carriage. Head better formed than most Indians, with a broad brow, rather an oval face, a strong determined jaw, a small well-arched nose, and very flexible nostrils. Large liquid eyes, more like a red deer's eyes than any eyes I ever saw in any other man. Broad in the shoulder and narrow in the hips, like most of his tribe ; feet small, and moved with remarkable grace and perfect balance.

" Bonnet Plume explained that this man's wife had had her first baby a few hours ago. She had had a bad time of it, and being a high-strung nervous girl had refused all nourishment and collapsed. Francis had come to ask if I could give him any medicine, as the squaws all thought that she was likely to die. I gave him liberally of what I thought would be best for her. Unfortunately we had no luxuries of any kind, but I got together two or three cupfuls of rice, a cupful of fine tea, five pounds of sugar, and a tin of condensed milk. This last was considered a tremendous luxury in the North. I never saw a look of more profound thankfulness on any man's face—that was reward enough in itself.

" As soon as I was relieved from guard I went up to the Fort, got hold of Bonnet Plume, and made him take me to Francis' teepee. I had in my pocket a small silver hunting-

flask of brandy, and I believe that it was a couple of tea-
spoonfuls of this that really saved her life. I didn't go into
the teepee, as I had a notion—which I found out afterwards
was quite right—that the Indians had a certain antipathy
to any stranger's presence at such times ; but there was an
old man there whom I came to know very intimately later
—his name was Colin—and I left a wineglassful of the
brandy with him, telling him to give her some of it in case
of collapse.

" You wouldn't believe that this little act of more or less
unintentional kindness was worth seven sleigh-loads of fresh
caribou meat to us in the scurvy time, and saved I don't
know how many lives in that way, to say nothing of my own
life every day for months later on. But there it is ! "

During his days of waiting at Fort McPherson Mitchell had
the good fortune to come upon a very fair map of the Peel
river, which had been made by a French explorer, the Comte
de Sainville. It has already been said that the Peel was
almost virgin territory at that time, and in fact de Sainville,
who made his survey in the course of a hasty canoe-trip in
1893, seems to have been the only white man who visited
the valley at all between its original exploration by the
Hudson's Bay Company in 1839 and Mitchell's own expedition. Mitchell pounced on this map and made a careful
copy for himself. His copy still survives in a split and dog's-
eared state, and I have reproduced it here as an important
material exhibit. The copy is made on a sheet of coarse
buff wrapping paper from the store, and shows the main
stream of the Peel from Fort McPherson to the junction of
the Peel and the Wind, with de Sainville's notes on the
natural features transcribed in Mitchell's hand. The note
on " hot springs " at the inflow of the Bonnet Plume river
turned out to be perfectly right, as the Indians told Mitchell
later that ducks and geese found open water there all through
the coldest winters, and Mitchell again found coal seams
burning in the region where the map marks " fires ".

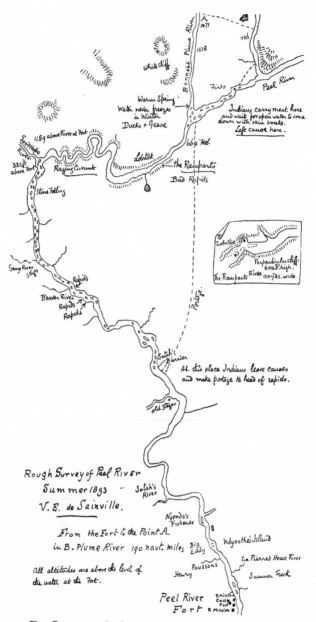

DE SAINVILLE'S SURVEY OF THE PEEL RIVER.

His study of de Sainville's map made Mitchell keener than ever to have a local guide. With the experience of river navigation that he had now acquired he saw very clearly the kind of difficulties that would confront them on the Peel, and how a good guide could save his party from accidents, delays and much unnecessary labour. What worried him particularly was the danger of mistaking a tributary for the main stream—the Company's first explorers had done this, following up the first large tributary, the Snake (which is called the " Good Hope " on de Sainville's map), instead of the Peel itself. This Snake, or the Bonnet Plume, or the Wind, were evidently considerable streams and might easily mislead him, and he understood that there were at least two other tributaries, the Hart and the Blackstone, which were beyond the edge of the map. As yet, of course, he had not been able to discover whether the Pass was at the head of the main river or of one of the tributary streams.

The map held plenty of other unpleasant promises besides the embarrassing choice of waterways. He read " rapids ", " rapids ", " rapids ", " raging current ", " bad rapids " and " whirlpool ", as de Sainville's information on current conditions alone. Then there were " the Ramparts " which looked ugly enough in the large-scale sketch that de Sainville had inset—Mitchell did not like the sudden constriction of a great river to a breadth of a hundred yards, nor the small curly arrows that indicated whirlpools in the gorge. Even the islands in the lower reaches meant trouble—right channels and wrong channels, sand-banks, shallows and endless delays. And next to losing himself outright or being drowned in a whirlpool Mitchell was most anxious to avoid unnecessary delay ; he had made all his preparations for wintering in the wilds, but if his party could make a quick journey up to the Pass there was a definite, though slender, possibility that they might still get down to Dawson before the rivers froze.

One morning, after waiting for some days, Mitchell received a note from Firth to come up to the Fort as soon as possible, as he had found him a guide. Mitchell accordingly went up, but the place was temporarily in an uproar as the Eskimo chief had chosen that moment to try to sell his wife to Firth, and business was impossible until his passionate oratory and very obscene drama had been brought to an end. Finally they got him thrown out, the patient wife following him without complaint, and then Firth turned to Mitchell's affairs.

A suitable guide had been found. Bonnet Plume, the interpreter, had consented to take on the job, and Firth was confident that he would do it properly. He spoke English well and was a very honest man, but Firth thought it would be well nevertheless if he was made to sign an indenture, as anything like a written contract had a very strong hold on the Indian imagination. Firth had questioned him about the Pass, and he had answered readily enough ; it lay at the head of the valley of the Wind river, and Bonnet Plume knew the whole of that country perfectly as he had hunted in it all his life.

But this was not by any means the most important part of Firth's communication. Firth had been considering Mitchell's whole project in the light of his knowledge of the Indians, and felt bound to warn him that, unless he got the Indians' permission to go through their country, he would run a very poor chance of arriving at the Pass. Frankly, he believed that they would murder every man of the party. Mitchell argued, but Firth stuck to his point. When Mitchell cited de Sainville, he said that de Sainville had come back in remarkably quick time, and implied that he would have pushed his exploration farther if something had not gone wrong. His last word was the same as his first —" I'll no be responsible for your lives." Consequently there was nothing for Mitchell to do but to open pourparlers with the Indians. Firth refused firmly to act as go-between, and rightly, as the matter was no concern of the Company, and for the same reason he stipulated that negotiations must take place outside the Fort. Mitchell accordingly fell back on Bonnet Plume to carry his request to the chief, but Firth supported him to the extent of giving Bonnet Plume a solemn and formal assurance, to be transmitted to the chief, that Mitchell and his friends were loyal subjects of the Queen and were good and trustworthy men. He also undertook that Mitchell would be personally responsible for any outrage that any of the white men might commit, and this was a very large order seeing that Mitchell thus became responsible not only for members of his own party but also for any and every scamp among the crews of the other boats that were following the *Amisk*. Mitchell, of course, had actually nothing whatever to do with these other parties ; they had followed him of their own volition, and he was unable to prevent them from doing so although he would have preferred their room to their company very much indeed. Consequently to hold him responsible for their misdoings was quite uncalled-for, and would, indeed, have been simply futile with ninety-nine men out of a hundred, as he had really no means of controlling other parties than his own except sheer force of character and a total absence of fear. However, no doubt Firth knew that the Indians would not be satisfied with any lesser undertaking.

At this point Mitchell made an important discovery : Francis, the young Indian whose wife he had doctored a few days earlier, was no less a person than the chief. Bonnet Plume had not mentioned this fact at the time, but brought it out now as surprisingly as a conjurer's rabbit. The old man Colin, too, proved to be a member of the council, so Mitchell felt confident that his standing with the Indians was good—for whatever that might be worth.

Bonnet Plume also told him of Francis' history. One winter, while Francis was still a baby, the band to which his mother belonged missed the caribou herd and all died of starvation. A party of hunters who were travelling light happened to come upon the lodges, and found everyone dead inside them except this baby, who was still at his mother's breast. (Francis' Indian name was *Tuttha Thsuga* —" one little suck "—on this account.) The hunters carried him away and gave him to a foster-mother, and in due course he inherited the chieftainship through his mother's right, as inheritance among the Loucheux goes by the female line.

After the Indians had had time to think over Mitchell's proposal, Bonnet Plume arranged for him to have a conference with Francis and two of the councillors—Colin and another old man whom he knew very well later on. The Indians debated for hours ; Mitchell sat by understanding no word of what they said, but occasionally answered a question or put in a suggestion through the agency of Bonnet Plume. In the end they decided that the white men should be permitted to go through, but they laid great stress on the condition that Mitchell must be responsible for outrages.

When the conference was over Mitchell invited the chief and councillors to a feast. It was a very simple affair, as it consisted only of tea and unlimited quantities of tobacco. At the same time he asked each man what he would like for a present, and was astonished to find that they were most moderate in their requests although they might well have seized on such an opportunity to be grasping. Francis, for instance, asked for a four-point Hudson's Bay blanket, that was worth thirty dollars ; Colin wanted some tea, a copper kettle, and a few bottles of pain-killer, perhaps worth fifteen dollars in all ; and the third man was quite satisfied with a few steel traps, which he needed to equip his young sons. Mitchell threw in pipes and tobacco for good weight, and the ceremony came to an end with profound courtesies and high satisfaction on both sides. It turned out later that the tribe never forgot about these presents which Mitchell gave to the chief and councillors, and his action in asking them to choose their own presents impressed the Indians as being generous beyond all precedent. Indians seem to accept presents in this way without loss of face or any feeling of beggarliness, regarding them, in fact, as ordinary rewards for good service and as marks of honour.

CHAPTER XV

THE PEEL RIVER

EVERY obstacle seemed now to have been removed and it was urgently desirable to start without further delay, but a new difficulty arose over the engagement of Bonnet Plume as guide. He had already consented to act, but Firth had advised Mitchell to insist on something more than a verbal promise, and as soon as a contract was mentioned Bonnet Plume became as elusive as a wild bird. Mitchell and Firth spent days in fruitless persuasion ; everything would be settled in the evening, and next morning Bonnet Plume would come back with some perfectly fresh suggestion, and the whole business had to be gone through again from the beginning.

Meanwhile the miners were growing impatient seeing the Indians setting off up-river after finishing their season's trading and knowing that the winter might come down on them at the end of another two months. So at last Mitchell, who was determined to have Bonnet Plume for his guide but was equally determined to have him tied up with a written indenture, sent off the rest of his party in the *Amisk* and bought himself a Peterborough canoe in which he would be able to follow up quickly with Bonnet Plume, when he had got him.

It was almost a week later that he finally succeeded in catching Bonnet Plume in the proper mood and securing his signature—or rather his mark. The document which cost so much eloquence consists of fifteen lines written in indelible pencil on Firth's office foolscap, and is now much creased and blurred with sweat. It reads as follows :

Peels River House,
21st July, 1898.

I, Andrew Flett Bonnett Plume, agree to guide the Mitchell-Merritt Co. to the Head Waters of the Stewart River by water up the Peel River and across the mountains, also to work for the said Company and give any fresh of game to them and all information and experience and disclose nothing of importance to other parties for the following considerations the said Company agreeing to feed me, give me One Hundred pounds of flour, one Hundred pounds of Bacon and 25 pounds of tea for my family, also they agree to give the pelts of all animals I may kill and all gold I may personally discover and allow me use of picks, shovels etc while I am with them. They further agree to give me a present of Twenty Dollars should I be able to cross to the waters of the Stewart before 30th September 1898

Andrew Flett X Bonnett Plume
George M. Mitchell

Witness
John Firth.

Mitchell remembers that he drafted the contract in wild haste for fear that Bonnet Plume should change his mind again before it was ready. But once he had put his mark to it he had no more nervous crises, and was always a perfectly true and reliable servant. The clause in the contract which provided that he should receive a present if he brought the party to the Pass by the end of September put him very particularly on his mettle, and though they did not actually cross the Pass that autumn he brought Mitchell up to it and so won his twenty dollars by giving him, as it were, a sight of the promised land. Bonnet Plume ended by becoming one of Mitchell's most valued friends, and this thumb-nail sketch, which I took down from Mitchell verbatim, was given entirely without malice.

" Bonnet Plume was a typical Indian in all respects but his characteristics indicated some Scots ancestry very clearly.

For instance, he learned English, was very shrewd, and had the good Scots knack of absorbing other people's goods without actually stealing them. A small very active man of about sixty—untiring on the trail, but when it came to manual labour he left that to George."

Mitchell and Bonnet Plume made good progress up-river in the canoe, and soon overtook the flotilla, which was moving very slowly. For the first fifty miles above Fort McPherson the Peel is a dead sullen stream some six hundred yards in breadth, running between low banks of clay with occasional sandstone bluffs. The current may average a speed of about two miles an hour, and there are few islands. On either bank lies a flat moss-covered plain dotted with swamps and small peaty lakes—a region of " muskeg ", as such country is called in Canada. The level is broken here and there by patches of stunted spruce. But at the point where the Satah river flows in from the east there comes an abrupt change in the lie of the surrounding country, as a steep escarpment rises six hundred feet from the muskeg plain to a high plateau, which extends to the base of the foothills more than a hundred and fifty miles to the south. The valley is generally about a mile in breadth through the plateau country, and the river makes its way among wooded or bushy flats and bare banks of gravel. The sides of the valley are steeply cut in clay and shale, which rise in some places as much as a thousand feet above the river. Where de Sainville's map marks " falling stones " the river flows closely along the eastern bank, and the undercutting of the bottom of the bank constantly causes landslides and falls of rock. In the bottom of the valley there is some fair growth of spruce, poplar and birch, but on the upper benches the timber becomes very sparse indeed, and falls off into the occasional scrubby growth of the northern barrens. Mitchell retains a vivid mental picture of the moose as he saw them on these high benches—" they showed up like elephants," he said, " among the patches of dwarfed black spruce."

Swift water began at the inflow of Trail Creek, which is so called because the Indians, when bound up-river, often leave the main stream there and make a traverse across country to the inflow of the Bonnet Plume, in order to avoid the strong adverse current of the Peel. Boat-work became terribly hard from this point onwards, as they were tracking day after day among shoals and savage rips of current, and the weather was intensely hot. Sometimes they made only two or three miles a day, and never more than ten under the most favourable circumstances. Long before they reached Trail Creek it had become clear that the *Amisk* was far too heavy and cumbersome to go up through the rapids and narrow channels that lay ahead, and though she was the largest boat in the flotilla many of the others were also too big for the work. (The whole flotilla amounted to perhaps fifty boats, and the crews may have totalled about two hundred men.) So when Mitchell one Sunday suddenly decided to cut the *Amisk* in half, a great many of the other parties followed his example, and something like a shipbuilder's yard was organized on the spot. Eventually the whole force turned to and helped, for the crews of the smaller boats were unwilling to go on by themselves and get out of touch with Mitchell and the main body, and felt that their own best interest would be to get the whole force moving as quickly as possible.

The plan which was adopted for shortening the boats was to cut them in half amidships, build a new bow for one half and a new stern for the other, and at the same time reduce them in breadth proportionately—or as far as was found needful. But the planks taken out in reducing the breadth of the boats were not sufficient to make the new bows and sterns, so that trees had to be cut down and fresh timbers and planks sawn out. This meant a saw-pit, of which Mitchell says that it is the most ghastly thing that any human being could work at.

" We fixed up four strong poles," he explained, " six feet

high, and put a platform on top. Then we'd pull out a good tree, broad-axe it flat top and bottom, and mark the lines for two-inch boards. Then one or two men stood on the platform and two poor devils down in the pit, and pulled the saw up and down following the lines marked. Eventually we made rather good boards. But it was terrible work, especially at eighty or ninety in the shade."

When they started again with the two smaller boats things went a good deal better. The boats kept together, and at bad places all hands would get to work on each in succession, hauling on the line or heaving at the craft when they stuck on gravel-bars. The other boats worked together in the same way, doubling up the crews at need. Mitchell's party still kept to a regular routine, as they had done on the Mackenzie; usually starting at four in the morning and running till four in the afternoon, with breaks every two hours and a stop for a rest and a good meal about nine or ten o'clock. The stove was kept going all day, so that beans and boiled bacon should be ready at every stop, and as before each man was cook for a week at a time by turns. They always kept Sunday as a day of complete rest.

Some of the other parties appear to have been much less happy in their internal economy. " We always found it far the best plan," said Mitchell, " to take all sorts of jobs in turn, and then nobody had any come-back. But the other gangs would often pick on some poor devil and make him the cook, and beat him and turn him into a slave. Oh, the cook in most parties was a most broken-hearted man !

" One Sunday I saw my friend Fife holding something down in the water. There were bubbles coming up, so I said,

" ' What the Hell have you there, Fife ? '

" ' My cook,' he answered. The cook was a nasty surly brute, and this was Fife's way of regulating him. But it was fortunate that he pulled him out then, when I spoke, or he would have been up before a miners' meeting for murder. A splendid boy, Fife."

More or less serious accidents used to happen fairly frequently. Inexperienced axemen would chop their feet and legs, and several men were nearly drowned in rapids. One day Craigie, who was poling on the forward platform, broke his pole in the middle of a thrust and fell backwards off the platform into the bean-pot that was boiling on the stove. He was treated with a cataplasm of tar and was not very much the worse—tar for a burn and salt for a cut or wound were the only curative agents that the miners knew. But a real tragedy was the death of young Tim Orchard. This lad was tracking with his party across the face of a very steep bank of slippery shale when the steersman suddenly lost control of his sweep, the boat swung outwards into the current, and the whole crew was swept into the water. The others slipped out of their nooses and came up clear, but young Orchard had tied himself firmly into his noose, though he had been warned not to do so no longer ago than that morning, and in consequence he was drawn under the boat and was crushed as she bumped over a sand-bar.

Thus between the labour of tracking and the cares of a party chief, Mitchell already had his hands full to the point of overflowing. Nevertheless, the miners had not been on the Peel very long before he found still further trouble coming his way, this time from the direction of the Indians. The undertaking that Firth had given on his behalf, that he would be responsible for outrages committed on the Indians by the white men, came home to roost with deplorable certainty and speed. This was the story.

" Bonnet Plume came in one morning with a message that some Indians wanted to see me—it appeared that there was some trouble. All right. But they wouldn't come down to our camp—would I go to them? I didn't want to, but it seemed there was nothing else for it, so off I went with Bonnet Plume, who said he knew where to go. He led me about five miles up a river, going fast, and he wouldn't say a word, black or white. I didn't like it a damn bit.

" Then we found the Indians and their story was this. Two sons of bitches from one of the boats had chased some Indian girls and caught them, but before they could do them any harm the Indians had appeared and driven them away—they had fired all round them so as to frighten them, not to kill. They asked me if I was responsible for the doings of the white men, as they had heard, and I said I was and promised to straighten the matter out.

" When I got back to the river I went immediately, with Bonnet Plume as a witness for the Indians, to the boat where the men belonged—the Indians had given me their description and I knew God-damn well who they were. Their crowd was the dirtiest lot of hounds on the river ; and the men themselves were one of them an Italian, a dark murderous-looking devil with yellow teeth, and the other a big red-bearded Russian—both of them terrible for women and cruel and wicked to everyone.

" I began by speaking quietly to the chief of the boat, but he blew right up and wanted to know what the Hell this, and why the Hell that, and how the Hell the other thing, until at last I told him that none of that was any of his business at all, but that I knew a great many things he didn't, including a lot about him himself, and that I was responsible for keeping the peace on that river and that kept it was bloody well going to be. If there was any more trouble with the Indians, I said, I and my pals would bloody well take the men who did the wrong and kill them ourselves, whoever they were. We were in the Indians' country and the outrages had got to stop as a matter of self-protection for all—otherwise the Indians would take the law into their own hands. In the meantime, they had better all of them get it into their heads that I was the police on that river, and I would see that there was no more God-damned monkey business from anyone.

" That was the kind of talk that those bloody swine could understand, and we had no more serious trouble—or not for a fairly long time, anyhow. They mended their manners a whole lot, and at the same time the Indians took their womenfolk twenty miles back from the river and kept them out of harm's way."

CHAPTER XVI

THE UPPER PEEL RIVER AND THE VALLEY OF NOISES

FROM Fort McPherson to the inflow of the Snake the valley of the Peel lies practically due north and south. Above the junction of the rivers it is the Snake that occupies the rest of the north and south valley, while the main stream enters it at right angles from the west. Up to the inflow of the Snake and for forty miles above it the Peel runs through the same wide steep-sided valley that has been described, the plateau lying four to six hundred feet above with its small scattered timber, its lakes, and its cover of frozen moss.

The miners found the current of the Peel a good deal stronger after they had passed the Snake, and the stretches of easy water became fewer and shorter. De Sainville had marked " raging current " against a part of this reach. The labour of tracking consequently became harder and more continuous, and the men were worn down by poor food, fatigue, and general exasperation. The bad element seemed to be growing more inclined for devilry every day, and by a most unfortunate chance some Indians turned up and provided an occasion for another brutal outbreak.

Nobody had seen anything of the Indians since the last unfortunate affair, and in fact at that season the whole tribe moved southwards into the higher mountains, following the migration of the caribou. However, soon after the flotilla had passed the Snake a small band appeared on the river with their wives and families, having come down with the

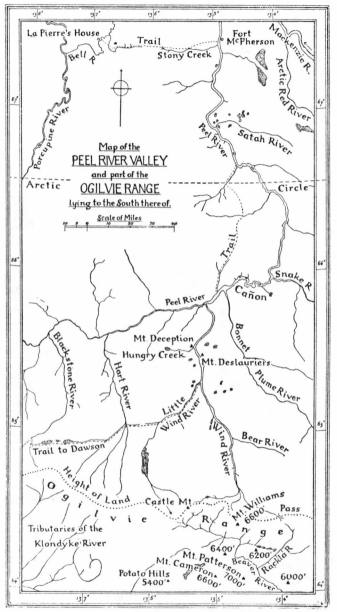

Map of the
PEEL RIVER VALLEY
and part of the
OGILVIE RANGE
lying to the South there of.

Scale of Miles

Base map from the Department of the Interior, Canada.

neighbourly intention of helping the strangers on their way. They offered to pilot the boats through the rapids and shallows and to keep the whole company supplied with fresh game ; and their help would have been of the greatest value to the miners as fresh meat would have put heart into everyone after the interminable pork and beans, and expert pilotage would have saved many groundings and an enormous amount of unnecessary effort on the tracking-line. But the bad element was incorrigible where Indians were concerned. Several of the boats' crews cheated the Indians who were working for them, starved them, ill-used them, and finally tried to ravish their women. It was a very unsavoury business in every way, and might easily have ended in murder on a large scale ; but fortunately the Indians applied to Mitchell for arbitration, and were magnanimous enough to go back to their hunting-grounds, as he advised them, leaving their vengeance untaken.

Indian hunters were all the more necessary to the white men owing to the singular scarcity of all the larger game. If there had been herds of caribou on the plateau the miners could have devoted some of their Sunday leisure to hunting on their own account, or if moose had been plentiful along the riverside some scouts could have picked up one or two pretty frequently as the flotilla advanced. But as it was they saw very few animals except an occasional bear, and even these were uncommon until they reached the upper Wind. But though the hunting was bad on the Peel, Mitchell had one interesting adventure of another kind. He used to amuse himself in the evenings by making Bonnet Plume tell him the Indians' stories, and once, when he pressed to be told " something strange ", Bonnet Plume came out with a story about the Valley of Noises.

The Valley of Noises was somewhere near the Peel Ramparts, a short distance ahead of them ; Bonnet Plume knew the way to it, though neither he nor any other Indian

had ever been there or would ever go as they all held it in
the liveliest possible dread. The valley, as he described it,
was full of the most terrible noises of roaring and rushing
and crashes, which could be heard miles off ; but the worst
thing of all, from the Indians' point of view, was that the
bottom of the valley was strewn with the bones of strange
gigantic beasts, such as had never been seen or heard of
by the oldest and most experienced hunters. Mitchell was
a good deal intrigued by this story, as it seemed to him to
possess some faint air of being founded on fact. He thought
of the reports that he had heard about corpses of mammoths
being found in Siberia in beds of frozen peat, so well preserved that sleigh-dogs could eat their flesh, and it occurred
to him that as far as high latitude and *tundra* went the Peel
river plateau was very much the same kind of country. He
made up his mind to investigate the " monsters' bones ",
and took a day off for the purpose when the boats arrived
at a convenient point on the river. Bonnet. Plume was
quite willing to direct him, provided that he did not have
to risk his own body or soul—whichever was in question
—anywhere too near the valley itself.

They started early in the canoe, landed at the mouth of a
small side-stream, and went up-country by a narrow wooded
ravine. After walking some three or four miles Bonnet
Plume stopped and refused to go any farther, but told
Mitchell that he would come to the valley if he followed the
little stream up to its source. Mitchell accordingly went
on alone, and at the end of another two miles came out of
the woods on to the open *tundra* and found a large cup-shaped
hollow—really a small valley—opening in front of him. It
was a kind of Devil's Punch-Bowl with high steep sides of
bare gravel and stony scree ; no water ran into it from
the higher ground beyond, but the stream trickled out
from a spring in the middle of the valley-bottom. Mitchell
understood at once why the place should be a " valley of
noises ", as he saw that the gravelly sides of the cup were

obviously loose and unstable, and that landslides must have happened very frequently. Indeed, he had hardly had time to consider this explanation of the Indian's tale or to look about him for the gigantic bones of which Bonnet Plume had spoken when a big piece of one of the cliffs came crashing down, and sand, stones and debris clattered all round about him.

Mitchell was just chuckling over this proof of his theory regarding the origin of the supernatural roars and crashes when he suddenly realized that he had got a confirmation of the other story as well. As the dust of the landslide cleared he saw that there was a huge animal's skeleton lying on the floor of the valley where the tail of the slide had carried it. There were great arched ribs, and long-bones, and an immense skull with tusks curving upwards and outwards and back upon themselves—clearly it was some kind of elephant or mammoth. But while he was looking at them the bones began to crumble away : the ribs collapsed, the skull caved in, and soon everything except the tusks had disappeared into dust. The tusks, as he handled them, still seemed solid enough though he was very much afraid that they would crumble too, and he determined to save some of the ivory if he possibly could. He accordingly hurried back to the river, looked out a cold-drawn hack-saw from among the stores on the boat, and returned to the valley the same afternoon ; he found the tusks intact, and sawed off a two-foot length from the end of one of them. But by the time that he had finished this work darkness was already coming on and prevented any further exploration of the sides or floor of the valley ; everyone is consequently free to form his own picture of a herd of mammoths engulfed in an ancient quicksand, and to speculate upon his chances of finding a rich deposit of fossil ivory.

I have often seen the fragment of the tusk in Mitchell's house in Quebec. It is four inches thick at the saw-cut and the tusk from which it was sawn was seven feet in length measured along the curve ; this must, however, have been much less than its original length, as the fragment bears clear signs of the loss of the tip of the tusk during the creature's lifetime—the end is roughly squared off by an old-standing fracture, the outer casing is cracked, and the inner pulp

SHALE CLIFF IN THE PEEL RIVER CANYON.

has hardened into wrinkles, like cold pitch. Mitchell was determined to preserve this piece of ivory through thick and thin and kept it by him in all his later wanderings, though after he was wounded he had the greatest difficulty in preventing the Indians from jettisoning it. They disliked it on the material ground that it added a good fifteen pounds to the weight of his equipment that they had to carry or haul, but they feared it too, and hated it accordingly, on account of its uncanny origin. So far from admiring Mitchell for having braved whatever terrors the Valley of Noises contained, they were disgusted at his common stupidity in running such risks.

At the point where de Sainville marks " The Ramparts " the lie of the land changes. The plateau passes into a range of hills, and through these hills the Peel has cut itself a canyon flanked by precipitous walls of coarse black slate. The canyon is two miles long by less than a hundred yards broad, and the water, hemmed in as it is between the precipices, seems to pile itself up into a hog's-back in the centre of the channel. Mitchell got out de Sainville's map and explained to me how the boats negotiated the canyon.

" You see, my dear Graham, the main current comes down here along the right bank, and on the left bank there's a kind of backwater eddy—that's what de Sainville means by one of his ' whirlpools '—and the hog's-back of smooth racing water in between. We started up the left bank as far as the eddy would carry us, and then had to row like Hell up the slope of the hog's-back and over into the main stream on the right bank. Then, when you get across there's a regular cauldron in the face of the rock with another whirlpool in it, and you have to keep out of that at all costs. Though it's a funny thing, when the Indians are coming down in spring in their big heavy skin boats they don't try to keep out of the cauldron—that's too dangerous, for fear they should be swept in sideways and swamped—the method is to go right into it and then turn and come out again. But I'll tell you about that later. In any case we kept out and we got up past, but we had a nasty time fighting the current just outside that place until we drew clear. I remember there was a cavern shaped like a keyhole about a hundred feet up in the side of the cauldron, and there were tree trunks and debris from the floods stuck about in corners at all heights. There was a lobstick up on the top of the cliff above the cauldron ; that's on the map too—I daresay it's there still."

" What is a lobstick, Mr. Mitchell ? "

" A lobstick ? Don't you know a lobstick ? Why, a lobstick is a tree that has had its branches trimmed in a particular way—it's generally a big spruce or pine tree standing in a conspicuous place, and they leave the head on, but cut out some branches below the head, and then perhaps another four or five rings of branches lower down, so as to make a distinctive landmark. The idea is that people shall point to it and ask whose it is. They are only granted to celebrated Indians or white men : you can't buy one, the Indians come and tell you you've been granted one, and then you give them a banquet. I had four lobsticks—one on the Athabasca, one on the Mackenzie, one on the Wind opposite Wind City, and one up by the Pass, where I broke my leg. I think the one at the Ramparts belonged to some old chief."

What with the stories that they had heard at Fort McPherson about the fate of strangers who trespassed on the Loucheux hunting-grounds, and what with their remembrance of the very bad treatment that the friendly Indians had lately received, the miners had come to be thoroughly afraid of the Indians and were always discussing the prospect of being attacked and massacred. So when an alarm was finally raised one peaceful Sunday morning a first-class panic followed.

" I shall never forget that morning," said Mitchell. " There were twenty boats or more aground on a sand-bar somewhere above the Ramparts, and the boys were all asleep or sitting round smoking quietly. I personally had just boiled up some water and was sitting in my big gold-pan trying to wash some of the lice off myself. Suddenly there were some shots from round a bend of the river and somebody shouted, ' The Indians are coming ! ' Everyone jumped up and began to yell, and there was considerable firing, so I pulled on some trousers and told Cecil and Jack to get out their shovels and dig a pit for cover behind some drift-wood—just the same as entrenching, eh, Graham ?

" And then when we were all keyed up and finger on trigger it turned out to be only some God-damned Yankee Americans who were trying to scare the boys. They were celebrating some Lincoln's birthday or I don't know what —gone on ahead and turned back, and pretended to be Indians raiding. I never shall forget McQuaide as they came down to us along the bank. He called them God-damned fools and every other name that he could lay his tongue to, and told them that they were lucky not to be all full of lead, as they deserved. They tried to laugh it all off, but they knew it was a pretty near thing that they didn't get properly shot up—I certainly should have fired at anything that looked like an Indian moving in the bushes. We were all pretty scared of Indians, Graham, I can tell you, and some of the crowd had damn good reason to be. And I was no braver than the rest—I didn't know the Indians then."

CHAPTER XVII

GOLD

IMMEDIATELY above the canyon the Peel becomes broad and shallow, and runs through a low basin, while the mountain range through which the canyon has been cut sweeps round in a semicircle to the north and west. Then about fifteen miles higher up the valley the mountains again come down to the western bank, and the river has to pass through another narrow cut. But this upper canyon is a good deal less spectacular than the lower one, as its sides are much lower and it is nearly three times as broad. The Wind runs into the Peel, on its right bank, a mile above the mouth of this upper canyon.

It was in the second week of September that the miners arrived at the junction of the rivers and turned off southwards into the Wind. Getting the boats up the lowest reach of the Wind was the hardest piece of tracking that they had had in the whole of their journey. Mitchell was very emphatic about this day's work.

" You swing to the left out of the Peel between very high ramparts of shale and sandstone, and the water comes through just like a sluice. We had to have twenty men on one tracking-line and there was next to no footing on the rocks along the bank. It was a most dangerous place, and we nearly had several men drowned. I slipped myself once and went right under—at least we'll say I slipped, but I know damn well that the man behind tripped me. I hit him twice when I got on shore again, but there was nothing doing—he wouldn't fight.

" Once we were above these ramparts the valley opened
out to a couple of miles broad, and the water ran in a
whole lot of small channels among bars and was very
shallow except at flood-times. Then it would narrow up
again for a bit, and sometimes you'd be on slippery shale,
and sometimes on a low bench, and sometimes you'd be
poling or trying to work impromptu sweeps when the foothold petered right out. Then there were freshets, too, that
used to come down in the damnedest way—it might not be
raining at all where you were yourself, but perhaps there'd
be a storm somewhere a hundred and fifty miles off up in
the mountains, and down it would come off those rocky
slopes like off a roof. I've seen the Wind rise ten feet in
an hour when there wasn't a cloud in the sky—woke up to
find my canoe floating on its end, and only just in time to
save my stuff ! A bloody freaky part of the river, that was,
one way and another."

For some little while the weather had been breaking up
for a cold and early autumn. By the beginning of September the sun was getting low and the days were shortening
fast. The water turned icy cold ; sometimes ice formed at
night where the water was still, and cakes of ice began to
float down the stream. Tracking in the cold proved to be
worse even than tracking in the heat. The men found
their legs breaking out into boils on account of the constant
soaking in ice-cold water, and they suffered terribly from
the cold at night in their drenching clothes. But nobody
thought of stopping, as the gold-fever forced them forwards.
At last so many men were absolutely unable to work that
Mitchell pulled ashore in a backwater and called in the
other boats' crews for a miners' meeting. As the boats
came up they all pulled into the backwater and a camp was
made for the night. And when they woke up in the morning the first storm of winter had begun and there were two
feet of snow on top of everything. This was the last straw ;
the miners agreed that it was impossible to get over the Pass

that season, and they decided to stop where they were and build log cabins for their winter quarters.

The gravelly bars and benches that they had passed on the Peel had naturally moved the miners to thoughts of prospecting, but the experienced men did not think much of the lower reaches of the river and nothing was done beyond a little desultory scratching and half-hearted panning during Sunday halts. However, after they had passed the Ramparts the experts began to look about them with an interested air, and by the time that they reached the wide-bottomed valley of the Wind everyone was panning for dear life. The decision to halt and go into winter quarters did not by any means bring the prospecting to an end. The weather cleared up after a couple of days of storm, and as long as the permanent snow held off and the ground remained unfrozen parties of miners continued to scour all up and down the Wind and the Little Wind rivers and Hungry Creek, and some even reached Bear river—which they called Bear Run Creek. (I find that Mitchell's account refers to the whole of the autumn's doings, and so I have not tried to keep a chronological order.)

The kind of prospecting which Mitchell was doing on the Wind has of course got nothing in common with the prospecting which goes on in northern Ontario and Quebec. In the east of Canada gold is in its natural state, intimately embedded in a vein of quartz or of some other mineral that has bubbled up liquid and hot from the nether regions and has brought the gold along with it in solution. There is very little gold indeed in a very great deal of the ore, so that prospectors and interested persons begin to throw out their chests when they can say that they have got five dollars' worth of gold in a ton of rock. Prospecting for this stuff means hunting the veins through the rock with pick and dynamite, after having first burned down the forest to let the surface of the rock be seen. The prospector fingers no money until he sells his claim, and no real gold can be produced without a mine-shaft and a mill and all sorts of heavy expenses. But the free-gold mining that Mitchell proposed to practise was a totally different affair. The gold for which he was looking had started its career in a vein somewhere among the summits of the Rocky Mountains ; but as centuries of frost and hot sun crack up the surface of the rocks, and ice scrapes off the debris and water carries it away, the gold is washed out of the quartz and begins to travel free in the form of dust or nuggets. As the gold and pebbles and trash go down the streams the gold, being six or seven times heavier than the rest of the debris, gets down to the bottom and stays there. The larger nuggets may get caught anywhere in crevices, but the general mass moves forwards until the slope flattens out, and then, when the rush of the water slackens and its carrying power falls off, the gold comes to rest and collects as a deposit on the bed-rock. The longer the process goes on the richer the deposits will be, and when miners come along at the end of a few million years they hope to find the gold that was originally distributed through some cubic miles of mountain-tops conveniently concentrated and laid down for them in the gravels of the streams down which the eroded remnants of those mountain-tops have been washed away.

Success in hunting for " placers ", as these deposits of gold are called, calls for great nicety of judgment and a long experience. Some placers are found in the steep narrow valleys that lie at high levels among the mountains ; the gold in these high gulches is usually heavy and coarse, but the deposits are narrow. Others are found in the lower-lying flat-bottomed valleys, sometimes in the flood-plain and sometimes on the terraces and benches. Bench-placers are difficult to spot, though McQuaide and the other old-timers would occasionally find one, while the most elusive of all are those that lie quite off the line of any streams —the streams that originally laid them down having changed their courses or vanished. But the men on the

Wind concerned themselves chiefly with the bar-placers that they found in the main stream as they passed up. Wherever the current was checked on islands or bars the material moving with the water tended to check itself, and if gold was present the heavier pieces would tend to be dropped, along with the larger pebbles, at the heads of the bars, while the finer gold and smaller pebbles and sand tailed out down-stream as the current continued to slacken. So it was always on the nose of an obstruction, or on the inner sides of sharp bends, that they stopped to pan the gravel.

Panning, as Mitchell describes it, appears to be a simple matter. " When we came to the head of a bar that seemed to look promising, we'd take out our pans and our short-handled picks and do some prospecting. I used to like a sand-bar with bed-rock showing at the head, then gravel, and then soil with trees. Sometimes we tried up side-creeks, and these were often rich gold-ground too. You fill up your pan with gravel and water and work it with a rotary left-to-right motion, gradually sloshing out the gravel and sand with the water. The nuggets and flecks of gold are heavier than the sand, and stay behind in the pan when the rest of the stuff is sloshed out. The nuggets we found were sometimes pin's-head size, up to peas, and beans, or perhaps the top of your thumb. You can't mistake a nugget—they're rounded and sometimes pitted, never two the same shape, and a rich gold colour—and we were never misled by iron pyrites, because that's got prisms and facets on it and is harder than steel—you can strike a light with it. Then we had lots of mercury put up in tubes, and if we found too much flour gold in the pan we'd collect it on a blanket and run mercury on to pick it up, and then we'd burn the mercury and extract the gold like that. The gold comes out molten, and you can use the mercury over and over again.

" One day we were tracking up along a bed-rock ledge

that had gravel on top of it, and I suggested panning. It looked good to me. So we snubbed up the boat and I cut in with my pick down on to the bed-rock, and put the gravel from the bottom of the cut—right off the bed-rock —into my pan. I sloshed her round, and as the gravel cleared out I heard ' chunk, chunk, chunk ' going round at the bottom of the pan. ' There's a bloody hen in this pan,' I said as I heard the clucking it made, and all the boys crowded round to see what was coming.

" Well, that very first pan-off was the richest that anyone struck on the Wind. There was a nugget in there that was over an inch long, and half an inch thick, shaped like a potato. There were eighty dollars right in that one pan !

" Wild excitement on the river ! All the boats stopped, and the boys cleaned off that bed-rock as if their lives depended on it. They got some excellent pans, but it seemed to peter out somehow as we followed down-stream. I think myself there was a flaw in the bed-rock below where we were stripping that may have trapped a lot of free gold and so accounted for the petering-out, and I'm sorry we didn't stay there longer ; but everyone was always too ambitious and we deserted the place when we lost the first rich showings. We all staked claims there, and God only knows how many claims were staked all up the Wind at different times ; for all we knew the Wind might have been another Klondike. We figured that we might rush over to Dawson and register our claims, and then get back somehow, if we decided in the end to settle down on the Wind for serious mining.

" Generally speaking, we were much too ambitious and always went ahead too fast. The place round the next bend was always going to be better than the place we were at. We panned all the time, and though panning's all very well for very rich places, you leave a lot behind, and we ought to have done more with cradles and sluice-boxes.

The sluice is what they use on big operations, and you must use it when there's a large volume of gravel to deal with. Say you want to work a bench, up on a side-hill, and there's a crick available for water-supply. You build your sluice-box any length you like from fifty yards to a mile and a half—it's just a wooden conduit with riffles (that's cross-bars) across the bottom. Then you divert your water out of the crick, shovel in gravel, and let it wash down along the sluice-box ; and after a certain time you stop the water, clear out the gravel, and clean up the gold which has lodged in the riffles. We built short sluices once or twice, and we set up cradles once or twice—they're really glorified pans on a wooden frame, which you rock backwards and forwards to slop out the water and gravel. But we all had the damned gold-fever, and nothing would hold us but what we had to push on and on.

" It was a most extraordinary thing, Graham, to see how the different men reacted to the gold. It took them all different ways, just like too much liquor. One would be cold and calculating, and as wicked as Hell ; another would be delirious with pleasure ; some showed themselves up as the lowest type of killer ; and many became open-handedly generous. You'd see one fellow dancing and hurroo-ing, and another looking murder at everybody—it was just like the difference between polite-drunk and fighting-drunk. But the old experienced miners took it all as ordinary business, and showed no excitement at all.

" No, there was never any scrapping over claims or stealing of other men's gold. We packed our nuggets into moose-hide pokes, and each man had some extraordinary private method of hiding his poke—down his trouser-leg or somewhere. I guess everyone knew that the majority ruled and they couldn't get away with any claim-jumping or killing or stealing, it was too damned dangerous. Naturally there were seasons of excitement, and there were other seasons of intense gloom—always a feast or a famine. But the seasoned men were very quick to stop any rumblings and grumblings, and would start up card-games or anything to divert attention. It was most fortunate that there wasn't any liquor : rum in that crowd would have been just like a match to powder."

CHAPTER XVIII

THE WINTER CAMP

GOLD-FEVER, like other agues, has cold fits as well as hot ones, and after the miners had spent a few miserable days in the snow and rain considering the prospect of a winter to be spent on the Wind, a cold fit took them in a way that was most unpleasant for Mitchell. The memory riles him still, after thirty-five years.

" When the miners found that they would have to winter on the river a damn nasty thing turned up. As you know, Graham, they had followed me uninvited because they thought I'd got Government information : I hadn't wanted them, and I'd never told anybody anything about my business—it had just leaked out that I was going up the Peel. And now they turned round and claimed that there wasn't a pass over to the Stewart, and that I'd lured them up there, and that they were going to lose a year or two years on the way and would probably all die. In fact they laid the blame for the whole God-damn thing on my head.

" As the days went by the men were getting uglier and uglier, and finally they held a mob-meeting and accused me publicly of having brought them all to disaster. Well, I didn't have to do it, but I knew the bad feeling would have gone on all winter and got worse and worse, so I just called their bluff. I got right up in the meeting and spoke.

" ' I don't know what you bloody fools are talking about,' I said. ' I didn't ask you to come up here and I didn't advise you to come up here. I didn't want you up here one damn bit. If you chose to butt in on my business that's your look-out—you came up of your own wills and now you can bloody well freeze and starve for all I care. But just to stop the chin-music I'll bloody well go up to that pass myself and show you. How I'll go, or when, that's no concern of yours, but I'm bloody well going.'

"And I bloody well did go. I took my guide Bonnet Plume, and we carried light packs and did that hundred and forty miles to the Pass in quick time. We met some Indians who came with us for part of the way, and we bought a small light skin boat from them which took us up through water where a heavy canoe could not have gone at that state of the water. We left it at Bear Run Creek and did the rest of the trip from there to the Pass on foot. We ran into masses of game in the last twenty miles below the Pass. The caribou seemed to be massed up there, and plenty of moose too in small lots. They looked like specks down below us in the valley as we travelled along the high benches. The game-trails were worn down two feet deep into the moss, and there were great numbers of dropped horns everywhere. It was on that trip that I shot my first mountain sheep.

" When we got to the Pass we found no great gash through the mountains, just a kind of twisty corridor that ran both ways. The Wind petered down to a rivulet, and up at the top there was a wide flat marsh with another rivulet going out the other way, south of west. Bonnet Plume said that this was the head of the Stewart, and we followed it down far enough to make sure that it was developing into quite a river. Then we turned in our tracks and beat it for home, as we were afraid of getting caught by the winter.

" When we got down to where the Wind river was a big stream again Bonnet Plume led me into a certain thick patch of bush, and there was a damn fine two-man canoe cached up on poles. It was a regular Loucheux canoe, up by the bow and down by the stern, with a nearly flat bottom—as

tippy as Hell, but Bonnet Plume managed it like a bicycle.
Once we put that into the water it didn't take us many hours
to reach camp—we went along like a chip down a sluice.
Tremendous cheering when we arrived! The situation
was saved."

After this story was finished Mitchell went on to set up a
monument to Bonnet Plume.

" I want you, Angus," he said, " to put in the book how
much I owed to old man Bonnet Plume. He got me to the
Pass as he had promised, and he proved, both on this trip
and on many other occasions, his absolute faithfulness and
loyalty—almost affection. He was the trickiest old son of a
gun you ever met : he might disappear for a couple of weeks
at a time, but he always came back, and I got to look on
him as a real friend. I guess he had the gipsy call, and
couldn't stick round too long in one place without a change.
And I'm sure he was afraid of the miners—afraid of their
wickedness and wild savage ways of going on."

The next urgent job was to build the winter camp. The
weather turned warmer after the first storm had passed,
but nobody knew how soon the winter might shut down
with lasting snow, and the first heavy fall had been a clear
warning that it was necessary to get under cover without
delay. So everyone started to build good solid cabins of
spruce-logs. Oddly enough, the place where the floating
ice had driven them ashore was as good a site for a camp
as they could have hoped to find anywhere. Just above the
backwater there was a long broad bench, high enough up
from the river to be out of the reach of floods, but not so
high as to make access to the water troublesome. There
was excellent timber on the bench and on the slope above,
and enough of it to build all the cabins that were needed
and yet to leave a good scattering of trees for shelter.

Mitchell and his party were determined to make their
camp warm and comfortable and proof against any kind of
weather. They built it against a dry gravel bank, digging

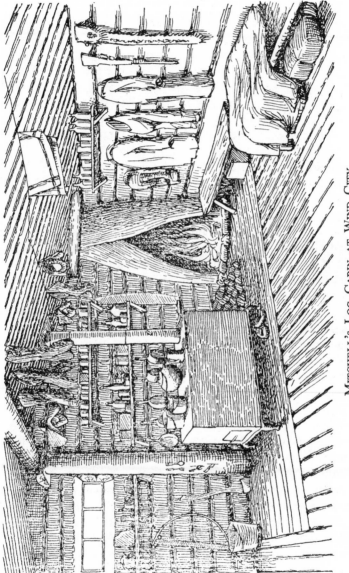

Mitchell's Log Cabin at Wind City.

away the bank to an up-and-down face so that no back wall was needed. The cabin was a little bit deeper than it was broad, perhaps about twenty feet from front to back and eighteen feet across inside. The walls were of good straight logs, adzed flat on the inner side, and packed with moss. The side walls served as party-walls for the adjoining cabins. The roof was made of poles, with smaller poles laid between them, supported on a roof-tree that ran the long way of the cabin. On top of the poles was a good thick layer of moss, and sods on top of all.

For inside carpentry they drew on the planking of the boats. This made the door, the bunks and the shelves, the top of the table, which was collapsible, and part of the floor. The rest of the floor, like the walls, was of timbers adzed flat. The stove was the same one that they had used in the boat from the beginning, and the little glass window, of which they were particularly proud, had been brought all the way from Edmonton in a wooden case. Two bunks were set end to end along each of the side walls, and another crossways at the back of the cabin ; packs and tools and heavy goods were stored under and between the bunks and guns and spare clothes were hung on the walls above. Food was kept outside in a little tent, and the bacon was cached in a tree.

The finest feature of the whole cabin was the open fireplace, which they built in one corner on McQuaide's instructions. Nobody else had ever thought of installing an open fire-place in a wooden cabin—which is a sufficiently inflammable structure even without this added temptation. But McQuaide had a plan for a bottle-shaped affair that was a fire-place and flue combined ; it was made of willow saplings set up on end and was puddled inside with clay, and never threatened the least danger to the walls or roof. It helped out the stove enormously when the cold weather came, and was a great attraction to visitors from the other cabins.

As before, Mitchell's party conducted their life according to fixed rules. " We had military discipline for sleeping, feeding, and the rotation of duties. We cooked, cut firewood, cleaned up the camp, and hunted by weeks in turn, while the other parties would eat when they felt like it, and sleep all the time, and observe no rules of life whatever. Our diet was beans, pork, bacon, flour, tea, dried apples and potatoes, and a few prunes, and we made a kind of *tisane* of spruce buds against the scurvy. The other miners laughed at us for that and said it was an old wives' tale, but they got scurvy later on and we didn't, so they were welcome to have their laugh.

" There was a two-man cabin a few doors off from us which always seemed to be unlucky. It was built first of all by two men who were always scrapping between themselves. One night somebody who was passing heard a fearful noise inside, so he raised the ' police call ', and everybody turned out and rushed over. The door was barred, but we broke it down and found the men rolling round on the floor, biting and gouging and with their knives out. When knives are going quick it is as hard to do anything with men as it is to break up a dog-fight, so we hung back a bit ; but they were cutting each other to pieces, and so at last I took an axe-handle and laid one of them out, and his pals tied up the other. That ended the scrap, but then we discovered that the man I had laid out wasn't coming to again. Some of the nastier specimens began to grin and ha-ha me—' You've done it this time, Mr. Smarty,' and all that. However, we douched him with cold water and did some artificial respiration, and in the end he came round all right.

" After that the two of them wouldn't live together any more and wanted to break partnership, but they couldn't agree over dividing up the goods. They were at odds about the cabin, because both had worked on building it, and worst of all about the stove, which they wanted to cut in half. Finally the miners held a meeting to regulate the business, and made them abandon the cabin altogether and leave the stove inside it. Later on the cabin was taken over by two Swedes from Ontario, two brothers, who took scurvy and died. One day I was looking after the one in the lower bunk, who was dying—he was in a terrible state, smelt fearful—when the one in the upper bunk said, 'Throw the damned swine outside, can't you, if he's dead?' I came near throwing him outside, and told him so ; but he went crazy later and had to be strait-jacketed in a canvas bag, till he died too. But all that happened in the winter, when it was dark."

About the time that the building of Wind City was finished the miners had one of their periodical scares of an Indian raid. One evening two lads who had been down the river late after beaver and muskrat rushed into the camp with a wild report of an Indian war-party, that they had seen dancing madly round an immense bonfire a little way down-stream. The miners immediately fell into a frenzy, and were all for rushing out on the spot and massacring the Indians while they were off their guard. But some of the steadier men suggested that it would be well to send some scouts out first, to find out what was really the matter. McQuaide was ready to go out himself, and asked for a few volunteers ; but though everyone had been eager enough to make a sally *en masse*, nobody seemed anxious to go scouting in the dark by himself, or with only one or two of his pals in not very close support. At last a few of the Kootenay and Idaho men, who were accustomed to Indians, came forward, and Mitchell went too to support McQuaide.

" We certainly found an enormous fire," Mitchell said, " and there were figures passing backwards and forwards in front of it, but nobody was dancing and we heard no war-whoops or drumming. Then suddenly out of the silence we heard a splendid baritone voice begin to sing in French :

Sur nos chemins les rameaux et les fleurs
Sont répandus dans ce grand jour de fête,

and so on—a French hymn for Palm Sunday, called ' *Les Rameaux* '. I knew it perfectly well, but I didn't do anything beyond whispering to the others to lie low a bit and let me go on alone. They could make nothing of the situation at all, and thought I was a damned fool ; but I waited till the singer had finished his last verse and then slow-marched out of the bushes into the glare of the fire holding my rifle like a palm branch with the butt upwards, and singing the chorus as loud as ever I could :—

> Hosanna ! Gloire au Seigneur !
> Béni celui qui vient sauver le monde !

" The strangers were utterly amazed and came crowding round to see what kind of apparition I might be. They turned out to be a fine husky lot of French-Canadians from Montreal, pretty well equipped, and the singer was a man called Millais who said he had sung in a big Jesuit church ever since he was a boy. I called in the scouts and we were given a warm welcome, with two or three rounds of whisky-blanc that they had managed to smuggle through somehow, and then we made a night of it together. They joined us next day at Wind City ; built themselves a good shack and turned out to be excellent neighbours."

CHAPTER XIX

PROSPECTING AND EXPLORATION

NOTWITHSTANDING the early storm, which had checked the miners' progress soon after the middle of September, winter held off much longer than anyone had dared to hope. Mitchell made the most of his chances for prospecting and hunting during these weeks of autumn, and often committed what the Indians assured him afterwards was a consummate folly, in going away to explore entirely alone. The Indians regard solitary travel as next door to suicide, as a man who breaks his leg or has any serious accident when he is by himself in the woods can only crawl miserably for a day or two, and in the end is certain to starve or to be picked up by wolves.

However, Mitchell was innocent so far in the matter of wolves, though he got a penetrating lesson before the autumn was over, and he continued to scour the country until frost and deep snow made it impossible to pan any longer. His ordinary outfit for a prospecting trip was a blanket with an oilskin cover ; three days' provisions of cooked beans, pork, sugar, salt and tea ; a billy-can ; a rifle and ammunition ; and his miner's tools—a heavy pick, a light pick, an axe, a pointed steel shovel, and a pan. It was quite a formidable load to carry for days at a time, but Mitchell was a great traveller, and managed to explore the whole of the Wind and Little Wind rivers at one time and another, either on foot or with a boat or canoe for his base. He lost himself once for two days at the head of the Little Wind, wandering among innumerable dried-up watercourses that were equally indistinguishable from one another and from the principal stream.

I gather that everyone found gold on a modest scale during the course of the autumn ; but the Wind was no new Klondike and nobody thought it worth while to stick by the claims that they had staked. Besides the gold in the gravels Mitchell saw a good deal of gold-bearing quartz in the higher mountains ; the gold ran through the veins in little wires and knots that looked like many dollars to the ton of ore, but he naturally had no means of dealing with solid rock and so the gold is still there for anyone who cares to build a crusher on the top of the Rockies. Some of the miners tried to sink a shaft at Wind City, thinking that there might be a heavy deposit of gold on the bed-rock right under the bench. But all the gravel in that country is permanently frozen at a depth of two or three feet, so the shaft-sinkers found themselves committed to the terribly tedious business of thawing it out as they went down, by means of fires built on the surface. A good hot fire, covered and left all night, would thaw the gravel for about four inches down ; this they would clear out and pan, and then light another fire and repeat the process. They found no gold, and gave up the project long before they reached the bed-rock ; but their shaft was most useful later on when a big common grave was needed for the victims of the scurvy.

Bonnet Plume was also a keen prospector, and as he possessed two pokes that seemed to be well filled with dust and nuggets, Mitchell believed that he must know of some good rich creek. But he was always as silent as a clam, and there was consequently great excitement one day when he came secretly to Mitchell and offered to lead him and his friends to a " creek of pure gold "

" We all three stole out of camp separately," Mitchell said, " and met the old devil at a certain dead tree, which was an easy mark to find. Then he ran eight or ten miles up-country and turned into a gulch down which a crick ran rapidly over beds of gravel. Then at a certain point he stopped and raised his hand, and when we caught up with him he pointed to the crick without saying a word.

" Well, that gravel actually looked like a bed of pure gold—so much so that we dropped everything and jumped right in and took up handfuls of the shining metal with wild whoops of joy. But when we scrambled up on to the bank again, to our horror we saw that the nuggets were not roundish, nor a dull gold colour, but sharp-edged and highly polished, like clean brass. We didn't even have to bite them to try the hardness : we knew them at once for iron pyrites—not worth a damn ! And that, my dear boy, was one of the shocks in life that it takes some time to get over ! "

As a result of all these journeys Mitchell gradually acquired a very good knowledge of the country, and on the strength of it he made the first map of the upper Peel and its tributaries. The Wind and the Little Wind he mapped from his own observations, and for the other rivers he used such information as he could pick up from Bonnet Plume and the other Indians who visited Wind City. The map is drawn in indelible pencil on a sheet of ordinary foolscap, and its air of lost secrets and dead men's chests could hardly be bettered by a pirate captain mapping his cache of treasure. I have had it reproduced here, and the legend, which I left out of the reproduction for lack of space, reads like this :—

Map of Peel River and Head
Waters of same. Showing
Wind City our Winter Home
Lat. 66 Longtd. 135^{40} and Pass
to Stewart River 150 miles South
South East of Wind City.

But besides its flavour of romance this map possesses the virtue of being fairly accurate in most of its principal

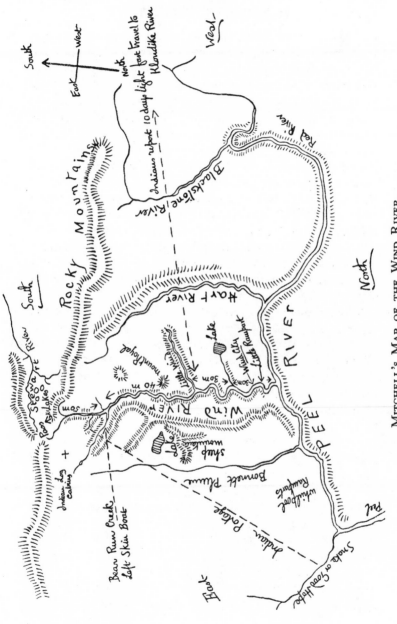

MITCHELL'S MAP OF THE WIND RIVER.

features. Anyone who has had much to do with home-made maps—particularly if he has ever got lost through believing what one of them showed—will understand that this is real praise ; and comparison with the copy of the Government map, which I have also had reproduced, will show that praise is thoroughly well deserved. For instance, Mitchell has got his Pass quite right, and the chain of small lakes that lie close by to the west. Bear river, or Bear Run Creek, is correctly placed at fifty miles from the Pass, with an unnamed mountain lying westwards beyond the Wind at about the point where the slopes of the main range of the Ogilvies rise up from the plateau and barrens. " Mount Royal " and " Sheep Mountain " are also in their proper places in some foothills called the Illtyd Range, through which the Wind passes in a gorge ; they represent the two parts of this range that abut on the valley of the river.

Mitchell described Mount Royal as " a freak of Nature— a gigantic pyramid of a mountain that rose right out of the valley of the Wind. It was such a peculiar shape that we all compared it to Quebec Cathedral spire. In September, although the sun set early and the nights were dark, with no aurora, the top of the mountain stayed lighted up long after sunset with the most beautiful shades of golden and scarlet and pink." Sheep Mountain Mitchell named after the wild sheep which he could see with his field-glasses from across the river ; Bonnet Plume told him that on one of the high benches of this mountain there was a range of caves, and that the sheep regularly used these caves as stables in very cold weather. He is rather less successful with the mileages to Little Wind river and Hungry Creek. The Little Wind is really only thirty-two miles from Bear Run Creek, against his forty, and Hungry Creek nineteen miles, against his thirty, from the Little Wind. But these are his only serious mistakes, and he is practically right again with his thirty miles from Hungry Creek to the Peel.

He has put in the large lake at the head of Hungry Creek, and if he has made the course of the Wind a good deal twistier than it should be he has only exaggerated the sharpness of the bends of the river, as everyone does who tries to make a traverse by eye. The note about the trail to Klondike was obtained from an Indian, who said that very good travellers with very strong dogs could make Dawson City in ten days from the mouth of the Little Wind. Mitchell disbelieved this report and no one attempted the journey ; but the Indian was certainly right, as the Government surveyor has thought fit to mark the trail, and the Mounted Police have used it for winter patrols.

On the back of the sheet on which the map is drawn there is a nominal roll of the men who wintered at Wind City, with their addresses or the names of their native towns. When Mitchell showed me the list he went off into a running commentary on the manners and morals of the different men, whom he seemed to remember perfectly, and on the reputation of the various towns from which they came. The commentary was very interesting, though far too libellous to print ; but it ended with some general remarks on the camp's bad characters, which I am safe in quoting. (Mitchell had been elected " camp captain ", and so bad characters concerned him closely.)

" There was far too much pulling of guns," he said, " among a certain section of the miners. We had a nasty little clique of what I call ' killers '—regular gun-men, shoot you as soon as look at you. I never made play with my gun—an old miner had advised me never to do so, and said that if I wanted to practise, to practise inside somewhere, and say as little as possible about it, and let on that I was no good with a gun. But these people were always practising in public, and bragging about what they could do, and it fairly intimidated some of the quiet-living chaps.

" I remember one day I was coming down the trail with

one of our bad bunch, the worst type of a killer, who began
questioning me about my powers with a gun. I made
some very modest answer : the man began to brag, but I
wasn't going to be drawn. Then he pointed to a whiskey-
jack that had perched on top of a dry rampole close by,
and asked me if I could hit it. I said I thought not, and
made quite a song about being a very poor shot ; but
in the end I consented to try. So then I fired. Much to
the joy of the killer, the bird fluttered up into the air, and
he began to grin and ha-ha me. But then it fluttered
down again and fell stone-dead—I'd hit the top of the
rampole just underneath it, and a splinter had been driven
up into its body and had killed it after a few seconds. So
that was the collapse of the killer, and a permanent collapse
too.

" Actually our man Craigie was the leader of all this
bad element. He was what we should call the ' bolshy '
type nowadays. We began to have trouble with him first
when we were building our cabin, as he was damned in-
subordinate and couldn't or wouldn't get on with Cecil,
who had offended him with his rather military English
ways—wanted Craigie to clean his boots, and all that.
This led to a lot of unpleasantness, and of course Craigie
upset Smith, who wasn't bolshy but just a damned stupid
strong work-animal, and finally it came to shooting. I
was coming back from hunting one evening, that being my
task that week, while Jack was cooking and Cecil was getting wood. As I came down the trail I saw Craigie leaning
against a tree taking very careful aim at something with
his rifle, apparently in the direction of the camp. I thought
this was pretty queer, and when I looked in the direction
he was aiming I saw Cecil coming along singing, with a
load of firewood in a tump-line over his forehead. I was
too far away to do anything, so I fired at the barrel of
Craigie's rifle, hit it near the chamber, and exploded the
cartridge, so that it was wrecked in his hands.

" Cecil came running up, and there was a Hell of a palaver and quarrel about the wrecked rifle, Craigie pretending that I'd tried to murder him. I refused point-blank to discuss anything and said that we must have a miners' meeting. So I called some of the chaps in right away and put the case before them : I explained that I'd seen Craigie aiming, had been surprised to see him pointing his rifle towards camp, had looked along and seen Cecil in line, and couldn't find anything to do but to fire quick.

" Craigie had no credible explanation to give at all : he just said I'd fired at him and spoiled his rifle, and tried to make a sad mouth about his loss. But the meeting found him guilty and put it up to me to assess his penalty ; so I put him on good behaviour, which meant that anybody might shoot him at sight if he went off it. This was all I wanted, as it put me all right in cases of any future trouble : there would have been no difficulty then, you see, if I'd dropped Craigie one fine day—I should have had the gang's authority for doing it.

" After this row we naturally threw him out of the cabin, and another miners' meeting ruled that this was justifiable provided that we paid him the balance of his grub-stake— and that of course we should have done anyhow. He took Smith with him, and he got his grub-stake too ; and the two of them built a small cabin and set up for themselves. From that time on Craigie was at the bottom of all the trouble in camp—trouble about shooting and cards and thefts and fights and so forth. Also he persistently talked against the Queen ; and we had a lot of trouble over the flag, you know, handling the riff-raff element, the foreigners, etc. The better fellows were consistently against anything like that, wouldn't stand for it at all. However, he continued to be pleasant enough to me through it all ; I believe he really liked me or respected me in a kind of way. Once I remember he came to me and said—' Mr. Mitchell, in case there's war, my men won't touch you : you'll be all right.' Damn polite of him, eh ?

" In the end the miners threw him out themselves for some matter of shooting at people or theft, I forget now just what it was. They gave him two days' provisions and told him to clear out of Wind City—a pretty harsh verdict under the circumstances—and they never heard anything more about him. He just dropped out into the atmosphere ! But oddly enough I heard later on what happened to him. When the miners fired him out he was lucky enough to run into some Indians before he starved, and then he was plausible enough to get them to take him on. After I joined the Indians I heard that there was a white man living with another of their bands near by, and that he was very clever and strong and that they thought a great deal of him : it never occurred to me that this man might be Craigie, but then one day he turned up at Francis' camp and came in to see me—all bygones were bygones by then ! I suppose he got over to Dawson in the end, by one means or another."

CHAPTER XX

BEARS AND WOLVES

HUNTING, which had been so bad on the Peel, improved very much on the upper reaches of the Wind —in fact it improved to the point at which the quarry would often go after the sportsman as readily as the sportsman went after the quarry. Grizzly bears were quite plentiful, and when he was on the main river or the larger creeks Mitchell used to see one or two of them every day, grubbing among the roots of the willows by the stream-side. The young bears live almost entirely on willow roots and tender bark ; as they get older they begin to dig for gophers, and pick up the young of caribou and larger animals. Sometimes they take to man-eating in their old age, and the Indians say that they will do anything to get human flesh once they have acquired the taste. Young grizzlies are not grey, but a tawny brown ; they turn greyer as they grow older, and some of the very old bears are almost white.

Once, when he was travelling with Bonnet Plume, Mitchell landed from the canoe to prospect in a certain creek. He left Bonnet Plume to put up the tent, and set off up the side of the creek with his prospecting tools and rifle. It was a perfectly windless day, but he happened to notice the willows in front of him moving ; as he peered through an opening among the bushes he saw a nice young grizzly grubbing among the roots. Mitchell whistled ; the bear sat up on its haunches, and Mitchell put two shots into the big white mark which showed on its chest. He waited a moment to see if it would charge, but it was too badly wounded to move, and could only claw at the willows like a man pulling up handfuls of grass ; so he walked up close and killed it with a shot below the ear, congratulating himself on a neat and efficient piece of work. But at that moment Bonnet Plume suddenly arrived in a terrible taking —he had dropped everything when he heard the first shots and rushed up with his rifle. As soon as he saw the dead bear he began to curse in his own language, calling Mitchell all kinds of names and fulminating against everything in general. Gradually it came out that he was cursing Mitchell for a tenderfoot, as experienced people never tackle a grizzly alone—Indians like to have support from several rifles, or to surround the bear and smother him with fire from all sides.

They cut up the bear, which was a nice big one with a fine golden-brown pelt, rolled up the meat inside the skin, and cached the whole in a tree. The fur was on the outside of the bundle, and they tied four heavy stones to the corners to keep them from being raised by the wind. But when they came back from their prospecting three days later Bonnet Plume remarked, as they approached the cache, " All meat gone," and pointed to a raven that was sitting on a rock, too much gorged to fly. And all the meat was gone : the ravens had torn the heavy hide to pieces and picked the bones clean, and a dozen of them were still sitting round the wreckage.

On another occasion victory rested with the bear. Mitchell was going up the Wind towards Bear Run Creek with two or three miners and some Indians : they were tracking a canoe, and Mitchell was ahead on the tracking line. Just as they came to the mouth of the creek Mitchell saw something white in the bushes, which he took for a mountain goat ; so he signalled to the others to stop and to hand up his rifle, and took a shot at the white spot without making out the shape of the animal clearly.

" Greatly to my consternation," he went on, " about ten feet of pure white grizzly bear, an old patriarch and probably a man-eater, reared up in front of me out of the bushes. I pumped in two more shots, and some of the boys behind me did the same. The bear looked like charging, but changed his mind and set off up the creek, keeping near the top of the farther bank. Two of the boys went after him, but I kept to the bed of the creek, thinking that he would probably come down off the bank higher up.

"And that's just what he did, but he came tumbling down right on top of me in a shower of earth and stones, and I had to dodge into a hole to keep out of his way. Then, after he'd fallen right over the top of me, he picked up the trail of the two miners and started in pursuit of them—they doubled back over the top of the bank, and I followed the bear and had another shot at him as he chased them. In the end we all got back to the boat and the bear disappeared—God knows where, because he must have been full of lead. We were all cut and torn and grimy and roaring with laughter at being beaten by a bloody old bear, but I suppose we were fools to play tag with him the way we did ! "

Then there was another hunt in which the bear was the aggressor. Mitchell's own account is again the best.

" One time in the autumn I had gone off by myself— very foolishly, as I know now—to prospect in a side-creek off the main river. The creek was about a hundred yards wide and was evidently a bank-high torrent in spring, but then there was only a trickle of fast-running water in the middle of the channel. The banks were perhaps ten or twelve feet high and were covered with bushes : the land above was barren, and there was no timber anywhere except some clumps of scrubby spruce a quarter of a mile away. I had gone off on foot and was carrying my tools and provisions and camping kit. It came on a pouring

wet evening, so I decided to camp on a small ledge some
little way above the bed of the crick—cut some boughs for
a bed, and sat down on them with my blanket and rubber
sheet over my head and shoulders. Then I made a little
fire and cooked some bacon and a muskrat.

" After I had had my supper I made my sheet into a
kind of bivvy and lay down underneath it with my feet
outside. In the morning I woke up in the way one does
in the North—quietly and quickly, with no yawning and
stretching about—and moved gently out of my bivvy feet
first, with my hand on my rifle. (All this sort of thing
becomes second nature.) It was a dark grey dawn, just
breaking, and as I got outside the bivvy the first thing
I saw was the God-damnedest big grizzly sitting up on
his haunches looking at me, with his hands hanging at
his breast. I figured that he was about six years old—
a beautiful golden tawny beast, with a pure white waistcoat.

" Now he was only about twenty feet off, on top of the
bank, and I thought that the next thing the son of a bitch
would do would be to drop on to all-fours and right down
on top of me. So I got on to one knee and fired three
rounds rapid into the white of his waistcoat. He pivoted on
his hams and made off straight up the bank and through
some bushes ; I thought this was pretty damn good business
and followed him up with my rifle in one hand and my
axe in the other. I found lots of blood and a regular
track through the bushes as if he made a practice of coming
down to the gravel-bars to fish. But I hadn't gone many
yards, poking slowly along with my eyes and ears going
overtime, when I heard a grunt *behind* me. This was a
nasty jar, and I looked round and saw the bear's head
poking out of the bushes only about five feet away. So
I dropped my rifle and took the axe and chopped at his
skull, and split it open and killed him. He was badly hit,
as all three bullets had gone through his heart and lungs

and into his spine, which just shows the vitality of the brutes.

" I'm pretty sure now that he'd smelt the bacon of my supper overnight and had come down to prospect—bacon will bring them for miles. And no doubt the son of a bitch was just on the point of dropping on top of the bivvy when he saw feet coming out, and being unused to the sight of feet he sat up to consider matters. The Indians told me afterwards that they had found his body untouched a few days later, and had been able to reconstruct the encampment of the white man and what he had done to the bear. They considered him a damned fool, whoever he was. I told them it was me, and protested that there was really nothing else to be done under the circumstances —you can't shoot at a bear's head at a range of five feet, and so I really had no choice but to take the axe. But no doubt I shouldn't have been out there at all without a partner."

Later in the day, while the idea of bears was still rather vivid in his mind, Mitchell was ploughing along a game-trail on the plateau, knee-deep in moss. It happened that his pack was unusually heavy, so he had slung it over his forehead with a tump-line, and had his rifle packed cross-ways behind his neck. Just as he was passing through a clump of small trees and bushes, where there was cover enough for an animal, the air was suddenly filled with a noise of roaring and sharp explosive reports. He got a terrific fright, as he supposed that he was up against another grizzly, but he was so bowed by the tump-line that he could see nothing until he had struggled out from under his load. Then he got hold of his rifle as quickly as he could and looked about all ways at once to face the bear— only to find that the noise had been made by a covey of ptarmigan rising from among the bushes.

Mitchell, as I have said, started his hunting without much experience of wolves. As the herds of caribou were up in the mountains and round about the Pass during the autumn season the wolves had drawn off after them, and until the snow drove both caribou and wolves back into the valleys for shelter he saw little of either except when he was on the high ground to the south of Bear Run Creek. And it was up in that region that he got his first lesson in wolves —the wolves, in fact, providing him with a three days' course of instruction.

There were two kinds of wolves in the Peel river country, small grey wolves and timber wolves. The grey wolves lived by hunting the caribou in packs of twenty or thirty ; in the winter Mitchell used to see them ranging round the herds baying and snapping while the caribou horned them away, keeping the cows and calves inside a kind of hollow square, while big bulls would sometimes charge out from the square and attack the wolves with their forefeet as well as their horns. But the wolves generally managed to pick out a few weak animals or calves, and were so cunning that they would sometimes drive the caribou over a cliff, where they would break their legs or be killed outright. Grey wolves would only attack a man if he were helpless, and a strong dog could stand up against three or four of them at least. Their method of attack is to slash with their long teeth as they race past, and they prefer not to get to grips, as a dog would do, until the other animal has been thoroughly bewildered and exhausted through loss of blood. But the timber wolves are much more formidable creatures, being so big and strong that two of them can easily pull down a moose. They hunt alone or in couples, and do not bay their prey as the grey wolves do but only call to one another now and then to keep touch as they work through the woods. The Indians used to value their pelts very highly for trade, but even the most skilful Indian hunters found them almost impossible to trap or shoot as their sight and hearing seemed to be supernaturally keen. Sometimes a trapper would get one with a dead-fall set over a kill—they have a habit of returning to their kills after their first feeding—but a dead-fall never succeeds unless fresh snow comes down to cover up the traces of human work, and the trapper must always keep his hands dipped in fresh blood while he is arranging the falls.

This is Mitchell's story of his first encounter with timber wolves.

" I had gone off prospecting by myself, and made a little camp for the night a few miles down-stream from Bear Run Creek. Before I turned in for the night I hung up my gold-pan on a bush—McQuaide had told me that the tinkling of a pan against the branches of a bush would keep me safe from wild animals anywhere. But the next morning, when I went down to the river to fill my billy-can, I was horrified to see a dog's tracks that were bigger than my fist. If it was a dog I figured it was too damn big, and if it was a wolf that wasn't healthy either, so I turned back to my tent, made my breakfast, packed up and got started. But just as I was leaving I saw two prick ears showing up over a bush—it was a wolf all right. The brute shrank down out of sight as I looked, but when I moved on it followed me, keeping under cover, and presently I found that there were two of them, working the hunt together.

" Every now and then one of them showed itself in the open and I had a shot at it, but they were as quick as the devil—you'd think they saw the flash and dodged the bullet, almost—and I never touched them once. After I'd had several cracks at them I happened to look at my belt, and I'd only got two more rounds left ! I'd come out with a heavy pack, and had cut down my ammunition to six or eight rounds to save weight. ' God,' I said, ' no more shooting, Mitchell ; you keep those rounds for yourself ' : if they'd got me, I tell you I wasn't going to be torn to pieces alive !

" As I went on without firing the wolves gradually realized

that there was no danger, and they got more and more cheeky, keeping closer and closer to me and calling to one another to check up on my movements. They didn't often show themselves out and out, and must have bellied across the open spots like an Indian, but there were always the pointed ears showing over a boulder or a bush, or a flash of grey fur between tree-trunks, and the feeling that you were being watched.

" The worst thing of all was the eyes in the fire-light after dark. I got no sleep that night, as I was keeping up the fire the whole time, and every now and then those eyes would draw up until I had to throw a burning stick at them. All the next day the same thing went on, and no rest again the next night—fire-light, and eyes, and I tell you I was getting pretty God-damn rattled. Then on the morning of the third day I saw they'd get me sure if this thing went on, and I thought it was about time to build a raft and go wherever it would take me. So I got hold of some driftwood, strapped it together with my pack-straps and tump-line, and launched myself—and I bloody well had to use up one of my two last shots on them as I was pushing off. They followed the raft down along the sands, but eventually it fetched up on the other side of the river, and I got away. Of course, the Indians said afterwards that it was my own damn fault for going out alone."

After he had finished this story Mitchell suddenly bent forward and banged the arm of his chair. " Graham," he said, " there are no words in the English language that I can use to convey to you the horror of feeling yourself a hunted animal. I shall never forget it—the eyes in the darkness, and the fear of something that *lurks*. I have been familiar with wolves for years since those days, but I've never got used to the sound of their howling, which is enough to make anyone shudder. Yet those devils that hunted me, they didn't howl—they ran a still-hunt, and that was almost worse in a way. You felt them always pressing on you, always just behind you, always just round that boulder, always watching for the moment when you would stumble or nod asleep—and then leap in ! "

CHAPTER XXI

THE WINTER NIGHT

A S winter closed down the daylight became shorter and shorter until it finally gave way to permanent night. Mitchell continued to hunt even after the last of the sun's light had disappeared, as the scurvy patients craved for fresh meat and the aurora was so magnificent that its light was often quite sufficient to show him his way along a line of traps. The moose and caribou were still very scarce, but beaver were plentiful, and ptarmigan, and the great arctic hares.

"Without exaggeration, Angus," he said, "there were plenty of days when we could make a good shape at hunting by aurora-light. (Apart from that you may say it was pitch black all through December and January, and that was what sent men crazy!) Sometimes the aurora was simply a kind of radiance in the north ; other times it was like a succession of lace curtains of all imaginable colours, or again it might be like spears. Sometimes we could hear the rustling of the aurora—that terrifies the Indians, as they think it's made by spirits. And in times of intense cold we'd sometimes see the whole air filled with the most beautiful tints of rose-pink and madder, as if the low light was striking through a haze of tiny frozen particles. The same pink light appeared again in the spring, when the sun was beginning to come back ; that was our first warning that the long darkness was getting over, and after that just a little edge of the sun used to appear along the horizon. When it got up a bit and the rays struck the snow crystals almost level it damn nearly put out your blinkers—just like millions of diamonds at your feet !

" That was when fellows used to get snow-blind, with that terrible dazzle. It's a fearful pain, like spears stabbing into the eyes, and I've seen men actually fall on the ground and writhe. We used face-masks of duffle with slits cut for the eyes, and that checked the dazzle : the Indians blacken round their eyes with charcoal, but the face-masks were better, and we had to wear them anyhow in the very cold weather, particularly in the terrible cold winds, to save our faces from freezing as much as we could. We used to get terrible cracks on our faces from the constant freezing across the eyes and cheekbones and ears ; and fingers the same way—we were in constant pain with the cracks in our fingers all through the cold weather."

One day, before the sun had finally gone, when Mitchell was prospecting among the higher benches with McQuaide and one of the Gecks, they saw a fantastic figure in the distance that might or might not have been a man. A mist which had risen from the river was making things look unnaturally big, but as the creature approached they made out that it actually was the remains of a man, though he was only half clothed in some tatters of skins and fur and was obviously a raving lunatic. Possibly he was a pro-spector who had lost his wits on account of the darkness and solitude. He fled when he saw the miners, and they followed him hoping that they might catch him and at least save him from dying of cold ; but although he had no show-shoes he kept away from them for hours and finally disappeared on a steep rocky hillside. They had to give up the pursuit, and Mitchell supposes that he must have crawled into some hole and died, as nobody ever saw or heard of him again.

There must have been many destitute white men wintering at large through the North, and no doubt they suffered heavily from scurvy, starvation, and sheer freezing. One man at least was rescued by Indians somewhere on the upper Wind : the Indians told Mitchell how they had found him lying helpless in a shack with his partner's dead body outside—he had food and cut firewood beside him, but was too weak to get out of his bunk and had been starving slowly for days. Another time two boys from Wind City got the handsomest fright of their lives when they were scrounging in an abandoned cabin, and, on pulling out a roll of rags from the bunk, found that it contained a corpse.

Mitchell himself came across the traces of the same kind of disaster when he was returning home by the Hudson's Bay Company's steamer the following summer. The steamer had stopped to load firewood somewhere near Fort Good Hope, and Mitchell hobbled ashore to take a little walk on his crutches. Following a trail that led back into the woods from the river-bank he came to a small log cabin, which he could see had been run up roughly and hurriedly by very inexperienced men. It was a ghastly looking dark little hole, that smelled horribly of decay and dampness ; there were no signs of life, but some old bones of caribou and the skulls of some beaver and a bear showed that the owners had lived in the winter by hunting. Mitchell went in, lighted the stub of a candle that he found on a shelf, and saw that he was in the presence of two dead men. One of them was lying in the bunk—no more than a skeleton covered with a few scraps of skin. The other had evidently been sitting at the table when he died, as his skull, arms, and ribs were lying on the table and the rest of the bones were hanging to them by the sinews. No doubt they had been caught by the winter, had dug themselves in with a few provisions, and had starved when their hunting failed. The one who was sitting at the table had a kind of rough diary before him, which he seemed to have begun to write when they realized that they were not likely to come through the winter. Mitchell looked it through in case it should give the men's names or any messages for their people ; but it simply alluded to " Pete " and " myself ", described the finishing of the food, the absolute silence and lifelessness of the whole country after the coming of the deep winter snow, and Pete's appalling illness—evidently scurvy, which had led on to complete insanity. The writer of the diary, as Mitchell says, must have been a very kind-hearted as well as a very plucky fellow, as it was clear that he had spent all his time in nursing and feeding Pete. His last words were, " The trail is pretty damn nearly finished."

Scurvy was the chief cause of sickness among the miners, as they had hardly any fresh food and most of them were too ignorant to understand the virtue of spruce *tisane*. The disease took a firm hold at Wind City ; Mitchell believes that a good three-quarters of the whole company were affected, though probably not more than ten per cent actually died. Having kept himself and his party fit with *tisane*, he dropped into the position of doctor to the camp at large, and describes a sufficiently gruesome state of affairs.

" The first sign of scurvy coming on is a weakness and bending of the knees ; then the upper part of the body gets emaciated and the lower limbs inflate tremendously. It's ghastly to see how they go—you poke your finger into a leg and the hole you make stays there, it doesn't fill out again like healthy flesh. Then the gums swell till the teeth drop out, and there is a most loathsome smell. (The scurvy smell, Angus, is like nothing but the sewers in Sous-le-Cap Street.) After the loss of the teeth they generally die.

" Some of the meaner bastards, when their pals went down with the scurvy, would go away and leave them helpless in the cabins, so the rest of us used to divide them up amongst us and nurse them. We would wash them and clean up the cabins, and let in some air to ventilate the awful stinks, and force them to drink *tisane*, which did them lots of good. They were all craving for fresh meat, but we could only get the odd caribou or bear now and then, and in the dark-time hunting was all the more difficult. But it was extraordinary to see how some of them recovered with *tisane* and fresh food, when it came along, provided they still had their teeth—men who had had their ribs sticking out like hoops, and their legs inflated like posts.

" All through the scurvy-time there was a regular oppression resting on the camp. Every man would be secretly testing out his knees, to find out if they were beginning to give way, and every man eyed his neighbours with horror, looking for the first signs of the disease. Most of them thought that it was something catching. Everyone's temper was on a hair-trigger, with nerves all gone—if you looked at a man, or if you didn't look at him, it might equally be taken as an offence, and a man might quarrel with his pal because he talked, or because he didn't talk, or for any childish reason that was no reason at all. You must put all that in the book, Graham, to show how we were affected by the strain of waiting, and the darkness, and the horrible disease."

Most of Mitchell's stories that refer to this time are remarkably grim. There was the case, for instance, of a man called Harris, which should go on record.

" Harris and I had gone up the river to cut fire-wood, and were coming back dragging our loaded toboggans. Harris was ahead, but not far enough ahead for safety, and suddenly the ice gave way and put us in the water five feet below. The river had dropped, you see, and left the ice and snow without any support. Luckily it was a piece of dead water, so we weren't drawn under the ice, but we were pretty wet about the feet and legs. I made a bee-line for the bank, where I saw some dry brush and tree roots, and made a good bonfire out of them : then I stripped and rubbed down, and put on the dry socks that I always carried slung on my chest, under my shirt. Harris, of course, thought he knew better—laughed at me for a tender-

foot, and hung round without changing or drying his socks ;
but before we'd gone a mile he was down on his back in
the snow howling that his feet were frozen.

" Well, I rolled him on to the toboggan and got him back
to camp somehow. Then I stripped his legs, and put him
in a big chair and lashed him in, so that he couldn't move
hand or foot. Then I got a basin of coal-oil and put his
feet in it to draw the frost, and of course that was absolute
agony. After that we got him into bed and chafed his feet
with snow. The left foot responded and gradually got the
life back into it, but the right foot, from the knuckles of the
toes down, and the butt of the heel, was solid. I dressed
it for days, but one morning when I was dressing it the skin
of the toes came right off like a glove, leaving the purplish
decayed flesh behind. And an awful stink ! McQuaide
and some of the old hands talked the thing over and decided
that someone must cut the toes off, or he would die of
gangrene, but who would do it ? Of course, nobody ; so
in the end it came back on me.

" Somebody had a hack-saw, and we sharpened up some
knives and got hold of some sewing-silk, and I got Harris'
permission in writing—signed and witnessed. Then I pro-
ceeded. McQuaide advised us to look out for the arteries,
and when a great spout of blood came two men were told
off to seize the worm with callipers, pull her out, and tie
her with a bit of silk. I allowed enough skin to turn over,
and sewed it all up, and then we had to cut out the butt
of the heel and scrape all round to remove the gangrene.
I don't know how long we were at it, but it seemed long
enough for a lifetime.

" Harris was a fine chap with any amount of guts and
cheerfulness (though he damned everyone to Hell during
the operation !) and in the end he survived and went down
the Stewart to Dawson with the rest of the crowd. But I
never shall forget the first day he was well enough to get
out of bed and hobble on some crutches that we'd made

for him. By that time the sun was beginning to show its rim over the horizon, and when we helped him to the door of the cabin and he saw the sun he raised one crutch in the air and cheered, and promptly fell down and cut his left hand open on the head of an axe. It was us who damned him then, and I tell you we damned him properly !

" I guess I saved another man's life there too. He had an internal stoppage, and we figured he'd die unless we could fix him up somehow with an enema. There naturally aren't any such things in a miners' camp, but at last I got hold of an old revolver barrel, and when I'd filed off the foresight and lashed on a caribou bladder for a reservoir it answered well enough. We made a strong liquor of soap-suds and black plug tobacco, and that fixed him up in fine style."

Another bad accident happened when two men tried to go down to Fort McPherson on snow-shoes. The miners had been told that the Hudson's Bay Company regularly sent out a mail by dog-team in the course of the winter, so they decided to send their own mail down to Fort McPherson and every man was allowed to put in one letter, of not more than half an ounce in weight. Two of the best snow-shoe runners in Wind City believed that they could get down to the Fort and were willing to try for two hundred dollars each. The experienced miners assured them that they were committing suicide and did their best to prevent them from going with arguments about blizzards, deceptive ice, and the certainty of taking a wrong direction ; but they persisted, and started off well enough with a blanket each, flour, pemmican, matches, and tobacco. They were a pair of big sturdy fellows, in excellent condition and full of confidence and heart. Two or three days after their departure, a man rushed up from the water-hole saying that some strange animals or a party of Indians were coming up the river. The light of the aurora and a winter haze combined to make things look queer, and when the miners turned out with their weapons it certainly seemed as if some large beasts were ploughing along through the snow out in the middle of the river. Then somebody realized that they were two men in distress, and when the miners got out to them they found that they were the two mail-carriers crawling on their hands and knees and reduced very nearly to their last gasp. It appeared that they had lost their way in a haze of fine snow raised by a whirlwind, and that they had then run into a place where, as they said, the surface of the snow rose and fell as they walked on it—probably it was a sphagnum swamp carrying a thin skin of ice improperly frozen under the snow. This terrified them, and their feet were wet and then frozen before they could get back to firm ground. They were terribly frost-bitten about the knees, hands, and faces as well, but they actually recovered without any amputations and in the end were none the worse.

Finally there was the appalling death of Johnny the Slovak—or " Slave-'Awk ", as his cockney partner made it. Fire-wood was running short near Wind City itself, so Mitchell had taken a party of five men with toboggans to cut down a stand of dry rampoles some miles up-river. The " Slave-'Awk " struck his axe into a certain tree that must have been under some heavy internal strain, perhaps from ice that had formed in the cracks of the dry wood ; and at the blow the tree exploded with a loud report, splitting from top to bottom and shooting out long spears of wood in all directions. One of these sharp pointed slivers struck the unfortunate man sideways in the belly, passed through him from left to right and disembowelled him in the twinkling of an eye.

The party were naturally horrified, and decided to leave the wood and take his body back to camp at once. They lashed him to a toboggan and started, but stopped on the way to boil a little tea—as Mitchell said, to quiet their nerves.

" I had made a little fire," he went on, " and was bending over it boiling the tea when I suddenly heard a yell, and turned round to see the others beating it off in all directions. I didn't know if they'd been attacked by wolves or Indians or what ; but as I looked about I caught sight of the toboggan, which had unfortunately been drawn up too close to the fire.

"There was my bird, sitting bolt upright like a half-opened jack-knife ! His legs were tied to the toboggan, but the heat must have affected some sinews, perhaps, and drawn the upper part of his body up at right angles. It was ghastly to see him sitting up like that with his terrible face—I was so frightened that I fell right into the fire ! Then I yelled murder for the others to come back, and we got him straightened out again and tied securely."

Deaths being so frequent the difficult problem of burial had to be faced. It was quite impossible to thaw out enough ground with fires to bury the dead in graves in the ordinary way, and ordinary burial is of doubtful value in the North because of the vile persistency of the wolverines, which will dig up a corpse from under a cairn or a massive slab of stone. Many of the scurvy corpses were put into the abortive mine-shaft, with a good layer of gravel on top which it was hoped would discourage the wolverines ; but the miners eventually found that much the best plan was to wrap the corpse up carefully in a blanket and put it in a tree, or on a platform between two trees, as the Indians did regularly with their own dead. The lower branches were cut off to prevent the wolverines from climbing, and sometimes a band of large fish-hooks was arranged round the trunk, points downwards, for the same purpose. Mitchell had with him a Church of England prayer book, and used to read the burial service for every-one alike, whether buried or set in a tree in the Indian fashion.

CHAPTER XXII

THE INDIANS' VISIT

ONE of the troubles which most afflicted the miners during the winter night, and which ranked with the scurvy itself, was the necessity of killing so many hours of unwanted time. Camp chores, of course, were always waiting to be done, but only the most energetic of the parties did any chores to speak of and the lowest types soon slipped down to the Eskimo standard of living. A good deal of carpentry went on, as sleighs had to be built for hauling stores and equipment to the Pass in spring ; there were clothes to be patched and boots to be put into order against the melting of the snow ; and some men carved wooden toys to trade with the Indians for moccasins and game. "Anything to keep ourselves sane," as Mitchell said.

The darkness itself was a great handicap in all these jobs, as the supply of wax candles soon ran out and only a few of the parties had had the foresight to bring in candle-moulds with them. Mitchell's party used to render down all the spare fat from their rations into tallow and did quite a brisk trade in candles ; and their own cabin, where there was always light of some kind as well as the marvellous luxury of an open fire, was a place of common resort for time-killing, story-telling, and cards. Cards were the standard form of amusement—" nice quiet games of poker, cribbage, and vingt-et-un, apart from wild parties "—with story-telling as an alternative when no candles could be had.

There was an old Scots miner called Campbell, with a

flowing white beard and a very sanctimonious look, who spent a great part of his time sitting on a bench beside Mitchell's fire-place. He never played cards and seldom spoke at all, appearing to be fully occupied on some kind of struggle with his own soul. One very cold day, when he was sitting there with his head sunk in his hands, Mitchell came in from filling his pails at the water-hole and remarked that he had just seen an extraordinary thing—dozens of gnats dancing over the frozen river. The aurora light was brilliant, and he had seen the gnats quite clearly, rising up like a column of faint smoke.

Campbell immediately raised his head and said devoutly, " Thank God ! "

" Why thank God," Mitchell asked him, " over a few gnats ? "

" Gnats be damned," answered Campbell, " I seen them masel'—I thought I was crazy ! "

Mitchell kept his sugar in a large square biscuit-tin, which used to stand—generally uncovered—under the bench that was Campbell's accustomed seat. Campbell tumbled to this fact, and every now and then they would see his hand grope down between his knees and then pass furtively across his mouth with the palm inwards. There would be a faint sound of sucking, and afterwards some research in the wispy druidical beard. When this performance had been repeated often enough to lose its humour Mitchell removed the sugar-tin and put in its place a duplicate, which contained salt. The old man duly took his mouthful and jumped up cursing ; then everyone laughed, and he strode out of the cabin purple with rage and offence. He never forgave Mitchell nor willingly spoke to him again.

One day in December, when the scurvy was about at its worst, the camp had yet another alarm of an Indian raid. Someone who had been out cutting wood rushed back in terror, with the report that a large force of Indians was advancing to the attack. The miners, who had really seen nothing of the Indians so far, were still in constant dread of massacre and mutilation ("Yes, Graham, I'm afraid they are rather apt to chop up "), and the whole camp immediately fell into its usual panic. Every man who was strong enough to stand turned out under arms ; everything was in an uproar, and everyone—as always on these occasions—was ready to start shooting at a moving shadow.

However, some of the seasoned miners managed to get the mob in hand before any actual damage had been done. They called a council, pointed out that it was sheer suicide for the white men to start aggression, and persuaded the others that their best chance was for someone to go out to meet the Indians unarmed. This raised the nice problem of finding an emissary, and nobody was very keen to volunteer ; but finally two men, whose identity Mitchell has modestly suppressed, went out on to the open river and held up their hands as a sign of friendship when the Indians came into view.

"And I'm bound to say," Mitchell went on to explain, " that the poor devil who rushed in with the first report had some damned good reason for thinking that we were going to be massacred, what with the uncertain light of the aurora and the noise that the Indians were making as they came down the river. There were seven dog-teams strung out in a long line one after the other—that meant fourteen Indians and thirty-five to forty dogs. And if you'd ever heard seven Indian dog-teams, with the dogs howling and the Indians yelling and cracking their whips and abusing each individual dog by name—well, you wouldn't be surprised that we jumped for our rifles !

"Actually, of course, there need have been no alarm at all. When the Indians reached our men they shook hands all round and a tremendous palaver began. It turned out that the whole thing was an act of kindness and courtesy on the part of the chief, Francis, who was leading the party himself. He hadn't forgotten what I had been able to do for his wife, and now he'd come in with seven good loads of fresh caribou meat—one was a present for me and my party and the other six were for trade with the miners. And by God we needed them for the scurvy ! That fresh meat saved many men's lives, and after we had got it the scurvy seemed regularly to lose its grip.

" Of course we had Francis in to stay with us in the cabin —we invited the drivers too, but he said that they could very well stay outside, and as a matter of fact they were all absorbed by the other miners. Now I want to tell you that although Francis had never sat up at a table in his life before, nor used a knife and fork in our way, his manners were damn well proper. And he did it too without any of us feeling that he was watching us. And then again, to let you see how keenly an Indian observes, I found out when I was with them months afterwards that he could describe clearly to the other Indians everything that was in the cabin, and where it was ; and yet he never seemed to be investigating anything in particular—not, my dear Graham, as I am now vulgarly investigating everything in your flat ! We could never marvel enough at this Indian's dignity and good looks.

" We still had the package of letters that our two postmen had failed to convey to Fort McPherson, so we asked Francis if two of his runners could take them down. He was delighted to let any of them go, but most unfortunately, before the full arrangements had been made, one of the Indians who understood a few words of English found out that we were going to have paid what they called ' eight hundred skins ' to our own boys, and be God-damned if they'd go for less ! Otherwise they'd have gone with the best will in the world for about forty dollars ! So we gave them a letter to Firth asking him to credit them with four hundred dollars, but only to pay it next year so as to ensure that they did their job properly. It was an easy enough trip, of course, for Indians : they were down to the Fort and back again almost before we knew.

" At last all the trading was over, and we said good-bye, and they went off ; but three or four hours later the whole damn bunch came pouring back again highly incensed. Then there came quite a nasty time, but before any trouble could start we called a council, with three a side, to find out what was really wrong, and it turned out, unfortunately, that a lot of the miners had palmed off trash on the Indians in trading for the meat—bad bacon, axe-handles with faults in them, and so forth. The worst case of all was one miner who had apparently been liberal in paying for his meat with twenty-five pounds of tea ; but when the Indians came to make their tea they found that it had been soaked with water and was worthless. No miner would acknowledge that he had done this trick, so we called on the Indian to pick his man. And he walked straight up to old Campbell, without hesitation ! Campbell swore ignorance of the whole affair, but several miners knew damn well that he had had this rotten tea, so the meeting forced the old blighter to hand over some of his own possessions and buy what he could from other men until he could pay the Indians up. The others were forced to pay up too, and in the end the Indians went off happy.

" Now I know it all sounds very easy when I tell you the story like that, but just the same it took one a Hell of a lot of managing to get both sides quieted down. Those Indians were properly sore when they found they'd been double-crossed, and our own fellows were none too easy to handle—some were blackguarding and some were for fighting, and any damned fool might have put the fat in the fire at a moment's notice. And besides the shame of it I knew all our lives were bloody well at stake if any of those Indians had happened to get shot."

While Francis was staying at Wind City, Mitchell took the opportunity of hiring the fourteen Indians and their seven dog-teams to transport his own party's belongings to the headwaters of the Stewart. He arranged that the Indians should come back as soon as they considered the snow to be in good condition for travelling, and that they should move the stores over the Pass and cache them at some point where boats or rafts could be built for the descent of the rivers in the spring. Cecil undertook to go up in charge of the first convoy and to remain on guard at the cache. Francis promised to guide him to the place where the cache was to be made, to build him a *wickiup* to live in, and to detail two good men to stay with him as his hunters and servants. Mitchell would then take charge of the later convoys, and travel backwards and forwards with them between Wind City and the cache, while Jack remained behind at Wind City until the last convoy left. Indians can be trusted never to touch a cache, but Mitchell would take no such risks with the miners.

Although the bulk of their stores had naturally diminished in the course of nine months, and they had also sold a good deal of surplus flour and bacon to miners whose supplies had run short, they still had between four and five tons of material to move. They estimated the distance to the Pass to be a hundred and forty miles, and as the Stewart only became navigable twenty miles down-stream, beyond the Pass, it seemed likely that the dog-teams would be kept busy for close on three months. Francis expected that the snow would be fit for hauling by the middle of January, so that there would be ample time to complete the move before the ice went out of the rivers.

The Indians came back punctually at the appointed time, "fulfilling their contract to the letter," as Mitchell put it, "with their usual absolute honesty." They brought down more fresh meat, and a good supply of snow-shoes and moccasins for trade—the affair of Campbell's tea was magnificently forgotten. Mitchell and his partners set to work immediately to organize their first convoy, and seeing the scurvy abated and sleighs actually loading for the Pass, the rest of the miners suddenly found themselves aware that the back of the winter was broken. The whole camp sat up and shook itself, as at the end of a bad dream.

CHAPTER XXIII

DOGS

FOR the next few weeks Mitchell was mainly occupied with sleighs and dog-teams. He had driven dogs of one sort and another in Quebec, but dog-transport as the Indians managed it contained a great many eye-openers for a civilized man. The Loucheux sleigh, or rather toboggan, was quite a notable piece of primitive craftsmanship. It was about nine feet long and three feet wide, made of thin narrow boards fastened together not with clamps or rivets but with a lacing of raw-hide thongs. The holes for the lacing were most skilfully arranged so that the thongs should never come through to the lower surface and wear against the snow. The cross-bars were laced to the bottom-boards in the same manner. The bottom-boards were turned up and over at the forward end to form a recurved prow, the corners being lashed backwards to prevent any flapping. A stout raw-hide thong ran along each side and was made fast to the floor of the toboggan at intervals of two or three feet, and other thongs were passed under this to hold down the load when it was packed on board. Yet another thong trailed loose in the snow behind, for the driver to grab in emergencies. The toboggan could readily be turned into a cariole by fitting two side-poles, running lengthwise and supported on short uprights, and closing in the sides and back with raw-hide curtains.

There were usually five dogs to a team, harnessed with traces in a kind of projected tandem and not simply attached to one long central trace in the fashion of the eastern dog-teams. Each dog wore a collar, made up of two or three strands of withy hooped together and carefully lined with caribou hide and packed with moss to bring the weight on to the shoulders without danger of galling. The outside of the collar was covered with moose hide and at each side was a stout tag of moose hide carrying a wooden toggle for the attachment of the traces. The traces were heavy solid strips of smoked and dressed moose hide two or three inches wide and long enough to extend from the collar of each dog to that of the dog behind him, leaving a little space between nose and tail ; the wheeler was thus attached to the toboggan itself, Number Four to the wheeler, Number Three to Number Four, and so on. The remainder of the harness consisted of a saddle with loops at the two sides through which the traces were passed to keep them away from the dog's feet. And then there were the dogs' moccasins, round bags of caribou hide with drawstrings, which were always put on to save their feet when the snow was frozen into cutting points.

Dogs' saddles were a very important matter in those days to the northern drivers. Collars and traces were always quite plain, but each man vied with his neighbour in crowding his saddles with ornament. The body of the saddle was of wood, padded inside with alternate layers of moss and soft caribou hide, the whole being encased in stouter moose hide. The top was generally covered with blue or red broadcloth, which formed the background for an elaborate decoration of beads or dyed porcupine quill ; and if possible the whole was topped off by the tail of a black fox, that stuck upright in the centre of the saddle with its white tip turned slightly towards the front.

Mitchell had a great deal to tell me about the dogs. " The leading dog is a vastly intelligent animal, and obeys all his master's commands instantly, except, my dear child, except when they run across a fox or an arctic hare, or even a ptarmigan, and then if the driver doesn't drop on the

leading dog and hold him down by force they are off for
good—perhaps miles before you overtake them, with the
load scattered and the toboggan broken and probably a
damn good dog-fight in progress at the end.   The second,
third and fourth dogs are irresponsible, though a good
driver is always on the watch to pick out a dog that he can
train for leader or wheel-dog.   The wheel-dog has to be as
intelligent as the leader, though in a different way, and
when the word is given to turn you see him steady down
on his fore-feet to check the momentum of the toboggan
while the rest of the team swing over to the left or right.
He works in like that with the leader, and I never saw any
trouble between a leader and a wheeler though there was
frequent trouble between either of these and any other dog
that they found loafing on the job.

" The Indian controls his dogs by voice : he has ' marche '
and ' whoa ' as with us, ' chaunipson ' for ' turn sharp left ',
and ' unipson ' for ' turn sharp right '.   He uses a short-
handled whip with a very long lash and a snapper on the
end that goes off like a revolver : he can make it tickle a
dog's ear, or cut it right off, and he can snap it so hard
anywhere on the body that the fur flies off.   The Indians
treat their dogs well, take 'em by and large : the dogs aren't
pampered in any way—no damn kindness—but they get
what is necessary.   The pups are highly valued, and litters
are culled over carefully and all weaklings destroyed at once.
The bitches are never worked immediately before or after
a confinement and at moving-times the women carry them
round in baskets on their backs.   They are well fed as long
as the Indians have food themselves.

" On the trail the dogs are well handled except for necessary punishment, but in case of a dog-fight or a dog snapping
at you you use the first thing that comes to hand—the flat
of an axe, or an axe-handle for choice.   You've got to put
that dog out of business as quick as possible—you know,
knock him cold, Graham.   Until I got used to it I thought

it was the most brutalizing thing I'd ever seen, but the fact is these three-quarter wolves only realize one thing, and that is *mastery*. Since I got back I've read all kinds of beautiful stories about love between master and dog, but I never myself saw an Indian put his hand on a dog with safety.

" The exception to this is harnessing, which the dogs understand. If you come to a dog with his harness he may yell blue murder but he takes it. Or his moccasins —it is extraordinary to see those wild God-damn wicked dogs come and lie down with their feet bleeding, holding them up to get their moccasins on. Otherwise it's whip or club with them all the time. For instance, when you're feeding the dogs you put them in a semicircle pretty far apart, chop up the bits of frozen meat or fish with the whip handy and throw them to each one separately. And if any one dog makes the slightest motion to go near the other chap he promptly gets the whip. Otherwise you're in for a dog-fight sure, and you may well lose a valuable dog before you get them straightened out.

" I had my first dog-fight one day when I was going up the river, just before I broke my leg. I had a fast team and a light load, and was running ahead of the convoy on a well-broken trail. I stopped for some reason or other, but forgot to call ' whoa ' and put my foot on the emergency thong, as I ought to have done ; and the first thing I knew was an awful row of yelling and yowling and snarling somewhere ahead. By the time I got up to them the team was one tangled mass of fighting dogs ; Number Three was of a mean disposition, and the leader had most probably turned to give him a nip and then he'd fought back, and as soon as he was down the whole bunch literally tore him to pieces. I could just about save his saddle and collar, and the rest was just paws and skin and blood. And I had to knock the leader right out. There's simply no stopping them when they get the smell of blood : the only way to do in a big fight is to hit as many dogs as possible on the head as quick as possible, and stun them—there's no end to it until they're all put out, unless the last one or two get scared and perhaps turn tail.

" I nearly got eaten myself one time in a dog-fight, when I was helpless with my broken leg in the Indian camp. The squaws had lifted me out of the lodge and propped me up against a tree in an open space where they used to work on their moose hides, and I thanked the Lord, for it was a perfect spring day with flocks of ducks going north and strings and arrow-heads of geese and swans. The men were all out hunting that day and the squaws had disappeared into the lodges when suddenly a tremendous dog-fight started in some part of the camp and came surging out on to the open space where I was. I fired my revolver in the air to call for help, but I didn't want to shoot any dog until my own life was actually in danger—otherwise my only weapon was a long crutch-pole, and I couldn't do much with that half lying on the ground.

"Just as I thought the dogs were going to close on me a young squaw arrived on the run and came and stood over me with the pole ; and with that and an axe that young girl kept the dogs at bay until some Indians turned up, called in by the revolver shots. Francis said afterwards that the dogs were attending to their own business, not trying to get me in particular, but that if the battle had spread on top of me I should have been involved and should certainly have got eaten. A very unhappy few minutes ! "

It was early in February when Mitchell's turn came to leave Wind City with the second convoy of stores. The weather was intensely cold, but very fine and still, and the sun was beginning to show itself at midday. The memory of the first night out on the trail has stayed with him.

" The day's run had been excessively trying, over the rough ice and obstacles in the river-bed. It really was literally a run, as the Indians were out to make a quick journey and ran all the time, one team vying with another

—they dress in very light furs for these trips, and wear special dog-running snow-shoes that are long and narrow and slide over the snow like skis. I was in good hard condition and didn't at all want to be beat by Indians, but by the afternoon I tell you I was feeling the strain. I just felt as if my lungs would *burst*. As you know, Graham, your breathing isn't improved by forty-five below, and we were at a high elevation which made it that much worse. About four o'clock, just as I was thinking I must give a signal of distress, the chief spotted a suitable place to camp on a bench above us and gave a certain call, at which the whole convoy turned uphill and stopped in a bunch of timber. The Indians immediately began to dig in the snow with their snow-shoes and hollowed out a pit about six feet deep and twelve feet across at the top, throwing up the snow into a rampart round about. Then they lined the bottom with spruce branches, leaving a bare space in the middle for the fire, and in a very short time had a fire lighted and tea boiling. Everything was done extraordinarily quickly and with no fuss or bother. The dogs were well fed with fish and disappeared for the night into holes in the snow—they say it's a trait in all dogs that have the wolf strain in them to know how to dig themselves *cabanes* in the snow, and the bushy wolf's tail keeps their noses from freezing when they lie curled up inside.

" You wouldn't believe how comfortable we were in that pit, the way the Indians fixed things up. The fire was kept going all night by means of two dry trees which were leaned up against the sides of the pit with their butts in the embers, so that as the ends burned away the trees slipped down and kept the fire supplied. The heat from the fire, combined with the number of people in the pit, kept us as warm as toasts all night in spite of the great cold outside : in fact it was so hot I had to take most of my clothes off, and even with that I was sweating.

" It was a most extraordinary experience to lie there

among all those wild people, looking up at the sky—dark and yet clear, like an ocean, with the stars like great electric lamps. And against the sky the grotesque shapes of the heads and joints of caribou that were hung over the fire to roast ! It was extraordinarily interesting too to watch the way the dogs behaved the next morning. There was no sign of a dog anywhere when we turned out, and when the Indians called them one only heard grunts and groans and moans and whining like creatures in agony. But in the end they all came to take their harness, though they had been run and beaten and abused to within an inch of their lives all the previous day.

" It beat me altogether to understand why such wild brutes stayed with their masters at all, and didn't just go off into the woods and live like the wolves. They were nearly all wolf anyhow by blood, as the bitches regularly crossed with wild wolves, and they had all the wolf attributes— prick ears, heavy furred throat, broad feet for running in the snow, a great bushy tail. They can't even bark like dogs : foxes bark, but these dogs can only howl like the wolves or sing-song, as they do when they bay the moon —you hear one start and then all the rest join in. It seemed to me they got all the kicks and damned few ha'pence, and in summer they weren't even fed, as they weren't being worked in the toboggans. Yet when the toboggans were uncached at the beginning of winter and the Indians called them they were always somewhere handy and ready to step into their places.

" Francis said the whole thing was that they were afraid of the real wolves. A bitch could go out into the woods with safety, but if a male dog went off too far the wolves would eat him sure, and so the dogs knew that their lives depended on keeping touch. It's odd, you know, Graham, to think of an animal that is really wild depending like that for protection on human beings."

CHAPTER XXIV

THE BROKEN KNEE

" I GUESS it was the fourth day out, at noon, that we reached a place the Indians call ' the hot water '. This, Angus, is a stretch of the Wind river, forty or fifty miles above the Little Wind, where the water never freezes for several hundred yards however cold the weather is. You can generally find some ducks and geese there all through the winter, though they're miserable starved birds, hardly worth killing—probably they're maimed birds that have been wounded by the Eskimo up north, as the Indians say they often find flint arrow-heads sticking in them.

" Francis called a halt on a bench just up from the river, and for some reason I set to work to cut down a spruce tree —a good-sized one it was, twelve inches or so on the stump. I'd cut almost right through it, and struck it higher up with the back of the axe to pitch it, when the damn tree butted the wrong way and the cursed butt hit me fair on the cap of my left knee, which was forward. I sat down hard in the snow, and was surprised to see the sole of my foot under my left elbow. My leg wouldn't straighten of itself, and the knee seemed to work both ways without any check. The pain, of course, was intense.

" Francis was simply wonderful. He lifted me gently up, laid me on a moose hide, and made me as comfortable as he could with fur robes. Then he had a Hell of a council with the Indians, which lasted for a long time with tremendous gesticulation and excitement. When this was over he told me very gently and kindly that he would take me away to his own winter camp, sixty miles farther on up-stream and back from the river, where he had removed the squaws to be out of range of passing miners.

" The Indians got busy at once, and in an incredibly short time they had cut me a pair of splints that reached from the thigh to the foot, and bound them on very firmly with moose-hide thongs—dog-traces I guess they were. Then they fitted side-pieces and a back to one of the toboggans to make a cariole of it, filled it well with furs for me to lie on, and lifted me and my leg in and tied me securely so that I shouldn't fall out going over rough ground. Francis himself covered me up most carefully with furs, and put a big moose skin on top of all—and I needed all that and a damn sight more as it must have been a good forty-five or fifty below.

" Then Francis harnessed up the six best dogs, took two more on leashes for spares, and started with his best runner for what I should think was one of the quickest dashes Indians had ever made. We did the sixty-odd miles in just about eleven hours. First we dropped down into the river-bed and then went up-river for miles and miles, sometimes on the hummocky ice and sometimes taking a short cut over the banks—the toboggan bumping and crashing and sometimes swinging round sideways like a pendulum when we crossed a bit of sloping ground. If I'd been compos I'd have been afraid of getting brained alive, the pace we made over those bumps ; but as it was I think I passed out pretty often though it seemed like eternity just the same. At last we turned off into a side-valley and climbed up the benches, and I remember coming back to consciousness as we topped a rise and getting my first view of the Indians' winter lodges.

" This was a semi-permanent encampment, where they might live for a week or two according to the time that the caribou herds stayed in the neighbourhood. By that time of year, you see, the caribou were coming down again from the high ground, and that is how it happened that the tribe

was in that region at all when I had my accident. The
lodges were large dome-shaped tents, perfectly round, and
about twenty feet in diameter. I learned afterwards that
they were built on a frame-work of alder wands, very strong
and bent permanently into the correct arched form, which
they carried round with them when they moved about.
The covering was tanned caribou skins with the fur left on
for warmth—the fur was clipped short, and was on the outside of the lodge. The door was a flap made of one big
moose hide. Inside the snow was excavated three or four
feet deep, and the floor was made of a deep layer of spruce
boughs covered with caribou skins and blankets of light
caribou or strips of rabbit-skin woven together. There was
a space left clear in the centre for the fire, and the top of the
tent above the fire was open to let the smoke out, which it
generally didn't do. Immediately opposite the door, at the
back of the tent, a small hole was kept open in the snow
under the tent wall, which was supposed to let in a current of
air to drive the smoke spirally up and out, but just the same
if you stood up in the lodge your eyes nearly dropped out
with the pungent smoke. A tent like this would house one,
two, or perhaps three families.

" We drove down the slope to the lodges at a break-neck
pace, with the men yelling like fury, and all the Indians
turned out to meet us in great excitement. Francis headed
straight for his own lodge, which was in the middle of the
camp, and after he had given his people instructions to clear
a space in the lodge the moose hide that formed the door
was taken down and the toboggan was picked up and carried
inside. The squaws rapidly cleared a sleeping-place for me,
tossed up the boughs and laid out clean fur rugs, and I was
carefully lifted out of the toboggan and deposited.

" Now I didn't know at all what the Indians had in mind
to do about my leg, but I thought that even if I came through
alive I should probably not be in shape to do anything
after they'd finished with me. So in spite of great pain I

got them to set me with my head and shoulders up, and before I let them start work I wrote a note to Jack at Wind City and another to Cecil at the Pass. These notes were short and to the point—' Follow this bloody Indian and come quick. Broke leg.' Francis sent them off at once, each with two good men, and then I said to carry on and do their damnedest.

" Now you must understand, Graham, that surgery, among my Indians, was entirely an affair for the women. Old Colin's wife Jane, and the young girl Flora, Francis' wife, were both surgeons—old Jane had learned the Indian medicine and surgery from childhood, but strange to say, though she would examine any case and give her diagnosis, the actual cutting she never would do, being much too kind-hearted. But this was very happily done by Flora, who loved cutting—the more she hurt the patient the better she liked it !

" First they removed the rough splints that Francis' men had made and old Jane gave instructions to two expert wood-workers to smooth them down and make them take practically the shape of the leg—one from the ankle to the groin and the other from the ankle to the thigh. (They worked this with their crooked knives, which are A 1 for that sort of carving and whittling when you know how to use them.) Then she ripped up my breeches—I had on two pairs of light caribou with clipped fur—and laid bare the leg, which was black, green, and purple, and so swollen that even the toes were standing out independently. Both women examined it very carefully and after quite a short parley decided what they ought to do.

" Then they began to talk at me and made a great explanation which I didn't understand practically a damn word of, but Bonnet Plume, who had followed us from the place of the accident, explained to me that they were going to take the skin back and bring together the two halves of the knee-cap, which they said was broken across the centre.

They began by putting on the splints, before they did any cutting, with a covering of duffle and old blanketing above and below the knee that left the region of the knee itself well exposed. Then they broke some flint flakes with sharp cutting edges off a block of flint that they kept for striking lights, and Flora started her business. I asked Francis later why they used flint flakes instead of an ordinary knife, and he said that a fresh flint flake was clean while a steel knife-blade would have been dirty.

" Flora made her first cut, about three inches long, inside the knee and upwards : this didn't bleed freely and what blood there was came out clotted, but it gave a feeling of relief and I urged them to press the blood out. Then she made another cut cross-ways below the knee and a third like the first, up the outer side of the leg, and after these cuts the blood came much more freely. Then she seized the U-shaped flap of skin and flesh that she had just released on the two sides and bottom and flayed it up and back, exposing the knee-cap ; and just as old Jane had said, it was split right across from side to side with the two halves drawing away from one another upwards and downwards.

" Old Jane had evidently known what she was going to find and had set some men to make a lot of little pins out of caribou bone. Now she forced the two halves of the knee-cap together and the other little bird drove in the pins below the base of the lower half and above the top of the upper half, and then wound them very firmly together, figure-of-eight, with fine strong sinews taken from the back of a caribou and pulled out to about the thickness of the coarsest sewing-thread. Then they put back the flap of skin and bound it into place with thongs, without any stitching.

" I don't know how long all this pleasant process took : it may have been two or three hours—anyhow, it was dark all the time except for the firelight. I tried to carry off the first part of the game with a high head—had my cutty pipe and tried to pretend there was nothing wrong. But I must have passed out more than once, as I would waken up to find little bags of moose skin with hot ashes in them in the palms of my hands, which they used to revive me when they thought I had been out too long and perhaps might not come back otherwise.

" The inside of that lodge, as I saw it, was really rather a nightmare. Every Indian who could had squeezed himself in and thoroughly enjoyed the exhibition—a free show, packed to the doors and nobody excluded. It was just one mass of sweating excited faces, with the gleam of the firelight reflected from them. Francis told me months later that they were all watching me to see how the white man would bear pain, and that it was lucky for me I'd got through without giving any signs of fear or suffering. If I had I should have had no standing in the tribe at all—just like with torture in the old days. But when I got my pipe back after it was all over I found the end of the mouthpiece was gnawed right off !

" My first conscious effort after I came to properly was to get a drink, and they gave me a long quaff of good boiled tea. They pressed caribou tongues and kidneys on me too, but I couldn't touch food then or for days after. Then for the next month every second or third day one of the squaws would come and clap a bloody awful poultice on my knee —my God, it was worse than the cutting, d'you know that ? I can see Francis' wife now as she used to sidle up to me bringing the damn thing, grinning like Hell. It was made of herbs and the inner bark of some tree, and it drew like a bank-draft—you'll hardly believe me, but its drawing power was so great that the whole wound healed perfectly, without a trace of pus, in spite of no washing or sanitary precautions."

To finish one story at a time I may as well say here that when Mitchell returned to civilization the doctors found his knee-cap perfectly knit. His leg was naturally stiff, as he had worn his splints continuously, and a long spell of treatment was required to restore the withered muscles and to loosen the stiff joint. But the leg was eventually brought back to a perfectly sound condition—so much so that he was able to break it again thirty-three years later in a different place, having also broken his right leg, for good measure, in the interim.

CHAPTER XXV

THE LAST OF THE WHITE MEN

" NOW I want you, Angus, to put in the book a record of the enormous debt of gratitude I owe to Francis for the way in which he saw me through everything and supported me with continual kindness and sympathy. You must realize that I was in a pretty damn bad way after that operation, and it isn't the same thing to be laid on your back among savages in a skin tent as to spend a few weeks in a luxury ward at the Royal Victoria. For one thing, there were three bloody families already living in that lodge before I was introduced—Francis, with his wife and little Jimmy, the baby ; old Colin and Jane ; and another man with a wife and three children. And a strange Indian or two would often call in and stay for a couple of nights, so there wasn't any room to spare. And though the Indians are very kind-hearted and would do anything at all for me, they've got no ' nerves ' (as we call it) themselves and just don't realize that a sick person wants peace and quiet ; so they carried right on with their ordinary duties just as if there'd been nobody sick there at all.

" But Francis was just a tower of strength for me, and did everything he possibly could to make things easier. He remembered the way we lived at Wind City and told off one squaw to look after me all the time, wash me every morning and feed me three times a day. That seemed very strange to the Indians, as they never have regular meals. Then I found it terribly cold when they let the fire die out, as they usually did when they didn't actually need it for cooking ; so he made them keep the fire going all the time on purpose for me, which was another extraordinary new idea and I don't think they liked it altogether—getting in extra fire-wood, and all that.   He even made a little wicker cradle to put over my leg, for fear of the children and dogs.

" I slept a good part of the time those first few days, but I did some pretty damned anxious figuring too, on my own situation.   I knew I should certainly die if I tried to go on with my friends, as they wouldn't be able even to keep me warm.   And I didn't want to be a burden on them either, having to be hauled round everywhere on a toboggan. The only thing I could think of was to stay with the Indians if I could manage to persuade them to keep me, and get them to take me down to Fort McPherson the following summer.   I hadn't any real hope of ever seeing the Fort again, but the Indians could at least feed me and keep me warm, as they kept themselves warm, so this seemed on the whole to be the best chance.

" My plan was to take out my third share of the expedition's supplies from the common stock and pay the Indians with it for carrying me with them.   I knew my partners wouldn't object, and anyhow it would save them from having to transport that much surplus stuff, which might have been more than they could do.   So I put the thing before Francis, talking through Bonnet Plume, and offered to pay the Indians three hundred pounds of flour, a hundred and fifty pounds of bacon, fifty pounds of tea, fifty pounds of tobacco, and some other oddments—all that to be handed over immediately by one of my partners and delivery taken by the Indians, into toboggans, at Wind City.   Then I promised further to pay half as much again, in addition, or its equivalent in trade, if and when they delivered me safe at Fort McPherson.

" Francis jumped at this.   He was quite overwhelmed by the munificence of the first offer, and the second was beyond everything.   So I called for my bag of papers and made out a covenant with him—I'm sure Francis himself believed I would pay but he wanted something that he could show his people. Indians like a written contract, though not a damn one of them can read it, and it's the Hudson's Bay Company's normal practice to give them chits when they send them to do a job.

" As a matter of fact, when the food convoy eventually came up there was a tremendous orgy, and in about three weeks the whole lot was in their bellies so that they weren't one bit further ahead. Indians are like that about food, and when I questioned Francis about it he said it was quite natural as all the higher animals—by which he meant wolves and eagles and beasts of prey—went on the principle of starving and overeating turn about. They only ate when they wanted to, he said, while the ignoble creatures on which they preyed—by which he meant hares and caribou and suchlike—would eat at any time. I got up one toboggan-load of food for myself with the same convoy and kept that separate until the famine came ; then I shared it out among the Indians, only keeping some tea and tobacco for ready cash.

" We had a little trouble with the tribe while we were waiting for my partners, as they were overdue in that camping-place, and were very restless and anxious to get away. The Indians' whole life in winter consists of following up the herds of caribou just as the grey wolves do, and as they'd pretty well hunted out that part of the country they were keen to get after new herds. I guess there were about two hundred Indians all told in that bunch, the rest of the tribe being scattered about in small lots in the dif-ferent valleys, so they needed a lot of meat, and if they lost the caribou they very soon starved. (I figured out later that they probably used about fifty caribou per day for men, women, and dogs, that allowance including what they would dry and smoke for future use or trade.) So Francis had quite a job to hold them, and I think it was my promises

of food and the hope of unknown rewards more than anything that kept them quiet.

" At last my pals turned up—they really came quick,
both of them, but it seemed a long time to me ! It was a
marvellous feeling to see a friend's face in the doorway after
lying there in the darkness all those days with nothing but
wild strange faces all about. They were terribly put out
on my account, and at first they wouldn't hear of my plan
for staying with the Indians till the summer. You see,
they were scared stiff of the Indians still, as they didn't
know anything about them—I had been too, and was still
for that matter to some extent, though I was beginning to
change my ideas about them now seeing the great kindness
with which they were treating me. But my pals couldn't
see that, and they didn't understand my real friendship with
Francis which had begun with the presents I'd given him
back at Fort McPherson : to them the Indians were still
a bunch of black savages, and they swore by everything
they held holy that they wouldn't leave a white man, and
their own friend, in savages' hands. They would bloody
well take me over the Pass with them or bust.

" Well, I had the greatest difficulty in talking them round.
But I explained to them what agony it was to me to be
bumped about, and I persuaded them that they couldn't
possibly keep me warm—I said they might drag me about
perhaps for three or four days, but that after that I should
freeze to death sure, and there wasn't a hope of being able
to get me down the Stewart. On the other hand I showed
them that the Indians could keep me warm and feed me—
and they did feed me, too, until they lost the caribou and
everybody starved—and that there was nothing to prevent
them taking me down to Fort McPherson quite O.K.

" 'But don't you think they'll kill you ? ' asked Jack.

" ' No,' I said, ' I'll pay them damned well now, and
they'll keep me to get the second payment when they get
me down to the Fort '—though really I thought it most

likely that they would get fed up and kill me, as, in fact, they very nearly did.

"However, I got them persuaded in the end, and we left it at that. I tell you, Angus, it was a pretty God-damned doleful ending to all our prospects, and we weren't one bit happy."

This sad and dreadful time was varied by one major diversion that was created, oddly enough, by Bonnet Plume. Bonnet Plume continued to act as Mitchell's servant, except when he disappeared mysteriously in the manner that seemed to be natural to him, though Mitchell came to depend more and more on Francis as their friendship strengthened and Mitchell became proficient in the Indian language. However, at the moment Bonnet Plume was on hand, being a good deal in demand as an interpreter, and one day he made a secret confession that he knew of a gold-bearing creek. He assured the white men that this was a *real* gold creek, with no unfortunate mistake about it such as had attached to his other creek near Wind City, and he offered to take Jack and Cecil to see it at once. It was a tributary of Bear Run Creek, and they could visit it and be back easily in a couple of days.

They slipped away secretly, leaving Mitchell to enjoy this last possibility of hope, and came back at the end of the second day tired out and utterly discouraged. It was just the same story as before—a bed of iron pyrites that shone like gold from the bottom of the stream, and had again deceived them so that they had plunged right into the ice-cold water. Bonnet Plume was desolated at their disappointment, but remained honestly incorrigible as a mining geologist.

"Next day the good-bye came, and it was a hard one. After the others had gone I asked Francis to have me carried out of the lodge so that I could see the last of them, and the Indians laid me on a toboggan and drew me out in front of the lodges to the edge of the bench. From where I lay I could look right down the slope, and saw my friends and the dog-teams that were escorting them dwindle to specks in the wide bottom of the valley. I called for my rifle and fired three shots as a parting salute : three little puffs of smoke spurted from the rifles of the other party, and long afterwards the noise of the reports came faintly up to me. Then I asked to be carried back into the lodge, so as not to prolong the agony."

CHAPTER XXVI

THE INDIAN CAMP

"WITHIN an hour of my friends' departure the lodge had disappeared from over my head : the covering had been rolled up, the poles had been lashed into a bunch, and all the household effects, dried meat, caribou tongues, and everything had been packed up and loaded on to toboggans. The dogs were called up and harnessed, and we were ready to move off in an astonishingly short time.

"Francis had made most careful arrangements for my comfort. He had got the Indians to build me a regular travelling *berlo*—like a toboggan but much more stoutly built, and with good solid wooden sides and back. The floor was covered with furs six or eight inches deep, and I was wrapped up in one of their marvellous rabbit-skin blankets made of thin strips of the furry skin woven together. They lashed me down for safety, and then covered me with more furs and blankets and a damn fine moose skin over all—not a heavy old bull's hide but a light warm one that covered me right from my toes upwards, and I could pull it over my head too, if necessary in wind or snow. Under the moose skin and very much available was my carbine, also strapped in ; then I had my light automatic under my left arm-pit and a couple of extra mitts and a bag of pemmican on my chest. Weren't they thoughtful, those devils, eh? But I couldn't carry anything to drink, and I had no liquor anyhow—my God, what wouldn't I have given for a thermos in those days?

" Francis wouldn't let me be drawn by dogs for fear they might smell game and run away, and then I should have been bumped against trees and into crevasses and probably come a Hell of a cropper somewhere. That may always happen. So he got four young hunters to drag me with lines and a kind of harness : they were good boys and were glad to do it, but they must have had a Hell of a time, breaking trail and everything. As a matter of fact, we were lucky that first day, as we ran into a herd of four or five hundred caribou when we'd only been going for perhaps a couple of hours : the hunters very soon killed as many as would last us for a week or more, and the squaws made camp again on the spot."

It was while he was in this camp, after his first move, that Mitchell reached his lowest ebb of illness, pain, and discouragement. His accident had happened about three weeks before, and for the first week he had borne up fairly well ; but after that he had begun to get very much worse. His stores had not yet arrived from Wind City, and he could not bring himself to face the Indians' unvarying diet of roast meat, so that real lack of nourishment was added to pain, shock, and bed-sores. He often fainted, and the squaws began to look askance at him as if they had come to expect the worst.

" One night," he told me, " I was roused out of a coma or faint to find Francis sitting by my couch and a crowd of Indians all round, with Colin and Jane very much in the forefront. They were all jabbering like Hell, and at first I couldn't understand a word of it all, but gradually Francis gave me to understand that I was going to die—he kept on pointing upwards, and closing his eyes, and so on, until at last I got his meaning. Well, that wasn't very good for a starter !

" Then they took me and clothed me in the ceremonial garments of a chief—the most beautiful robe of white-tanned caribou skin you ever saw, and everything else complete right down to the embroidered gloves. I couldn't think what the Hell was happening, but I didn't like the look of things any too much, and then it suddenly dawned on me that this was my bloody funeral and that the white robes were the grave-clothes that I should be buried in. You understand, of course, Graham, that their burial is always done in trees : the body is wrapped up in very substantial coverings, practically like a mummy, and lashed upright against the trunk as high up as the tree will stand ; and afterwards all the lower branches are cut off the same as we used to do at Wind City, to prevent wolverines or any other climbing animals from getting at it.

" Why they held the service before I was dead I never made out. They may have thought it a pity for me to miss a good show, and so held it while I could still be present, so to speak ; or it may have been that they thought I really had died—perhaps more than once—as they'd seen my eyes roll and my jaw drop when I fainted off. Anyhow, they were weeping copiously, and I do believe they were sincerely sorry.

" The service was quite an extraordinary mix-up between Christian and pagan. Old Colin had a New Testament in Bishop Bompas' translation, printed in pot-hooks, and he read some bits of this and said Christian prayers in his own language. He was really and truly a Christian, and so was his wife. Then one of the other Indians would do a bit, and I guess their stuff was pretty well pagan though of course I couldn't understand a word of it. Then they started to sing ' Nearer, my God, to Thee ', which I recognized at once by the tune : their words for it are ' *Do nee nya quann deea, do nee nya quann* ', and I got to know it very well later. (As a matter of fact, I taught them the whole hymn in English, and they came out with it the first Sunday at the Fort as a surprise for the parson—he was amazed !) Then there were more prayers, and they carried on the service according to their own ideas for hours and hours

—singing and praying and weeping and wailing out loud all by turns.

" Now you may think that all this sounds foolish, my dear Angus, but I can assure you it was the eeriest God-damn proceeding I ever went through. It scares the pants off you to attend your own funeral service ! And it occurred to me, too, that if they thought I was dead they might give me a tap on the head or something, with the best will in the world, just to help me on my way and make everything right. I figured at all costs I must show them I wasn't so bloody dead after all, so when the service was over I called for my pipe and some tea in as strong a voice as I could manage, and drank off the tea with a great flourish to prove my vitality. And then we had tea all round and the whole thing gradually blew over.

" After that show two nursing mothers offered to breast-feed me, but I refused. I felt I really would rather die than that."

One of the things which troubled Mitchell particularly at this time was the fear that, if he died, Francis might come under suspicion or get into trouble of some kind. This seemed intolerable in view of all the kindnesses that Francis had shown him, and he accordingly wrote out and gave to Francis a letter addressed to Firth, in which he certified that the Indians had done everything that was possible in order to save his life, and that they were on no account to be held responsible in the event of his death. This action he now regards as " extremely foolish ", seeing that if Francis had chosen to murder him he could have done so in comparative safety, as he held what was practically Mitchell's own receipt for himself. However, Mitchell had such absolute confidence in Francis that this possibility never came into his head at all ; and to guard against the misuse of the letter by others of the Indians who were less well disposed, he gave it to Francis in secret, showed him how his own safety might some day depend on it, and warned him to say nothing at all about it to the council.

Another experience that belonged to the worst time of his illness Mitchell described to me in something of the following manner.

" I was lying awake one night a little while after they held my burial service : I was perhaps a little better than I had been, but I was still most terribly weak. The Indians were all asleep, the fire was out, and I was very cold and in extreme pain. I looked up through the smoke-hole of the lodge and saw the same old dark-blue sky there just the same as it always was, and stars as big as your head. I realized that I was four hundred miles from the Fort, and two thousand more from Edmonton, and then another three thousand from home, and what after all was the good of trying to play the game ? I could never possibly get home, and one pull of the trigger would finish it all for good.

" I'd got my automatic out, and what do you think it was, Angus, that stopped me ? It was the memory of having found a man once during the scurvy-time lying at the back of his shack just ready to pull—and I'd said to him, what the Hell was he about, the God-damned bloody coward, blowing out his brains when there wasn't anything in them anyhow ? And if I'd called another man a coward for trying to shoot himself then, how could I go and do the same thing now myself ? When that thought flashed on to me the pistol was back in its case in an instant—just snapped back on the spot. And I never once felt like doing it again."

During the first weeks of his illness Mitchell naturally could not take in much of what was going on round about him, especially as he had not yet learnt more than a few words of the Indians' language. Apart from Francis, Colin, Bonnet Plume, and the squaws who were looking after him, he did not have many dealings with the Indians at large, and consequently the accounts which he has given me of their characters and doings are all based on his later experience. However, to make his narrative more intelligible, it will be well to say something on this subject here. In the first place he has given me a description of old Colin, which I will quote in his own words.

" Colin and his dear old wife lived in our lodge. He was about sixty years of age ; a larger built man than most Indians, with tremendously thick silver-grey hair, heavy eyebrows, and tranquil thoughtful eyes with great intelligence behind them. He gave me an idea of great inward power ; probably he had been a Hell of a lad when he was young, but I always thought that some catastrophe had come on him, perhaps the loss of his children, or some great danger like the ice breaking under his feet, and that afterwards his character sobered down and ran like a great still river. He was very quiet, forcible, patient with bad Indians, and determined with quarrelsome ones ; I never saw him beat anyone up, but he controlled everyone just the same. He and his wife, who was an almost similar type, were absolutely and genuinely Christians, not only at the Fort but also up in the mountains where the great majority threw the cloak off.

" Colin was the chief councillor of the tribe, and was revered and looked up to by all the Indians for the advice that he gave. In times of danger he never got excited and always seemed to do the right thing ; and in cases of women squabbling about their men and their children he stayed quite cool and gave the Solomon's judgment—you know, that type of chap. That was the kind of thing that councillors were for ; quite apart from formal meetings of the council, men often used to come to Colin and girls to his wife and have long serious talks with them, and I'd see them going away again apparently soothed and in their right mind. Other times Colin would read his Testament aloud in his deep rich voice to a bunch of the other Indians, who couldn't read. They seemed to love that, and listened with great attention. Colin was so good himself that he could recognize and pardon errors in other people—bad girls, for instance, he recognized they were built that way and it wasn't their fault. Or a man or a squaw who was inherently cruel, vicious, dirty, etc., was not so much to be punished as to be shown where they were wrong ; it might take a month or it might take ten years, but Colin would try. And as I've said before, though Jane knew all about surgery and was appealed to in every case, she always got Flora to do the hurting, her heart was so damned good."

Then there were meetings of the council, at which Mitchell learned a good deal about the characters of the chief and his leading men. Colin was at his best in these meetings, being far wiser and far more experienced than Neil and the other members. (There were six councillors in all.)

Mitchell described the meetings somewhat as follows. " When any matter of importance was brought before the chief he used to call the councillors together and they discussed whatever it was in a most thorough and dignified manner—I never heard one man interrupt a speech or contradict another flat, in fact they always addressed the Chair, that is to say Francis, and didn't wrangle or argue between themselves at all. Some of the speeches were brief and pithy, but other men spoke at length and wandered rather round about the subject in the regular Indian way. I never heard Colin speak otherwise than tranquilly, searching every man's face as he spoke ; he would get up and begin very quietly, but with that dignified manner of his he'd soon rip up the bellies of all the previous speakers— cut all the wind out of them, see what I mean ? His word generally went, and though the other Indians generally argued the point, I figured it was more to save their own faces than anything else. All the same, Colin wasn't infallible, and when he was wrong he used to take his opponent's side very courteously, once he was convinced.

And he always came down on the side of the under dog. Meetings sometimes lasted an enormously long time—two hours at least, or sometimes up to five or six, and always with a very large consumption of tea and tobacco. Indians never will hurry a thing, and tea seems to be called for on every occasion. Some of the councils which I could understand seemed to deal with family blood-feuds, or perhaps one family group would accuse another of having trespassed on its hunting-grounds, or would say that cached furs or food had disappeared—meaning to imply, without quite saying so, that the other gang had stolen them. But I never saw a case like that proved ; it was always some damn foolishness on their own part—they'd forgotten the place, or something like that. Then there were quarrels over dogs, if somebody had shot or ill-treated another man's dogs or driven them over a precipice ; and complaints about the bad girls (made by the wives) or other matrimonial disagreements. Most of these were amongst the newly-weds, or a squaw complaining about excessive beating by her husband, but they all seemed to be settled up one way or other to the complete satisfaction of all parties. I've no doubt at all that the council had more serious cases now and then, and that it acted as judge and jury in a pretty stringent manner. For instance, there seemed to be no theft or lying or dirty talk, and I'm quite sure that state of affairs wasn't entirely automatic ; and I'm sure, too, that cache-breakers, when there were any, or liars spreading scandal about their neighbours, were damn well disciplined somehow. But I never heard anything about what happened owing to the peculiar reticence of the savage ; in fact, I was careful not to enquire too much into these matters as I had a good idea that there was a pretty definite line beyond which I'd bloody well better not poke my nose—nobody told me so, but I sensed it just the same."

At this point I made an enquiry about the powers of the chief, and Mitchell's reply suggested that Francis' position must have called for a great deal of policy and tact. As chief by hereditary right he seems to have managed all the ordinary affairs of the tribe, allotting hunting-grounds, ordering moves and halts, and acting for the tribe as its representative and champion in dealings with the white men or in any kind of emergency. He evidently possessed a certain social prestige—as Mitchell said, " he was the MacGregor "—though his outward circumstances were not in any way different from those of other well-to-do Indians. On the other hand, his power was by no means arbitrary, as the council could take up any question at will, and if necessary overrule the chief after discussion ; Francis' only privilege as against the council was to give a casting vote in case of an impasse, and Mitchell never saw anything debated further after it had been settled in this way. The chief appears to have had no religious functions, or none that appeared to Mitchell's purposely incurious eye. There were no medicine-men, and the spiritual leadership of the tribe seemed to rest with a certain old woman of whom a great deal will be said below.

So far Mitchell's description of his tribe would suggest something like a philosopher's ideal republic ; but actually the Indians were not all perfect citizens, and it is necessary to say something here about the " bad Indians " and their leader Amos, who were a constant thorn in the side of Francis and his councillors. I will again quote Mitchell verbatim.

" Some of the Indians were good by nature and some were bad—cruel, vicious and wicked in every way—and many were neither one thing nor the other, but liable to sway over to the bad element when occasion arose. Amos was the leader of the bad element ; he was a very cruel, wicked man with a nature thoroughly warped—I guess he was a hereditary throw-back of some sort, as all his instincts were so vastly different from the other Indians. He'd maltreat any animal, squaw, or child that he came across ; he'd

never got married and I guess the reason was that no
girl would trust herself with him. He was particularly and
vindictively cruel to dogs—if a dog was bad with him he'd
lead him quietly out into the bush, tie him to a tree, and
practically thrash him to death. Terrible, eh? That's not
done in polite society. He should have been just the opposite as he was a magnificent specimen physically and naturally clever at the same time, but his cleverness took the form
of doing evil in place of good. He was taller than the
average, and heavier ; he could lift and carry more than
any other Indian and could handle any two or three Indians
with ease. He had a handsome face, but it was entirely
spoilt by the evil showing through and the peculiar marks of
passion round the eyes and lips. No, he wasn't a half-breed,
but just a good Indian gone bad for some unknown reason—
someone said he'd had a regular devil of a mother who
would tie him to a tree and thrash him.

" However that may be, he was the champion of the bad
boys and the god of the bad girls. I'd met him first down at
Fort McPherson, but had never had anything to do with
him, as I'd taken a personal physical and mental horror of
him from the start, which he cordially reciprocated—I don't
know if anyone else had noticed our feelings towards each
other, but each of us knew the other had. Well, as soon as
I'd joined the Indians he showed he was my enemy ; he didn't
like the idea of carrying me around when they didn't carry
their own old people and invalids around, and he made no
secret of thinking the Indians ought to kill me and divide
up my blankets and food. I'll have a lot to tell you later
about all the trouble I had with him and how nearly he
did me in."

CHAPTER XXVII

CARIBOU

I HAVE already explained that the Indians spent the whole winter in following the herds of caribou, never remaining in one camping-place for more than about ten days. As Mitchell looks back at these months he seems to have been continually on the move, freezing by the hour in his travelling toboggan and suffering torture as his escort bumped him up and down banks and over rocks and crevasses. He has given me a very full account of how the Indians organized these hunting expeditions and the movements of their headquarters camp.

" When a move was due Francis used to make a public announcement the previous evening—he would stand at the door of his lodge and state the plans for the following day in a loud voice that everybody could hear, telling off certain families or groups to hunt in certain valleys, and giving them a rendezvous where the whole gang could meet together again. If anybody had anything to suggest he was at liberty to do so, but Francis' decisions were usually accepted in silence as the Indians knew that they were based on good reports received from scouts and had been discussed beforehand with the council. Early next morning Francis would give the order for starting the move—' *Tutt-suga cheetai tchayngit oneengi* ', which really means, ' everything take it quick outside '—and then the hunters would set off by themselves while the squaws took down the lodges, packed up their bundles and got the dogs and toboggans ready. They were extremely skilful at packing and unpacking ; I suppose they did so much of it that it came to them like second nature.

"My cariole was drawn by some young hunters, so I used to go off with them ahead of the main convoy, and I got a very good idea of the way they did their hunting. We were generally working along benches two hundred to nine hundred feet above the valley of the Wind and its larger side-valleys, climbing up and down the ravines or cutting across the plateau that lay above. There was good timber in the deeper ravines but nothing more than fifteen feet high on the plateau, and that very sparse and bunchy. In the distance to the west rose the immense barrier of the Rockies, and to the east we could see some high mountains which divide the Wind from the Red River, beyond which again is the Mackenzie running north. As March came on and the sun rose higher the light effects were positively startling, as the sun struck horizontally across the benches and mountain-sides, emphasizing and magnifying to an extraordinary extent any foothills or smaller elevations which wouldn't have shown up at all in ordinary light from the sun high overhead. All these features were exaggerated in a peculiar ghostly sort of manner.

"The main body of the hunters used to keep together on a single trail, with scouts out in front and flankers to right and left. When the scouts or the flankers spotted a herd of caribou they came back quietly and warned the main body, and then the whole gang would work round to leeward of the caribou so as to be able to approach them within short range. Generally they got up to within fifty yards or less and would be able to kill several with arrows before the others knew what was happening—bows and arrows are capital for that sort of work as they make no noise, and don't cost anything for ammunition. You'd be surprised too, Graham, to see what an arrow will do ; it goes right through a caribou's body, and can plunk pretty well into a moose. Caribou get stunned in an emergency and lose their heads, so that gives the Indians a chance to pick off a good number with their rifles while they are milling about and when they start to make off ; the survivors of a small herd once blundered within ten yards of where I was lying in my toboggan—the Indians always left me just where I was when they started their stalk—and I dropped one with my carbine.

" I can assure you, my dear Angus, that nobody could feel more absolutely alone and abandoned than I did on those occasions. Sometimes I'd lie there for hours before anybody picked me up—generally it was the squaws who found me when they came along with the heavy baggage. I had my pipe and my little bag of pemmican tucked into the neck of my caribou skin shirt, but otherwise I was quite helpless until someone came for me. I remember particularly one time when I was left in this way in very cold weather : the hunters had been gone for hours, and I heard no firing, and I might have been the only living thing out in the middle of nowhere. It seemed an eternity, and the cold began to strike through my fur clothing and the robes with the intensity of needles running into one's flesh. After I'd lost all idea of time I dozed off to sleep, and when I woke up I found the squaw who looked after me standing beside me with a pannikin of hot tea and some freshly roasted caribou kidneys ; she'd come after me and found me, and she'd been so careful that she'd made the fire without ever rousing me until my tea was ready. I remember how I lay there and dozed off comfortably after the tea had warmed me up, and how the squaw's little fire gradually sank down into the snow by its own heat and disappeared."

While their chief interest was in caribou the hunters pretty often encountered moose as well, either single animals or small groups. Moose are not really designed by Nature for very high latitudes and suffer from two serious handicaps during the arctic winter—firstly, that their feet sink down into the snow; and secondly, that their digestions demand the tender bark and shoots of deciduous under-growth and will not be satisfied with a diet of lichens and moss. Consequently, while the caribou's deeply splayed feet, with their auxiliary attachment of stout bristly hairs, carry the animal over the snow with much the same freedom as snow-shoes carry a man, the moose, which possesses a foot very like that of the domestic cow, is reduced in winter to laborious ploughing and plunging and can generally be run to a standstill in a mile or so in spite of his colossal size and strength. In order therefore to reduce their mile-age and at the same time to provide themselves with sus-tenance, moose spend the winter in " yards " (or what the French-Canadians call more adequately " *ravages* "), that is to say small feeding-grounds on which they work backwards and forwards, stamping themselves paths through the snow and nibbling at the shoots of the underbush that project above the surface. If the Indians came upon one of these yards with moose in it they generally managed to get one or two without much difficulty; and if they found a track leading across open country they were often able to follow it and run the moose down when the deep snow finally broke its heart. For this latter method of hunting they had evolved a special type of snow-shoe, which a hunter would always put on before he set out to pursue a moose. These moose-hunting snow-shoes were between six and seven feet long and were designed to give great speed, as the moose could move fast for a short distance in spite of the snow; the hunter could also use them as skis, for making quick swoops downhill from bench to bench, if he sighted the moose below him in one of the valleys.

Actually the Loucheux had no less than three kinds of snow-shoe, all of which were evidently quite different from anything that we use in the East and were much nearer in their conception to skis than to orthodox snow-shoes. Their ordinary shoe, about four feet long, was used where no great speed was required and a longer shoe would have been awkward. Then there was the special shoe for dog-running ; this was longer than the ordinary shoe, as it reached from the ground to the owner's forehead. Finally, there was the very long ski-like shoe for moose-hunting, that has just been described. All three types were narrow, no more than ten inches across at the broadest point, and all were used with the sliding motion of skis instead of with the deadly pounding and lifting that is called for by a roundish or wide lozenge-shaped shoe.

Mitchell considers that snow-shoe making was the prettiest of all the Indian handicrafts. He describes the operation as follows. " Each snow-shoe frame was made of two pieces of wood, not of one piece bent round the way ours are, and they're made from rods, not wood cut out of a piece of lumber. The Indian takes two seasoned rods, prepares an end of each, and joins them together with a kind of scarf joint. This joint makes the toe of the snow-shoe, the middle of the front. Then he bends the rods back on themselves to form the two sides of the frame, and inserts cross-bars to keep the breadth and shape right—very narrow, as I've told you—one just ahead of where the toes come and the other considerably back of the heel. The back ends of the rods are fastened together with a very tight lashing Then comes the shaping of the front end, which is quite peculiar to the Loucheux—they raise the part that's forward of the toes at quite a sharp angle, and then bend down the extreme tip again so that it's horizontal and about three inches off the ground. This is done by steam-ing the end of the frame and bending it over a strong cross-bar, and that's when they sometimes break the God-damned thing. The meshing in front of the toes and behind the heel is done with the finest *babiche* (caribou, of course) and with very small openings, but the central part is of coarse *babiche* with large openings—the Indians figure you pick up the least amount of snow that way. The frames

are all carefully bored, to let the meshings through instead
of being whipped round and round like ours are ; and
that leaves a sliding surface on the polished wood, you see,
so that you can ski along without wearing the *babiche*
against the snow. They do the whole job with their crooked
knives, and leave the wood just as smooth as if it had been
planed and sand-papered."

After a time the Indians decided that the plan of sending
Mitchell on with the hunters was a bad one ; possibly
the young men who dragged his toboggan found their
enthusiasm waning. So he was handed over to the squaws
to be brought on with the baggage convoy behind the
hunters : five dogs were harnessed to his toboggan and
he was put in charge of two boys, who were threatened
with the direst penalties if they allowed the team to run
away. Mitchell has kept a vivid mental picture of the
long caravan of toboggans as it trailed over the pure white
benches and slopes. The women who drove the teams
plodded along on their snow-shoes in long shirts of white-
tanned caribou skin, with fine red broadcloth leggings
heavily ornamented with beads pulled up over their trousers
to the knees. The smaller children rode on the sleighs,
the babies being strapped on for safety, while the larger
boys and girls rushed backwards and forwards chasing the
arctic hares and shooting at ptarmigan with their toy bows
and arrows. The howling, snarling, and scuffling of the
dogs, which numbered between two and three hundred,
hardly fell short of pandemonium.

There were continual possibilities of danger on these
journeys. What Mitchell calls " snow tornadoes " were not
at all uncommon, sudden whirlwinds raising the powdery
snow in clouds and forming a kind of fog. Dogs were
always liable to stampede in these snow fogs unless the
drivers jumped on the leading dogs and held them down
by force, and a stampede, ending in an upset or a fall over
a cliff or into water, was naturally the least desirable of

all possible accidents for a man in Mitchell's condition. " I was scared positively blue the first time or two we got into snow tornadoes, thinking I was covered up for ever and ever. I could only lie there and just wait for God to clear things up, don't you know. Sometimes they lasted a minute or two or sometimes it might be nearer a quarter of an hour, and when everything had calmed down you'd see Indians and dogs popping out of hummocks of snow and shaking themselves clear, just like jack-in-the-boxes —the damnedest funny thing to see.

" Then you have to watch out very sharp for bad ice when you're crossing the rivers. The ice may form at high water, and then the water goes down and leaves a cavity under the ice, and down you go like I did that time with Harris at Wind City. Then you get holes in the snow formed round the heads of fallen trees ; there may be a thin skin of snow over the hole with nothing at all to show on the outside, and I've seen dogs and toboggans and everything disappear into one of them and a glorious dog-fight at the bottom to finish up with. Of course, if you fall into the middle of a dog-fight like that it's all over sure—dogs get so panicky in fights and emergencies that they lose all their reasoning power and just chew up anybody and everybody they can reach."

However, all these difficulties and dangers were taken by the squaws as part of the normal routine. The baggage convoy crawled slowly along the trail that the hunters had broken and sooner or later Mitchell would hear rifle shots ahead where the hunters had come upon the caribou. That meant that the worst of the journey was over, and then they would arrive on the scene of the killing to find the Indians butchering the carcases. The squaws made camp as quickly and skilfully as they had struck it in the morning ; the lodges were very soon standing, branches and furs were spread on the floors, fires were lit, and tea was ready for the hunters by the time they came in from their work.

Mitchell was always astounded to see how quickly the Indians could start their fires. " Fire-making is a bloody art with those Indians," he said, " the result of generations of work, I suppose. If an Indian wants to make a cup of tea or roast something he will make a very small fire that throws a tremendous heat with next to no smoke. He chops his sticks, we'll say, ten or twelve inches long, and splits them small : then he piles them lengthways on top of one another—parallel, you understand, not criss-cross—and then he lights them from the *top*. You know, Graham, the Indians do the God-damnedest curious things sometimes, and that's one of them ; if a white man made a fire like that it just wouldn't light, but with them the result after a few minutes is a splendid mass of glowing embers. I asked Colin about this once and explained that white men always lighted fires from underneath. Colin said that was the wrong way to light fires, they should be lighted from the top ; but when I asked him how he did it he couldn't explain at all—he just did it that way and that's all he knew about it. When I pressed him he reminded me of the difference between the work of a man and a beaver—when a man wants to put a stick upright in the mud he has to get an axe and hammer in the stick, and then it doesn't stay, while the beaver quietly swims up with the stick in his mouth and sticks it in, and it does stay. Well, we can't make fires in the Indians' way any more than we can put sticks in the mud in the beavers' way, so that's all there is to it.

" They make big fires with larger logs, for parties of eight or ten men, in just the same way, laying the logs lengthwise. They're most expert at finding dry twigs, and they know how to split dry wood out of the inside of dead branches even if they're soaking wet on the outside. As I've told you, their fires for cooking out of doors are pretty free of smoke, but if they want a signal fire they can make it smoke right up to Heaven and can make the column of smoke veer to north or south, or however they want, by fanning it with a coat, or a blanket. They never leave a fire burning by any chance—you won't find any burned land up that valley anywhere. And now we're talking about fires I want to tell you one of the oddest things about my Indians and see what you say about it. When they want to say in their language ' you make a little fire ' they say ' *Kunatcha* ', and when they want to say ' we two will make a little fire ' they say ' *Quanatchi* ', but when they want to say ' everybody make a big fire ' they say ' *Ignaz* '. Now it's curious enough that they should have quite a different word for making a big bonfire from what they have for making a little cooking fire ; but what I want to ask you, Graham, is why they should have that word for the big fire, ' *Ignaz* ', which is just the same as ' fire ' in Latin ! ''

Mitchell was at pains to explain to me how carefully the Indians made use of every particle of the caribou which they killed ; between dogs and men there was literally nothing wasted. When the hunters found a herd they seemed to see red and slaughter at random, but actually they never killed more animals than the camp could use during the time that the women were working on the skins. On butchering a carcase they immediately ate the contents of the second of its three stomachs ; this partially digested moss provided them with a substitute for the green vegetables which were otherwise quite absent from their diet, but Mitchell never quite steeled himself to the point of tasting it. Later they ate the tongues, liver, kidneys, and a few other tit-bits, unborn calves of both caribou and moose being regarded as a delicacy. The remainder of the meat was cut into strips for drying and smoking. The brains were carefully preserved in bladders and used later as a kind of soft soap for the tanning of the skins—Mitchell remarked on the appalling smell that arose from the decaying brains. Marrow-bones were eaten on the spot, or small quantities of the marrow were put aside to be used later in making pemmican ; a great deal of the dried meat was pounded and made into pemmican, with the addition of the marrow and certain dried herbs. The back sinews were always taken out entire, and sewing thread was drawn out of them as required in various thicknesses according to the work in hand ; for fine work on gauntlets and moccasins the squaws could draw these threads of sinew as fine as fine sewing silk.

The smoked meat that was not required for immediate use was invariably stored in a cache. The Indians never carried supplies of meat about with them on their migrations, but depended on picking up cached meat, as they needed it during the season when the caribou herds were not available. Permanent caches of meat were required particularly at certain convenient points for their supply during the autumn and early winter, when they were engaged on the trapping of fur-animals ; the trapping left them very little time in which to hunt for their own subsistence, and the caribou were only to be found on the very high ground at that time of year. These were the most important caches and might often last over from one winter to the next, but the Indians also made temporary caches of meat, fish, or whatnot at times when they had made a big killing and drew on them in case of scarcity or for trade with the white men at Fort McPherson. All these caches, whether permanent or temporary, were made with the greatest care to protect them from birds and animals, particularly from wolverines. The method was to choose a clump of three or four trees growing close enough together to support a platform based on logs that were made fast among the branches. The meat was packed very neatly and carefully in hides or canvas and lashed solidly to the platform so that it could not be disturbed even by the strongest winds. (Mitchell remarked that a platform built by Indians would stand indefinitely, while one built by white men nearly always fell down in the first storm.) As in the case of the tree-top burials the lower branches were removed and the snags smoothed off so as to provide no foothold, and shrubs and undergrowth were cleared away from round about so that no animal should be able to jump up to the platform from them.

Mention of the caches provoked an outburst from Mitchell against the wolverines. Wolverines, like the Eskimo, are such red rags to him that he can seldom pass either of them over without a release of emotional pressure. This time the wolverines got what follows.

" The wolverine, Angus, is bitterly hated and despised by my Indians because he has a devilish brain. If any cache is made that he can possibly reach by climbing, that's the end of it right off—he eats what he can at the time and fouls the balance. A favourite trick of his is to follow an Indian's trap line, sniff out the traps, and take a fox out of one and a marten out of another, or whatever there may be, and foul those he doesn't want. They work through the traps methodically, just like a hunter, and that's how the Indians manage to catch them sometimes by putting traps for them on the trap line itself after they have visited it once, because they know the wolverines will always come back and go over the line again. They're vicious devils, and wicked fighters when they have to."

CHAPTER XXVIII

THE OLD LADY

" FRANCIS, Colin, and the other 'better' Indians (as I call them) had warned me from the very beginning of my stay with them that although they would do everything they possibly could to see me through, as they liked me personally, the absolute and final verdict as to what was to happen to me lay in the hands of a certain old squaw. When I say 'verdict', Angus, I mean, of course, whether I was to be kept and carried down to the Fort, or thrown out into the snow, or knocked on the head right off. I couldn't for the life of me understand how a very old squaw could interfere with the chief and councillors, but there was no doubt about Francis being in earnest over it, so I just had to wait and see. And when I met her there was no doubt about the dominating brilliant spirit encased in that shrivelled little frame !

" I never shall forget the night she arrived at the lodges. It was some time fairly early in my stay with the Indians, but it can't have been right at the start because I know I was feeling stronger and I'd also begun to talk a little Indian. Francis knew she was due, and had advised me very kindly to be awfully careful with her, but he wouldn't for a moment indicate what it was he thought I ought to do or say—he may have been afraid of suggesting the wrong thing, or he may have been simply nonplussed and trusted me to get through the business best under my own steam. Anyhow, I remember it was one of those very cold still nights ; all the lodges were very quiet when suddenly

Francis sat up and listened, and then rose to his feet. He listened again, and then turned very solemnly to me and said ' She comes.' And that was all he damned well did say. I couldn't hear a thing—of course the Indians hear, see, and smell much more than we can—but eventually I did hear dog-teams in the distance, and then they ran right in among the lodges with a tremendous howling of the dogs. All our dogs howled too, in reply. I hadn't time to fix things up, but I felt for my bag and got out two unused pipes and some plugs of tobacco, and trinkets that I thought might go down well as a present.

" Then Francis signed to the women to lift down the big moose hide from the doorway, and I got the surprise of my life. A little white bundle came quickly through the door, hopped across to my couch, and plumped down beside me. I don't think the creature was really four feet high, and she was completely dressed in a snow-white cloak or wrapper woven out of strips of rabbit skin with a backing of some light material. She threw back her hood with a hand that was just a little claw and showed me a tiny wizened face just like one of those faces we used to make out of a hickory nut, with a little peaky nose sticking out of it. The handsome Indian features had all faded away with age, but the great luminous black eyes still remained, intensely intelligent—they were all that was alive about her. She was just a damned little mummy, do you know ; that was all there was to it—dried right up.

" She didn't say a word for an interminable time ; simply sat there gazing at my face, lifting up my hands, and studying their formation and the nails. Fortunately I was scrupulously clean, as I shaved every day and my hands and finger-nails were well looked after. Then she turned to the Indians and burst into a torrent of rapid-fire Indian words, so fast that I couldn't pick out one of them ; and then she bowed to me very ceremoniously three or four times, without getting up, and finally shook hands with great formality. After that I did my part—produced a new pipe and a plug of tobacco with all the dignity I could muster under the circumstances, and presented them to her. The old bird examined them carefully, took a valuation of them, and then stowed them away somewhere in her inner clothes. Meanwhile the squaws had set out the white caribou skin table-cloth which they used on grand occasions, and a big copper kettle of tea with tin pannikins—they dip their tea out of the kettle with pannikins, and drink it like that instead of having a teapot. The old bird didn't seem to like roast meat, so they gave her a bowl of pemmican softened with warm water ; I guess she hadn't a tooth in her head, just gums.

" She lived in our lodge for ten days or a fortnight, and very nearly beggared me in pipe-tobacco, tea, and oddments. She was a politician, that old woman, if ever there was one. But just the same, most fortunately for me, we really did strike up a perfectly genuine friendship—I liked the old blackguard very much, do you know that ? Francis told me as soon as he could what her tirade that first evening had meant ; she'd said that the Indians hadn't done nearly enough for me—that I was evidently a chief in my own country, and that if I reported anything bad to the Hudson's Bay Company they'd suffer. I wasn't very much impressed by this as I figured she'd got her eye on my tobacco and tea, and meant to pump me dry if she could, and she damn well nearly did. But her support clinched my position with the Indians, so it was worth paying for. I tell you I needed all the support I could get before I was through.

" Her dominance over the other Indians was quite extraordinary. She was treated with the greatest possible respect, really reverence, by both men and women—the way you'd treat a god, don't you know, whatever that is. The children weren't terrified of her but were awfully damn well polite. The Indians brought her all their family troubles and differences of opinion for solution while she was with them, and her verdicts were as clean-cut and hard as could be. About three words settled everything ; she told them just where they got off at, and whatever she told them they went and did right off, whether permanently or not I can't say. Her voice, as she spoke, was just as clear as a bell ; not sweet like a young squaw's contralto voice but distinct and very well enunciated—you felt the spirit was burning clear inside the shrivelled husk.

"You know, I had great fun with that old girl one way and another. She used to talk to me by the hour, and I found her intelligence very much higher than that of the ordinary run of Indians. I should say, judging by the way we discussed things, that we were much more nearly on a par intellectually than Indians and white people commonly are. Of course, if she was really over a hundred years old, as Firth told me afterwards he figured she was, she'd practically had two life-times of experience, if one can put it like that. She told me a whole lot of things about Indian life and Indian ways, especially about the old times, which was all most intensely interesting to me, and helped me no end in my own relations with the Indians.

"But the most amazing thing was that as her mind worked backwards into bygone days she suddenly dropped into French. I remember so well how she seemed to brighten up, as if she'd just had an idea, looked at me ever so cunningly, and began to say ' *la rivière* ', ' *la maison* ', ' *la montagne* ', ' *la hache* '—said the words just as they came into her mind, not in a sentence, and pronounced them very slowly and with great difficulty like a rusty door opening after a hundred years. This fairly amazed me as I'd never known that there had been any French-Canadian traders in that country ; Firth confirmed this later on, but said that about a hundred years before some French-Canadian traders had come down the Mackenzie and crossed over to the Rat river, as the Loucheux hadn't allowed

them into the valley of the Peel, so she might have got
mixed up with them. I guess she was rather a charmer
in her young days and she nearly went wild with excitement one time when I sketched her an old-time *coureur
de bois,* like a Kreighoff picture—I often used to make
little drawings with charcoal on white caribou skin to amuse

THE *COUREUR DE BOIS.*

the Indians. Anyhow, that picture of the old ruffian in
his tuque and sash seemed to bring back memories of old
beaux ; she was tickled to death with it.

"And then she told me a very strange thing about how
her tribe had met white men for the first time. They
came across some trees which had been felled, and were
astonished to find that the chips lying round about the
stumps were as big as a man's hand. Of course, their

little stone axes wouldn't take out big chips like a steel axe, and as they'd never seen chips from a steel axe before they didn't know what the Hell to make of it. So they followed up the tracks which led away from the place until they ran into a party of white men. Incidentally, she called these white men ' men who live under a stone ', and I had a Hell of a time finding out what she meant by this. At last I gathered that these birds were travelling light without tents, and used to spend the night in caves or under natural rock shelters. Or possibly there were no travelling tents a hundred years ago.

" Her going away was just as mysterious as her coming. One night Francis gently wakened me and I found the little old bird sitting beside me and the Indians standing round looking very much like people in church. She said she was going away—how, when, or where to she didn't mention—and bade me a very tender farewell with a lot of ceremonies attached which I really think she'd put on to impress the Indians, so as to leave me in good standing. A dear old blackguard ! I don't believe she could walk as far as the toboggan ; the old bag-of-bones just scurried to the door, and then I saw them lift her and carry her out. She had several people attending on her and some of the finest dog-teams I ever saw. I thought of getting carried outside so as to be able to see her off, but didn't do it as I knew it was very important to preserve my dignity."

Mitchell's story about the old lady's advanced age deserves to be considered in the light of what is known about early explorations in the Peel river country. Sir Alexander Mackenzie made the first descent of the Mackenzie river in 1789 : it is therefore quite impossible that the old lady could have met her white men before that date. Mackenzie did not visit the Peel river, his turning-point having been somewhere in the Delta, and it is consequently quite unlikely that his party can have been the ' men who lived under a stone '. Again, as Mackenzie's exploration was made a hundred and six years before Mitchell's meeting with the old lady, she would have been over a hundred and twenty years old at the time of Mitchell's visit if the white men of whom she spoke had really been Mackenzie's retainers, and this is an even greater age than has been suggested. (I assume fifteen as a convenient figure for the lowest age at which a young squaw might have been expected to take the lively kind of interest in a Frenchman that Mitchell deduced from her response to his sketch of the *coureur de bois.*)

The first white man who actually visited the Peel river was Sir John Franklin, who discovered and named it as he was returning from his exploration of the Arctic Coast in 1826—actually he mistook the Peel for the main stream of the Mackenzie, and ascended it a short distance before he discovered his error. But the old lady's description of the strangers does not by any means suggest Franklin's company of British sailormen ; moreover, some at least of the Loucheux must have been well acquainted with white people before that date, as Franklin found numbers of them trading at Fort Good Hope in 1825 and 1826, and consequently the large chips of wood cut by a steel axe would no longer have appeared to them as portents. This alternative therefore seems hardly more tenable than the other. It is possible, of course, that the particular band of Indians to which the old lady belonged in her youth lived so far up country that Fort Good Hope was quite beyond its ken, and that it remained in ignorance of white men's ways until the Hudson's Bay Company explored the Peel river valley in 1839 and 1840. But so late a date as 1839 hardly accords with her obviously very great age, as it would have made her no more than seventy-five, or eighty at the most, in 1899. Further, as Fort McPherson was established in 1840 and trade had been carried on continuously with the Indians of the Peel river district since that time, an Indian's report of a chance meeting with the Company's party of explorers would most probably have been stated in rather different terms, as relating to a first encounter with the Company's emissaries rather than with white men as such. On the whole, I am inclined to believe that the old lady's Frenchmen were an unofficial party who have left no other record behind them ; private traders, broken men, *coureurs de bois* in the exact sense of that phrase, who had drifted northwards to follow up the discoveries made by Mackenzie in 1793. I am also tempted to imagine that such an expedition might probably have been made quite soon after Mackenzie's own pioneer journey, while the memory of it was still fresh among the fur-trading posts of the interior, rather than, for instance, in the second decade of the nineteenth century. The upshot of this tissue of surmises would therefore be that the old lady might have been born about 1790 ; that she met her Frenchmen about 1805, or at any rate not later than 1810 ; and that at the time of her meeting with Mitchell she was close on a hundred and ten years old.

CHAPTER XXIX

FAMINE AND RIOT

SOON after the old lady had left their camp, and while the weather was still very cold, the Indians lost touch with the caribou. They expected the herds to move in a certain direction, following their usual habit, but they actually took an entirely different course, with the result that the Indians travelled first up one valley and then up another and found no caribou anywhere. They were carrying next to no meat with them and had no caches in that neighbourhood to fall back upon, and consequently they were very soon not only hungry but starving. In time they became too weak to undertake the labour of moving camp, and so remained where they were while the younger and stronger men ranged over the surrounding country to look for game. Every valley within fifty miles was searched, but the whole region seemed to be completely bare. As soon as the famine became acute Mitchell shared out the toboggan-load of his own provisions which had come up from Wind City, giving what he could to the women and children and a little to the very old men, but he had not enough to make very much difference. The children began to die first, then the women, and then the weaker men ; the two larger children in Mitchell's lodge died, and he thinks that there were probably two or three deaths in every lodge. The biggest eaters seemed to suffer most.

Mitchell told me a strange story of how some Indians appear to have died on purpose during the famine. His account of this ran as follows. " It's a very strange thing,

Angus, that Indians will eat enormously, or go without eating for a long time, but when we came down to famine and the women and children were dying from starvation I sometimes saw an Indian throw a blanket over his head, sit quiet for a few minutes, and then topple over—just go dead, give up the ghost, stop fighting. I saw several cases of this, all men ; I never saw a woman cover her head to die at all, though I've seen them fall down dead on the trail. It's just like the way an Indian will go to a certain point in races or tests of strength, but if he knows he's beaten he'll simply quit, and quit at a point where he wouldn't quit if he knew he was winning.

" Talking of people dying on purpose, I can tell you a very odd thing about old man Bonnet Plume. Once in the fall when we were going up the river in my canoe we came ashore to rest for a while, and as we were sitting quietly on the bank a little bird—some brightly coloured little bird, I don't know what it was—came and lit on Bonnet Plume's shoulder. I looked at him and smiled, thinking it was a sign of good luck for a bird to light on you, but the old man went ashy grey, his jaw dropped, and he turned up his eyes and groaned.

" ' What the Hell's the matter with you ? ' I asked him— I was astounded to see him go like that.

" ' Oh, I shall die before sunset : a bird has lit on my shoulder ! '

" I called him a fool and every other name I could think of, and roared with laughter at him, and gradually got him annoyed and then thoroughly offended. But it was only when he was thoroughly annoyed that he forgot to die ; the anger somehow switched him over, and I really believe it's quite possible he might have died otherwise judging by the ghastly face he showed when I first looked at him.''

Mitchell cannot say how long the famine lasted or how many days he himself went without any food whatever ; in fact, he believes that he was comatose for a time and lost his reckoning. The Indians sank into a condition of complete hopelessness ; they made no complaints or lamentation, and indeed Mitchell remarked that they were far too well resigned to their fate, as this quiet resignation was the first step to what he calls "dying on purpose". If they had continued in this frame of mind the whole band would certainly have died, and as it was their lives were only saved by the barest accident.

"One day," Mitchell said, "when we were all just waiting to die, Francis came and sat down beside my couch in a hopeless state, and as I looked at him sitting there with his head sunk on his hands I suddenly seemed to get a flare of energy.

"'Francis,' I said, 'have you got three boys who can walk?'

"'Yes,' he answered, rather doubtfully.

"'Can you walk?'

"'Yes.'

"'Then for God's sake go out just once more and see if you can't get some caribou!'

"The idea appealed to his imagination, and he brightened up for the first time for days ; otherwise he had quite given up any effort the same as the rest. He took a few boys and went out, and they'd only been gone a few minutes when we all heard a succession of bangs—they'd run into a small herd of caribou only a quarter of a mile from the lodges and had got six of them. Everybody staggered out with great manifestations of joy to get a bite and to drink the warm blood ; they brought me a hunk of meat as big as a good loaf of bread, all dripping with the fresh blood which was the most delicious part of it. I ate it raw, just as it was, drank two pannikins of tea and fell right over to sleep—I guess I slept for twelve hours on end. These caribou were the forerunners of a large crowd and we never missed them again for more than a few days all through the winter. It was really charming to see the Indians' native kindliness and good nature return, with their strength and ability to work, once they'd got some food into them.

"Before the worst came to the worst the Indians killed and ate several dogs. (It was always middle dogs that they ate, as leaders and wheelers were still too valuable even in that extremity.) But after a few dogs had been killed the rest all seemed to fade away, and I guess they'd realized that the camp wasn't healthy for them just about then. Actually there weren't three pounds of meat on one of them, because dogs aren't fed at any time when they're not pulling the toboggans, and certainly not when rations are short for the men. They turned up again, though, as soon as we'd struck the caribou ; probably they were hanging around somewhere close by and smelt the fresh meat and blood. Whisky-jacks were very numerous all through the famine, chattering continuously ; the noise used nearly to drive me mad. But there was nothing on them either if you shot them—perhaps they were starving themselves."

Though Mitchell's life had thus been saved again by a narrow margin, it was too much to expect that it should stay saved for very long at a time. After starvation came murder, attempted by that Amos who was the leader of the bad element in the tribe. Amos' original dislike of Mitchell had been greatly increased by jealousy when he saw the favour with which Mitchell was regarded by the mysterious old lady, and he probably felt that Mitchell was a powerful moral support to Francis and Colin in their resistance to himself and his disreputable associates. The upshot, in any case, was what Mitchell calls his " riot with Amos ", which he has described to me as follows.

"The riot broke out one night without any preliminaries at all. Francis had gone away for ten days or so, and the first night he was away most of our lodgemates were out visiting. The only people left in the lodge were old Colin and his wife and a couple of strange Indians, besides Francis' youngest sister who happened to be sitting by my couch sewing some moccasins. Suddenly the lodge door was thrown open and Amos stepped into the firelight—two strides, and he stood at my feet as I lay there on the branches. He had nothing on except a pair of leather breeches ; a long hunting-knife in a sheath hung round his neck by a cord, and his huge chest and arms and back were painted with war paint, yellow, red and black. But it didn't need that to tell me that he was out looking for trouble ; the devilish face he had on him was quite enough. He glared round the lodge like a wild beast and just stood there, heaving great breaths and clenching and unclenching his hands, and didn't say a word. Neither did I. I just watched him and wondered where he'd begin.

" Well, my tobacco bag was lying on my knees and the first thing he did was to snatch that up and fill his pipe lavishly, spilling the tobacco and not lighting his pipe. Of course this was unheard-of behaviour from the Indian point of view, but I took no notice. Then he picked up my tea pannikin and drank lustily, but I still took no notice. Then he spat at my feet very largely and audibly, and I took no notice of that either. Finally he reached across me, grabbed Francis' sister by her hair, and pulled her violently across my legs. Now I always kept a good pole beside me to keep the dogs off my broken knee—it must have been five feet long and an inch and a half thick—and almost before he'd touched the girl I sat right up, grabbed the pole, and hit him one good Hell of a swat right in the face. He was just standing at a nice distance for me to reach him, by the foot of my couch and on my left, and I laid the whole left side of his face open from the temple to the chin. The blood poured through his fingers as he laid hold of his face and ran all over my legs. Of course that put the fat in the fire. Quick as a flash he drew his hunting-knife and came right at me, but I was a little quicker than him on the draw and had him covered at once with my automatic that I always kept in my left armpit. My finger was just itching on the trigger, but good sense fortunately restrained me—it would have been a pleasure, but I knew that if I shot him his brother or next-of-kin would have been compelled by their code to do me in, so I denied myself. The suspense lasted for a few minutes, and it seemed like half an hour ; but then, seeing that I had the drop on him, he finally turned and went out as quickly as he'd come in, and the show was over. The wound on his face healed up into a great purple weal, and for weeks and months afterwards the Indians used to have a lot of fun walking up behind him, touching the scar, and saying ' Mr. Mitchell '—they roared with laughter at him about it ! "

" But, Mr. Mitchell," I said, scandalized, " didn't you have some kind of a show-down with him when Francis came back ? Surely, after an out-and-out attempt at murder like that, the chief might have done something, mightn't he ? I mean, your life can hardly have been worth an instant's purchase after a thing like that had happened, and to put the thing on its lowest ground I can't imagine it would have improved Francis' prestige with the tribe to have his friend nearly murdered and his sister insulted, right in his own lodge, and then not do anything about it ! "

" No, my dear boy, that's just where you don't understand the Indian mind. They've got no idea of the policeman for maintaining law and order. For them an affair like that was no business of anybody except the two principals until one or the other was actually killed, and then of course the family would have taken up the blood-feud. They wouldn't have acted any differently if I'd been one of themselves with brothers on the spot ; they'd have let the thing go from bad to worse just when you or I would have said they ought to nip it in the bud, if only to save the tribe from perhaps losing several damned good hunters. That's just the difference between their point of view and

ours. And the assault on the little girl wasn't serious enough
to be considered a crime against her, so there the thing
rested."

" Well then," I objected, " if Amos was left to do as he
liked, didn't he take the first opportunity of getting back
at you for that crack you gave him ? "

" No, Graham," Mitchell answered ; " I had no more
violent outbreaks with this bird at all, except that on two
or three occasions when I was outside a bullet would
whistle along a good deal closer to me than I liked. I never
could identify the shooter, but I knew damned well who
it was because the rifle always seemed to make the same
very loud heavy report, like a forty-five-seventy, and Amos
was the only man in the whole gang who had a forty-five-
seventy. (I had a good joke on him over that later, as I'll
tell you some time.) No, when he did try to take his revenge
he went about it in a much more dangerous way, and he
bloody nearly got me too. But that happened a long time
afterwards, so we won't rush into it now."

CHAPTER XXX

MITCHELL BECOMES AN INDIAN

MURDER apart, Mitchell's life with the Indians now began to be rather more tolerable. His wounded leg gradually became less painful, he picked up a good deal of the language, and when once he could speak readily he began to make some personal friends. His friendship with Francis was of course on a firm footing, and he had begun to feel that the Indians had a great deal in them while his partners and the other white men still regarded them simply as benighted savages ; but he obtained very little insight into their real characters until he had learned their language and established himself fully in their confidence. He believes now that the white men who were ordinarily in touch with the Indians, even missionaries and others who had had a good deal of experience in dealing with them, really knew very little about their intimate lives ; and he is sure that nothing was further from the Indians' thoughts than to give them unnecessary enlightenment. For his own part, as soon as he was well enough to take notice of what was going on round about him, Mitchell began to cultivate the Indians' friendship by showing them that he was interested in their daily affairs. For example, he would get old Jane to sit beside him with her needlework and explain to him how moccasins or breeches or whatever it might be were cut out and sewn ; or when the squaws were filling bladders with pemmican or marrow, or the men were making snow-shoes, bows, or dog-harness, he would get them to raise him on his couch so that he could

watch the operations. He used also to get out his prayer
book and compare notes about Christianity with Colin—
Colin was greatly interested, and recognized a good deal
of what Mitchell endeavoured to translate to him. In these
various ways Mitchell was able to pick up a great many
new words and also to break down the Indians' suspicion
and reserve. He always let the children play round him
too, though he found them an intolerable nuisance.

One of his most successful dodges for making friends with
the Indians was to draw pictures for them with charcoal
on white bark, as he had drawn the *coureur de bois* for the
entertainment of the old lady. He made a sketch from
memory of Fort McPherson standing at the edge of the
bluffs, with the Eskimo tents spread out on the sands below,
which came as a revelation to the Indians as their first
experience of landscape. They were also very much
intrigued by pictures of white men's houses and civilized
towns, though he suspects that they may have thought that
he was simply delirious when he drew a long street of three-
storied houses, with a church and steeple, and said that
his people built all their houses out of blocks of stone.
Horses, particularly harnessed horses, were very difficult
for them to swallow ; it puzzled them that the horses had
no horns, and they could hardly understand that white
men did all their hauling with horses instead of with dogs.
A world without working dogs seemed utterly impossible.
But the picture that caused most excitement and laughter
was one of a big fat sow with six little pigs, which they
considered the finest joke that had ever been made ; they
were very much impressed when they heard that this was
where bacon and salt pork came from, while the few of
them who had seen pig-skin leather immediately began to
tell the rest about its marvellous strength. Mitchell's
familiarity with such marvels soon gained him a considerable reputation for wisdom, and his position was made more
secure through the friendships which he struck up with the

rank and file of the tribesmen, who regarded his picture-drawing as an entertainment of the highest order and flocked in from all the other lodges to see the fun.

Another thing that helped to raise Mitchell in the estimation of the Indians was his skill (or good luck) as an amateur doctor. He began his practice with a few household medicines that he had happened to have in his kit, but what really established his reputation was an emetic compounded of mustard and a mixture of smoking and chewing tobaccos. The Indians had never seen an emetic before, and this mixture turned out to be sovereign in cases of a peculiar nervous frenzy to which they were very prone. Mitchell has described to me how an Indian would sometimes become morose, cruel, and dangerous—what Mitchell himself sums up as " wicked "—and finally fly into a violent rage, foaming at the mouth. The Indians' own method of dealing with these cases was to tie the patient to a tree until he either got better or died, but Mitchell's emetic proved to be very much more effective, and the men whom he cured by means of it used to come back and thank him for having saved them from bad spirits. (As he himself says, he had probably saved their lives.) Some of the Indians who were brought to him in these states of fury were so violent that they had to be pinioned, and even gagged to prevent them from biting ; to give them their mustard and tobacco he would have their mouths wedged open with a stick forced between the back teeth, so that the dose could be poured down their throats out of a pannikin.

" I had quite a windfall later on," Mitchell said while telling me of his clinical experiences. " My own stock of medicines got used up after a while, but one day some Indians who were coming up the main Peel river happened to pass over a patch of clear ice and saw a dump of stores lying on the sand four or five feet below the surface. The things had evidently been left on the sand-bar by some miner going up in the fall, and then the water had risen and it had all been frozen over. They chopped through the ice and found a regular treasure-trove, and what they brought me was a fine new medicine chest from the Army and Navy Stores. It had kept perfectly watertight and had everything in it you could think of up to surgical instruments and patent silk for sewing. But the greatest find as far as I was concerned were two or three glass bottles of Cockles pills—dozens and dozens of them—and after that I made them my staple remedy. The Indians were constantly applying for treatment for one thing or another, and I was always pretty careful what I did knowing that if anyone died on me things might go very badly indeed. But I thought Cockles pills were perfectly safe, so when anyone came in complaining bitterly of every possible ailment I used to give him enough Cockles pills to change his view-point immediately. (They'd never seen anything like so powerful as a Cockles pill.) And I guess they were really good for very severe headaches, which the Indians had very commonly from living on a constant meat diet. Their own cure for headache, by the way, was to bleed by slitting the eyebrows—they wanted to do this to me one time when I was suffering great pain but I wouldn't let them ; but they did bleed me in the back during the worst of my illness, while I was in a coma, and wanted me to take the breast afterwards.

" It was very touching sometimes to see how the Indians appreciated anything one could do for them with medicine and that kind of thing. They're great stoics in general about concealing their emotions as well as bearing pain, but I never shall forget the way some of them used to let me feel their gratitude. There was one boy of whom I was very fond, who used to come and sit beside me and talk—he was brought in very badly clawed by a bear, and I fixed him up as best I could, but he didn't live. Afterwards for several weeks his parents used to come into the lodge and sit by me quite silently, as if they were looking for sympathy from me because I had known the boy and been kind to him. The same thing happened with several other Indians and squaws whose children I had tried to help when they were dying : I can't say for sure that this was why they came to visit me, but I feel that they wanted to let me know that they appreciated what I'd done, and to be with someone who sympathized with them on their loss.

" One of the saddest cases that I had was a beautiful young girl who was brought in one night ; I'd never seen her before, so her people must have been hunting in some far-off valley. As soon as I looked at her I saw that peculiar greyness about her face and dead look in her eyes, and I was sure she wouldn't last for more than another three or four hours ; but her parents insisted on having some verdict, so I made a thorough examination. I found all the lower part of her belly was as hard as a stone with intense consti-pation : I'd have liked to do something for her but there wasn't the slightest hope. I could only shake my head and say with due solemnity that she was beyond human power and would soon be with her ancestors. They wrapped her up warmly in furs and carried her away, but after a very few hours they came back and said she was gone. I was very sorry for that girl and her people, but I must confess that my sorrow was somewhat abated by thankfulness that I hadn't attempted to do anything, as if I had her death might have been blamed on me. Actually this was the first case in which I had refused to do anything, and as the result worked out they thought all the more of me for it."

In due course, after Mitchell had won the Indians' confi-dence and respect, he was made a blood-brother to Francis and Colin. This was the highest mark of esteem that the Indians knew, and the effect was to give each man the responsibilities of the other in family matters, particularly in the vendetta. The ceremony consisted simply of making a small cut in each man's forearm and putting the two together so that the blood from both cuts should mingle. No rites were performed as the Loucheux are not given to what Mitchell would describe as " monkey business ". The completeness with which the tribe accepted him as one of themselves was expressed by the name which they gave him in their language—*Tingisuethli*. This means " the man " (in this case " the white man ") " who became an Indian ".

Even after he had been accepted in this way as a member of the tribe Mitchell found that the Indians remained very reticent about their personal philosophies and convictions, and he made a point of avoiding any kind of enquiry about their old religion. But he knows that they believed in something in the way of good and bad spirits, the function of the good spirit being to help them if they did right and that of the bad spirit to punish them if they did wrong. At the same time they regarded the plagues and epidemics which sometimes attacked them as penances inflicted by the good spirit, and not as vindictive attacks made by the bad one. They thought of the bad spirit as the extreme cold of the north wind, which would sometimes freeze a lodge full of Indians stiff, dogs and all ; and they also regarded the great heat of summer as an evil spirit coming out of a mountain to melt them into grease. Another thing that they dreaded very much was a certain huge wolf which nobody could kill, an incarnation of their devil. Although no ceremonies were carried out anywhere near the camp Mitchell did observe that Indians would sometimes go away for a few days professedly to hunt, but without seeming to be equipped for hunting, and he thinks that their real object may have been to worship the spirits in some retired place. But he was at pains to point out to me how thoroughly the tribe in general seemed to have abandoned most of the more or less unpleasant practices that are common among primitive peoples, and he considers that this must have been due to some natural fineness in their character, seeing that they were at that time very imperfectly Christianized.

This observation led me to enquire about the education and training of the children, and to ask whether they went through any kind of initiation rites. Mitchell replied that he knew nothing of any initiation ceremony for either boys or girls, and described to me how the children learned everything they knew by listening to and copying their elders.

" Indian children," he said, " were constantly at play, and were always smiling and happy when they had enough to eat. But their play was their education, because all the time they'd be making, we'll say, little tump-straps and practising carrying loads, or toy toboggans or snow-shoes or dead-falls, or weaving little nets out of willow bark. Sometimes they made beautiful toy bows, with bark quivers and a perfect assortment of arrows, or sets of dog-harness, and you'd see them harness up a pup and drive him about just like the kids on the Beauport Road. All these little works of the boys were overlooked unostentatiously by their fathers in the kindest way. And the girls went on the same lines, only they made dolls out of anything handy and dressed them in scraps, stealing sinew and sewing-needles from their mothers and working away at all kinds of miniature clothing. But just as soon as they grew big enough they were rigidly kept at work, both boys and girls—when the boys could carry a pack they bloody well had to, and when the girls could look after the younger children or make moccasins or clothes they had to do it, and do it well. Any undue meanness or lying or torturing of a puppy was suddenly and definitely punished—they'd grab them by the back of the neck and shake Hell out of them, or smack them with the open hand, or send them away when they were eating. Children were never allowed to lose or break anything and had to keep out of their elders' way, but when the Indians were sitting round talking of hunting, snowshoeing, pulling loads, and so forth, the little eyes and ears were very much alive. They had no books, and so they learned everything from the talk of the grown-up people and imbibed all the folk-lore and history of the tribe from hearing the stories told. All the time the boys were training themselves to hunt and trap by experiment, and there was no nonsense about that either as they weren't given any firearms and had to get them for themselves by trade. At a later stage a boy would be made a man when he proved himself very successful in hunting or performed some act of great courage or endurance. But he didn't finally graduate, so to speak, until he'd killed a grizzly, and not a young one either, but one that was old enough to have the long heavy claws ; these he was then allowed to wear as the insignia of full manhood.

" As far as reading and writing went I don't believe there were more than one or two men in the whole tribe who could do either. Colin could certainly read and write, and Francis could read a little. I really don't know how they learned, but I suppose they taught themselves from different printed books that came into their hands, like hymn-books, and selections from the Bible. But though they couldn't read themselves they loved hearing Colin read the New Testament aloud, as he very often did when a party were sitting round working in the lodge. The language and teaching appealed to them very closely ; but they could never swallow such ideas as a man herding sheep, which to them were wild bloody creatures, or gathering corn, which was absolutely outside of their experience."

Mitchell has fortunately remembered one first-rate Indian myth, which I took down from him as follows : " Once when I was talking very confidentially with Francis and a couple of elders about the ' bad element ' they told me their legend of the miraculous child. There were once two young Indians who had been married for several years but had no children. One night the woman woke up and called to her husband that she could hear a baby crying ; they both looked up and saw a papoose-case hanging on the pole at the top of the lodge. When they lifted it down they found a new-born boy baby, a beautiful child dressed in the most splendid imaginable furs—mink and marten—and the papoose-case itself marvellously worked with beads. The baby spoke to them with a grown-up voice and manner saying that he had been sent to them because they were getting worse and worse, and that he was to save them. The tribe assembled next morning and received the baby with the utmost reverence ; he repeated the same story— that he would be glad to stay with them as long as they were good, but that if they were bad he would be recalled. He spoke as if he were under orders. He stayed with them for some four or five years, living the ordinary life of a young Indian child, but always giving marvellously good advice, far better than their wisest councillors could have given. All this time the Indians remained good, were successful in their hunting and improved in health. But after a while they began to slip back into their same old ways ; the child warned them, and said that if they went on he would be called back to where he came from. Eventually the Indians had some really bad outbreak, and at that he told them that he had been recalled, but that if they improved he would return to them. He then vanished, and never reappeared."

Having heard Mitchell speak more than once of Indians who were believed to have a " bad eye ", I enquired whether the Loucheux believed in the " evil eye " as this expression is understood in Scotland. He replied that the Indians certainly had some idea of the " evil eye " as we know it— that squaws, for example, did not like strangers to stare at their children, and that the children themselves used to scatter like flies when strangers came too close to them at Fort McPherson. He thinks, too, that the old lady may have had a reputation for the " evil eye " in the Scots sense.

But in addition to this the Indians seem to have thought that certain people possessed a supernatural power by which they could force others to do wrong, and it was to this power of evil control that the expression " bad eye " applied. " There were several people," said Mitchell, " who could put the ' bad eye ' men in their places—Francis, Colin and Neil could all do it, and they did it by personality, not by hocus-pocus. And I want you to understand, Graham, that these strong good men were the only power for good that existed in all that country—the power of the Government meant nothing up there and there were no policemen for thousands of miles. Yet there was no debauchery or murder among the Indians when they were away back in the mountains, so what the Hell else was it that controlled them except just those few men's will ? "

CHAPTER XXXI

AN INDIAN "VEILLÉE"

HOWEVER reticent the Indians may have been about their gods they seem to have had plenty to say on worldly subjects, and Mitchell enjoyed nothing better than listening to the stories that the hunters told as they sat round the fire in the evenings. This is his account of what we should call a *veillée* in Quebec.

"When the hunters came in at the end of the day the first thing they did was to strip off and have a snow-bath, rub themselves down with pieces of duffle, and dress in dry clothes. My Indians were always very particular about washing, which is more than you can say of most tribes—I guess we all had those little lice, but that's natural in the woods, and in every other way you may take it they were clean Indians. They had no false modesty about it either; if a squaw felt like washing she'd get some snow and strip off and wash right in the lodge, whoever there was about. (However, that's a digression.) When they'd changed the Indians would settle in for a good feed—tenderloin, liver, kidneys, or roast head—rounded off with strong boiled tea, kept over and reboiled. Before the days of tea they made a brew of bark and the leaves of a small shrub that has a tuberous root. As I've told you, their meals were very irregular, but they always fed me at regular times and nearly every hunter would bring me in a tit-bit of some sort whenever he came back. Damn nice of them, that; wasn't it? At this time, after the famine, we were living on pure meat and nothing else except for the odd grayling caught through the ice, and marrow-bones—it's extra-ordinary to me now to think that I'd sometimes eat two or three pounds of meat at a sitting, even when I was taking no exercise, and I drank lots of raw blood. Our way of eating meat was to cut off a strip with a knife, take the end into the mouth, and cut it off at the lips. The squaws used to dish up the meat pretty nicely on bark platters that were clean except for cinders, and the copper kettles were clean—had to be, or we'd have been poisoned—but they'd no feelings about giving you a drink in an uncleaned bowl, with grease and hair sticking to it !

" The Indians never talked while they ate, and after the meal was over they'd sit round the fire in silence for some time digesting and thinking. Then two or three other hunters would drop in quietly and sit down, and then every-body would get out their pipes and light up. There was always a bit of ceremony over offering a man tobacco—when an Indian comes into the lodge you open up your smoke-bag and offer it to him to take what he wants, and then you both light up and smoke together. (If you're running short of tobacco you get some inside bark of the willow, what they call *kinnikinnick*, and mix it in.) I had a very fine smoke-bag made of black velvet lined with black silk with a pattern of roses on both sides and a heavy trimming of cut steel beads. It closed with a draw-string of plaited wool, with woollen balls at the ends made over centres of moose hide. In this I kept my cut tobacco, a short straight pipe, and a waterproof match-box made out of two brass cartridge cases fitted together. I was very proud of my smoke-bag—I guess the steel beads on it alone had cost the squaw who made it ten dollars in trade. (But all that's another digression.)

" I have the most vivid remembrance of the circle of keenly interested intellectual faces with the firelight rising and falling on them, and the boys in the background also listening intently—in fact, learning their business. I can't think why Indians are generally supposed to be glum : there was nothing at all glum about my Indians—all keenly alive. The stories were wonderfully told in particularly beautiful forms of speech, and were always illustrated in a most dramatic way. In the case of a bear-hunt, we'll say a man would describe the first sighting of the bear, then the cautious retreat to bring up reinforcements, then the manœuvring for wind and position, and finally every detail of the battle, which might often be quite a prolonged affair. It was all so realistic you felt you'd been there yourself ! They always gave more details, and more exact details, than French-Canadian hunters ; as you know, Angus, a Frenchman's rather inclined to tell that sort of story on the lines of bombast, letting you see how clever he was himself, while my Indians were much more interested in giving an exact record of the facts, and never made any special mention of their own performances.

" Grizzlies are so wicked that nobody tackles them with levity. If an Indian meets a big old bear when he's alone he just passes by ; it's far too dangerous to attack him unless there are two or three men together. And nobody ever touches the cubs, as that makes the mother frantic, and she'll chase a man and keep after him till she gets him. You may not know, Graham, but a grizzly's forearm is as big as a man's thigh, and he has such extraordinary powers of cunning that even experienced hunters never feel they know where they are with him. Sometimes he pretends to run away when he's just preparing to rush you, and if he's fired on too close he'll play coon until he can get within reach. I remember once four boys had shot one and he lay como like that, while they stood round him and began to praise each other—out of bravado or ignorance. Well, Mr. Grizzly suddenly sat straight up and took a swipe at one of them, and tore every bit of flesh from his arm and shoulder and shoulder-blade. I saw that boy brought in— there were just the bones left, with a few sinews holding them together—a most terrible mess. (A grizzly likes to get that downward smashing blow on the head or shoulder, unless he can get you in his arms to crush.) All the same, the Indians are very glad to get a bear when they can, especially in the fall when his fur is rich and the skin gets a big price, and he has a thick layer of fat all over him which they render down carefully and store up. Fat is a most essential item of diet in that climate, and they're generally pretty short of it. Then there's a tremendous mass of actual meat on a grizzly—a young one has light-coloured flesh, like mutton, but an old one's like shoe-leather. The paws are a great delicacy, and the fat, when it's boiled down, is the only kind of soup they know of. That's odd, isn't it? They never could understand when I wanted a meat broth! The way they usually kill a bear is not in open fight but with a dead-fall. If an old bear who looks like a man-eater is hanging about too much where he might be a danger to anyone—and old grizzlies are definitely man-eaters—they look for his regular trail and put a dead-fall on it. It seems hardly credible that you can kill a grizzly with a dead-fall, but it's true none the less : they arrange a very heavy butt-log to fall on him, and if it doesn't necessarily kill him he'll be pinned down helpless so that they can finish him off in safety. The killing of a bear is a great event for the tribe and they treat him almost with reverence when he's dead. I've told you how they sing and chant in his honour, and hold a cere-monial feast which the squaws are not allowed to attend. That's another odd thing that I never got to the bottom of, but I suppose it's to do him the more honour as a great warrior.

"It always beats me, Graham, to think of the courage of those Indians' forefathers—going after grizzlies with spears and bows and arrows before the days of firearms. Of course, when I was with them the younger men were getting good ·44 rifles from the Hudson's Bay Company, though the older ones still used to go round with old smooth-bore muzzle-loaders, carrying three or four bullets in their mouths. (The guns sometimes burst, ' but not often ' as they said !) But those old men's fathers relied on bows and arrows and a shortish stout spear, just long enough to keep them out of the bear's reach. In those days they used to go out in parties of five or six, two with spears and the rest with bows and arrows ; and this was because you can fill a grizzly with arrows—or with lead either, for that matter—and he won't die, but with a spear you can jab his heart. But it can't have been any damned picnic, when you think of an old bear's claws, something like railroad spikes, curved, and a good six inches long !

    " I remember a story they told me about one of their greatest hunters of bygone times. He disappeared, and was found several months later dead in the arms of a dead grizzly—his six arrows were in the grizzly's body, his spear was through it too, and his hunting-knife was in its belly ; but still it had managed to kill him before it died. The Indians thought a lot of the story of that old man, and they were always ready enough to describe other people's feats however little they boasted about their own. I always admired them for that.

    " But, of course, what they liked best of all were the stories of the old wars with the Eskimo and the Indian tribes on the Red river and over the mountains. War, to them, was the very height of hunting. The old-time battles were fought with bow and arrow, axe and spear—of course, all flint-headed weapons—and the very first demand the Indians made on the white men was for steel weapons and tools, and firearms. In their wars they killed everybody, men, women and children, except the few they kept out of the massacre for torture purposes : I guess they had too much pride in keeping their race pure to adopt prisoners into the tribe the way the Iroquois did. But the Hudson's Bay Company always put a stop to all those tribal wars whenever they could and there had been no real fighting for a very long time ; it was only the oldest of the Indians who had actually seen a battle, and the younger men had never done more than shoot up intruders, allowing them to get away with their wounded.

" Naturally there had been no tortures for many years, so it was only the very old people who knew anything much about them, but I remember the old lady told me a good deal about them one night when she'd got confidential. Common winter tortures, she told me, were to tie a man to a stake outside, remove his toe-nails and pour on hot pitch ; stick slivers of pine-wood between his toes and burn them ; strip lengths of flesh from his legs and pour on hot pitch or spruce-gum ; and cut off his lips, tongue, nose and ears and gouge out his eyes. Then they left him to freeze to death. In summer they would peg him out in a hot dry place and leave everything to the mosquitoes—several Indians told me that the shrieks of a man tortured by mosquitoes were simply appalling. Or again, when they had done a bit and the smell of blood was beginning to attract the ravens, they would bury the man alive up to his chin and then watch the ravens peck out his eyes and eat his face and head. Burning off the feet was a common preliminary to any form of torture. Another pretty trick, that was seldom used because it worked too quick, was to bend over two strong saplings and tie the man's legs to them—then take out the pegs and have him whisked up into the air and split in half. But they'd never do that if they thought they might get several hours' torture out of a man, or a day or two days—only if they thought he was likely to break down early. They never tortured women or children, and got no kick out of a man who broke down and screamed—that just didn't interest them. On the other hand they would rest and feed a man who stood it well, and heal up his wounds, so as to get more out of him later, though of course a wise man would never take anything from them. They had an extraordinary respect for a strong character that could bear pain like that and were extremely stoical about it themselves : that boy whose arm was torn away by the grizzly never whimpered, and I never saw one of them give a sign of suffering in all the gunshot accidents and axe-choppings that the squaws fixed up while I was there. And mind you, those boys weren't put through any artificial hardening process, like the Iroquois boys ; they were just several steps higher than the average Indian, having kept their race pure in that valley from the very beginning.

" But I set out to tell you about our *veillées*, and I keep on digressing from the narrow paths of war and hunting. As far as sheer skill in hunting went it always seemed to me that sheep-hunting and goat-hunting were the greatest tests of all. (Let alone doing it with bows and arrows, which of course nobody dreams of nowadays.) The point is that these animals live out on the open rocky mountain-sides, and stalking them may mean several hours' detour to get wind, cover, and direction for shooting. I remember once being planted in my toboggan on one side of a valley while the hunters stalked a bunch of sheep on the other : I was watching the sheep through my glasses—they showed up well against the black precipices where no snow was lying—and it was hours and hours before the puffs of smoke and the reports of the rifles came and I saw the sheep start off. They went straight uphill, as they always do when any danger appears, jumping from ledge to ledge and making their way up the most extraordinary and apparently impassable places. Goats do just the same thing when they're caught out on a slope.

" Goat skins make excellent short winter coats, that will shed rain, and the Indian children's winter caps are gener-ally made of white kids' skins. The goats go round in parties of eight or ten under one old billy, with a couple of young ones on the watch to drive him out when he gets too old—the Indians say they push him over a precipice and then divide up the nanny-goats. Anyhow, this same thing is certainly true of beaver ; when the old chief beaver gets past his duties, social and family, or gets too cranky, they drive him out, and he has to go and live by himself in holes. That's what we call a ' bank beaver '. They say too that the goats range farther to the north than the sheep, and they call the goat *tivi* and the sheep *avi*, which are the same words as they use for the north and south winds. They call the east wind *newsthum atri*, and do you know they have no word at all for the west wind, for the very good reason that no west wind ever blows in that valley !

" You wouldn't believe, Angus, what a lot the Indians know about every kind of animal and bird and fish. They've got our idea of the survival of the fittest—that's nothing new at all ; they often said to me that the grey wolves kept up the breed of caribou by killing off the weaklings. And they know all about the lean years that come once in every seven when the hares go off. They say Indians, lynx, wolves, foxes and marten all starve in that seven-year cycle, and they've got a name for the hare that expresses the idea that he's the staple food of every other animal—*eeti-tingi-onega-nepa*—that really means ' little man everybody lives on '. But they've no explanation why it is you never find dead bodies of animals in the woods in those lean years, or else they wouldn't give it. And for their trapping they're bound to know the habits of every fur animal or they'd never get anything—foxes, for instance, they don't follow regular run-ways, so if you want to set a dead-fall for a fox you want to know just where he's likely to go sniffing for ptarmigan and hares along the edges of the willows by the lakes and brooks. Otherwise you've got to set a steel trap with a bait, and a fox just won't go near a trap if there's the least whiff of human hands having touched it, nor will a marten. Or take a lynx ; that's a pretty fine business too. To get a lynx you want to kill a hare and put it sitting up in a little opening hollowed out of some willows, with a noose fixed just in front of it and attached to a bent-over sapling ; then the lynx comes along, leaps at the hare, and gets into the noose, and the sapling springs up and whisks him into the air. And to get all that just right, you know, Graham, takes quite a bit of knowledge.

" But the best thing that ever happened at one of our *veillées*, my dear boy, was the joke I had on Amos. You remember I told you a bullet used to whizz past me every now and then in a way I didn't like, and I suspected Mr. Amos ? Well, this was the way it happened. One day the squaws had kindly propped me up against a tree outside the lodge and I was just sitting there enjoying the early spring sunshine when I heard the roar of that same heavy rifle, and the whack of a bullet striking the tree close by my cheek. I called over a couple of boys to dig the bullet out, thinking I'd like to keep it for luck, and when I looked at it close and began to pick at it with my knife—be damned if it wasn't *silver*, not lead ! I put it in my smoke-bag and made a few tender enquiries, and very gradually I made out from the Indians that Amos had collected some odd bits of silver—coins and so forth, as best he could—and had melted them down and made a silver bullet in his mould. You see, he'd tried it on with lead bullets several times without success (being a thoroughly bad shot !) and now he figured that the silver bullet would be absolutely infallible ; when that failed too, he was quite sure I was bewitched and never even tried it again. However, to come on to the joke—after I'd found all this out I kept the bullet in my smoke-bag and bided my time until one evening Amos came into the lodge with some other hunters to join the circle. Then I quietly worked the bullet up with my fingers so that it lay on the surface of the tobacco, and offered the bag politely to Amos to take a fill.

" Well, Amos looked into the bag and there he saw his silver bullet, and that was enough for him ! He just took one look and then beat it right out of the lodge as if the Devil was after him ! If ever an Indian was upset it was Amos that time. When he'd gone I took the bullet casually in my hand, turned it over and looked at it—the Indians pretended not to look, but saw, and saw the joke damned clearly. They all chuckled quietly and glanced at each other in a meaning way. Not a word was said ! "

CHAPTER XXXII

WOMEN

THE Place of Woman in the Far North was defined long ago by Matonabbee, the Chipewyan chief who guided Samuel Hearne on his overland journey from Hudson Bay to the mouth of the Coppermine river on the Arctic Ocean. Hearne had been charged by the Hudson's Bay Company with the duty of verifying rumours regarding deposits of copper on a great river which the Indians called *Neetha-san-san-dazey*—" the far-off metal river "—" a river ", as his written instructions put it, " represented by the Indians to abound with copper ore, animals of the furr kind, etc., and which . . . is supposed by the Indians to empty itself into some ocean ". Hearne made two unsuccessful attempts in 1769 and 1770 to reach this river, and only escaped death through starvation and the ill behaviour of his Indian guides by a very narrow margin. As he was returning from the second of these expeditions, more dead than alive, he fell in with Matonabbee, who guaranteed that he could take him to the copper mines and the Arctic Coast in the following spring without excessive hardship, provided that some women were allowed to accompany the party. This was a reasonable suggestion enough, and in fact Hearne's former guides had asked for feminine support ; but it had been vetoed absolutely by Hearne's immediate superior, the factor of Prince of Wales' Fort, who, though he kept a considerable harem of his own, was unnaturally careful of the morals of his colleagues and subordinates. Matonabbee, however, stuck out resolutely

for his point, assuring Hearne that the lack of women had
probably done more than anything else to wreck his two
previous expeditions. " ' For,' said he," Hearne's journal
records, " ' when the men are heavy laden, they can neither
hunt nor travel to any considerable distance ; and in case
they meet with success in hunting, who is to carry the
produce of their labour ? Women,' added he, ' were made
for labour ; one of them can carry, or haul, as much as two
men can do. They also pitch our tents, make and mend
our clothing, keep us warm at night ; in fact there is no
such thing as travelling any considerable distance, or for
any length of time, in this country, without their assistance.
Women,' said he again, ' though they do everything, are
maintained at a trifling expense : for as they always stand
cook the very licking of their fingers in scarce times is
sufficient for their subsistence.' " Now it is far from my
intention to try to go one better than Matonabbee in anything that I may write about Indian women, for he, of
course, knew ; it is rather with the idea of amplifying and
illustrating his general statement that I have gathered
together into the present chapter the bulk of what Mitchell
has told me at different times about the Loucheux women,
their works and ways.

   The girls, it seems, began their married careers between
eighteen and twenty, or whenever they were recognized
as being fully qualified to run a household. Young men
were careful about this aspect of the question. A man
would be unlikely to marry before he was twenty, as the girls'
fathers were careful too, insisting that an aspirant should be
a good enough hunter and fur-taker to support a wife.
Mitchell remembers at least one wedding, because the feast
lasted all night and he provided the tea ; but beyond
attending the feast he was careful to remain outside the
whole affair as much as possible, as he realized how much
the Indians disliked the intrusion of any white man into
such intimately personal affairs. Consequently he does not

know which side paid which, or how the marriage-settle-
ments looked at the end of a long pow-wow that was held
before the feast began. Marriages that were made in the
woods were always put through the Anglican church at
Fort McPherson the following summer. Morals were good
and the Hudson's Bay Company were active in their preser-
vation, as it had no desire to be burdened with the mainten-
ance of more fatherless children than those which treacherous
rivers, grizzlies, gun-accidents, starvation and snow were
always throwing upon its charity.

That married life had its ups and downs appears from
a passage headed " wife-beating " that I find in my note-
book. " As regards punishing women," said Mitchell, " it
was customary to beat women when they needed it, and
they often did need it. I didn't ordinarily interfere in this
any more than in other things they occasionally did which
I didn't like—I wasn't a missionary and didn't consider
that those matters were within my scope ; and, my dear
child, as I've told you before, I had a skin to save and wanted
to get down to Fort McPherson. But once I remember a
man who was in a grouchy neurotic state seized his wife
and began to beat her up with a cartridge-belt full of cart-
ridges, practically half killing her. I yelled to him to stop,
but he was too mad to pay attention, so I hit him with my
crutch-pole—I was hobbling about then—and he turned
on me. I covered him with my automatic and called for
the chief and council, and then I explained that though I
recognized that women often required beating, if I saw
anyone beating them beyond reason like that again I
would shoot him then and there. It was damn dangerous,
but they took it, and I'm glad to say I never had to call my
own bluff over that ! "

Child-birth was taken very calmly, and on it I have
recorded what follows. " Fortunately Nature has relieved
the squaw of ninety per cent of the pain of bearing children,
because the rest of her life is God-damned hard. There's

an idea going about that young mothers are left quite to themselves, but this isn't right : babies might be born any-where, even on the trail, but if they were a couple of squaws immediately dropped out of the procession to stay with the mother—they grabbed a couple of blankets or a bundle of warm clothes and a papoose-case, and that's all the provision that anybody made. Then they all caught up again a few hours later or the next day ; they didn't put the mother on a toboggan or anything, she damn well walked and carried the baby too. I didn't know very much about these things, but it seemed incredible. Yet when I questioned the Indians they pointed out the way the moose and caribou did it and said that child-birth never gave trouble in the North-West.

" When it came to providing for their babies and looking after them those women were splendid mothers, and the fathers were just as kind and as proud of the youngsters as the mothers were. They say Indians have no feelings about that sort of thing, but they have just the same—you bet your life ! The women often nursed their children up to two or three years old, so they sometimes had two at the same time—I argued with one of them once that she ought to wean a big running boy and give herself a chance, but she said, how could she put him on to nothing but half-cooked caribou ? So I guess there was something in that. With a young baby the Indians always had a horror of breaking its back, so they used those papoose-cases to keep them stiff and flat."

Mitchell had mentioned a papoose-case before, but the expression conveyed nothing to me and I accordingly demanded an explanation.

" A papoose-case, Graham, is like this. First you must have a back-board, which is flat. Then on that you fix up a kind of pouch for the baby, rather like a swallow's nest on a barn-wall—you attach a piece of canvas to make the outer casing, line the inside with cotton and caribou calf skin, and fill it up with fine picked moss to make a soft nest for the baby. (All summer long you'd see the squaws picking over that moss and getting out the hard bits.)   This moss could be taken out and washed as required, and they carried round a square bag and dry moss to change.   Then on the outside there'd be a piece of silk velvet—royal blue, scarlet, or yellow, and highly ornamented. The baby would be carefully lashed in with just his face showing and stay there for hours without showing any signs of restless-lessness ; and he could be carried round on his mother's back or laid down or leaned against something or even hung up on a tent-pole with perfect safety, as he couldn't fall out and the stiff board prevented his back from bending. At irregular intervals she'd take him out, wash him clean in cold snow, and let him creep round on the boughs while she was changing the moss, but when Flora had little Jimmy out in our lodge I often heard him crying to be put back. My God, I never shall forget the day Jimmy sat on a live coal while Flora was outside and I was alone with him !   I grabbed him off it, but he yelled blue murder, and Flora came in looking as if she thought I was skinning him.   I dabbed on some salt from my salt-bag, which made him yell all the more, but when old Jane and the rest of them had examined him they said I'd done quite right, so I suppose I was forgiven !

" Taking it all in all, Graham, those women's work was never done. The men were concerned solely with hunting and trapping, and when they weren't on the trail they had plenty to do keeping their toboggans, harness, snow-shoes and so forth in order, so you may take it the women did pretty well everything else. Apart from packing and un-packing for moves and driving the dogs when required they had to keep the lodges in perfect order—and weren't there rows if the men found the spruce boughs lumpy or holey when they lay down ! They had to be prepared to cook for their men at a moment's notice, or perhaps for

many men, as visitors were always dropping in suddenly.
Then they had to manufacture pemmican, which meant
gathering the herbs as well as pounding and packing ; feed
and look after the kids ; make clothes for everyone, for
summer and winter, and especially moccasins, which wore
out at a tremendous rate ; and attend to the sick and
wounded. If a man had time he might leave some fire-
wood ready cut, but if not the squaw would have to rustle
that too for herself. And then there was the dressing of the
skins, which was the heaviest job of all. The men would
prepare the smaller skins, like beaver, mink and marten,
as it was easy to put these on small stretchers and scrape
them cursorily : but moose and caribou, bear, and mountain sheep and goats, which had to be strung up and scraped
at intervals for several days, were always left to the women.
You'd never believe, Angus, how many processes there are
to the tanning of a fine caribou skin—removing the fat,
removing the hair, rinsing and washing five or six times in
water, and rubbing in the brains. When everything's done
the skin comes out a beautiful snow-white—that's what
they use for the chief's official clothes or anything for cere-
monial occasions, but for their ordinary summer clothing,
that has to stand weather, the skin must be smoked to a
light amber-brown. And there again, if they smoke it too
much it burns, and if they smoke it too little it won't keep
out the wet. There must be generations of experience
behind all that skill, to say nothing of the damned hard
rubbing and drubbing !

" But though they were always working, and their routine
never stopped or started at any given time, just as they never
ate at any particular time, those squaws were happy indi-
viduals. They're not one bit stolid, any more than the
men are stolid. They might be silent on the trail, and
when the men were in the lodges the women always kept
to themselves, sitting in groups behind the men and making
their own conversation. But if some orator came out with

a funny story you heard their delightful gurgling laughter, and when four or five of them got together at one of their sewing bees there was constant chatter and joking. Being laid up as I was and constantly inside the lodge, I got to know them all very well indeed, and I'll go so far as to say, Graham, that they were as nice a lot of girls as you'd meet anywhere—good-looking, kind-hearted, interesting to talk to, and full of downright humour. Really charming girls."

Mitchell could never speak highly enough of the squaws' skill in needlework and particularly in embroidery with beads, coloured silks, and tiny slivers of dyed porcupine

EMBROIDERY ON A LOUCHEUX MOCCASIN.

quill. In some tribes it appears to be customary for the men to draw out the patterns of the clothes and for the women to do no more than the mechanical cutting and sewing up ; but among the Loucheux the women were capable of making everything themselves from the beginning —shirts, breeches, caps, leggings, moccasins, rifle-cases, haversacks, light summer gloves with fingers, or heavy winter mitts. Mitchell still has some samples of their work, notably the mitts that are illustrated on page 263 and a pair of embroidered moccasins. The mitts are of stout brown moose hide, warmly lined with duffle ; they have good deep cuffs to cover the wrists, and the thumbs are set on without

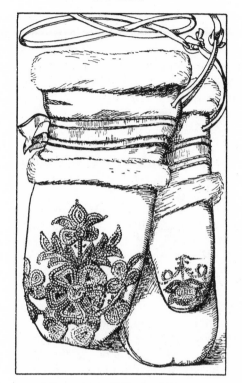

MITCHELL'S WINTER MITTS.

any seams across the palms. The backs are decorated with
a fine conventional design of rose and thistle, beautifully
done in very small coloured beads, and the cuffs are trimmed
with two bands of ermine with a red and blue striped silk
ribbon between them. The sewing is excessively neat, and
is done with fine-drawn sinew. The moccasins are of light
caribou skin, and are remarkable for the flowers that are
embroidered on their toe-panels in small silk knots. One
of these flowers is illustrated on page 262. The squaw has
used five colours for this flower—purple, red, pink, and a
darker and a lighter green—and has surrounded her panel

with three lines of piping in red and purple. The piping is enough in itself to establish her place among needle-women, as she has made it by laboriously whipping her coloured silk round and round a thread of her finest sewing sinew.

Mitchell also remarked on the excellence of the Loucheux basketry. The squaws used bark baskets and buckets for every conceivable purpose—fish-baskets, berry-baskets, panniers for a litter of puppies, and even pails for water. They sewed the joints with strips of willow bark and spruce root fibres, and the buckets held water perfectly.

Matonabbee makes no mention of surgery as part of a woman's duties, but the Loucheux women's surgical skill was so remarkable that it deserves some further notice in addition to the account that has been given of the treatment of Mitchell's knee. More or less serious accidents happened pretty frequently in the tribe, when men chopped their feet with axes, or got under falling trees, or shot one another at bear-hunts. (The tactic in use against bears, of forming a close circle and opening rapid fire towards the centre, naturally caused a good many shooting accidents.) Mitchell at first used to dress the Indians' wounds as best he could with such salves and bandages as he had with him, but he soon discovered that the squaws got just as good or better results with their herbs and poultices, and after that he left first aid to them. He has told me of some extra-ordinary cures which were made, particularly by old Jane.

" One man, for instance," he said, " was going to cut some wood, running fast downhill with an empty toboggan, when the whole team suddenly made a leap after some small game. The Indian hadn't time to catch the trailing thong, so he leapt himself, to land on the toboggan and get control of the dogs. Unfortunately he fell against the handle of his axe, which was lying on the toboggan in such a way that the handle was sticking up and the head fixed firmly ; and as the Indian axe handles are quite straight with only a very slight hook on them, this handle pierced right into his side just above the groin. He had on a red woollen shirt at the time, and of course there were pieces of that carried in too. Well, when they brought him back to camp old Jane promptly went to work and cleared out all dirt and pieces of cloth out of the wound, shoved his bowels back into place, sewed up the gash, and then strapped him with *babiche* all over his belly from the crotch to the waist. I guess she poulticed him too, with herbs. She didn't allow him to eat very much, and do you know in an incredibly short time that man was up and around again. He treated himself as a semi-invalid, of course, and did not work for a while, but it wasn't at all long before he was trapping, and running dogs, and doing everything just as before. I should like you to put it in the book that a very high tribute was due to old Jane for the way she saved that Indian."

Then there was the case of a boy who was shot accidentally in the mellay of a bear-hunt—a bullet struck him from in front, just above the heart, turned upwards, and came to rest in the shoulder somewhere between the shoulder-blade and the back of the neck. The squaws were a good deal puzzled when they found that the bullet had not gone straight through, but they probed for it in the approved manner with flexible slips of willow, and when they eventually found it they removed it through an incision in the back. Finally, they were evidently quite well aware of the danger of allowing so deep a wound to heal superficially while any possibility remained of trouble arising inside, as they left the probes sticking in the wound—no doubt to the most extreme discomfort of the unfortunate boy—and only withdrew them very gradually as healing progressed from the bottom. This boy also recovered completely.

But in spite of all their women's knowledge and skill the Indians consistently refused to countenance any kind of amputation. Mitchell observed this frequently, and pointed out as an example the case of the young man whose clawing by an apparently dead bear was described in the last chapter. Francis asked Mitchell's advice as to how this case should be treated, and Mitchell, seeing that the arm could never by any possibility be serviceable again, suggested that it should be cut off at the shoulder. Mitchell is convinced that the squaws could have carried out this operation with very little difficulty, especially as the bear had already removed practically all the flesh ; but Francis refused point-blank, giving no reasons, and simply had dressings applied. The lad survived, but was condemned to a miserable existence, having the withered limb permanently bound across his chest in such a way that it interfered with all his natural activities. Mitchell never managed to discover the real reason why the Indians so abhorred the idea of an amputation, but supposes that they were bound by some religious scruple rooted in their ancient beliefs.

CHAPTER XXXIII

THE CLOSEST SHAVE OF ALL

I HAVE now to record how a thunderbolt fell from out of a clear blue sky. Mitchell had " become an Indian ", and as " *Tingisuethli* " and the chief's blood-brother one might have supposed that he would have had nothing more to fear from savage jealousy and cunning. Yet before the winter ended he was betrayed to the very threshold of a violent death. He described what happened in more or less the following words.

"I've mentioned to you more than once, Graham, that Amos made another damned good try to get me murdered before all was said and done, and he bloody nearly brought it off too ! Well, now I'll tell you how it happened. One evening Francis came into the lodge, looking very grave, and sat down beside my couch, and then he said quietly that I was going to die before midnight. I tell you I sat up at that and began to take notice !

"'What do you mean, 'die before midnight'? I said. 'I'm God-damned if I'm going to die. I'm going to get better—I'm feeling fine——'

"But Francis shook his head. 'No,' he replied, 'you're going to-night.' And then he added, 'And I'm going with you.'

"I asked him what the Hell he meant—I'd never seen Francis like that before and couldn't make head or tail of it. Then he told me that Amos had been busy with propaganda against me for a long time ; that he'd been working not only on the regular bad element but on what

I call the 'intermediates' as well, that is the eighty per cent who were neither one thing nor the other but were ready to go with either side, and the result was that a great proportion of the ordinary decent Indians had gone in with the bad eggs and Francis couldn't control them any longer. He said he didn't want to hold a council meeting on it as he knew the council would be swamped and that would only make matters worse.

" Well, that was a pretty awful facer. I could see clearly enough that Francis had done everything he could and had only spoken to me after he'd given up all hope. All he meant to do now was to sell his life as dearly as he could alongside of me. I didn't say anything at all for perhaps half or three-quarters of an hour—you know, one never hurries an Indian—and then I told him quite quietly to call a general meeting of all the Indians for me to address them. Every man was to come, and it was to be my own personal meeting, not to be run by him or the council or anyone else. Then I told the squaws to prepare for a great feast which I would give after the meeting was over, and in the meanwhile I tell you I did some of the tallest thinking I'd ever done in my life.

" Soon the Indians began to assemble, and I'd never seen so many in camp before. I guess Amos had drafted in a lot of his own trusties from the other groups to support his side in the affair. The lodge was soon full, but more and more came crowding round outside, as close as they could get ; I seemed to be smothered with the press of faces all round me, some eager, some stolid, and some cruel, with the lights and shadows from the fire playing over them all the time. Francis wanted to sit beside me so as to be ready when the end came, but I made him take up his proper position with the council as I'd told him that this was my meeting and I was going to fight the thing out with the Indians myself.

" I started by giving them plenty of time. I said nothing

for an hour, until I saw the Indians were beginning to get
nervous and fidgety, evidently feeling that something big
was on the way. Then when the right time came I suddenly threw up my hand for silence and began to speak.
Naturally, Graham, I can't tell you everything I said, after
all these years, and anyhow I kept it up for God knows
how long, but my general line was more or less like this.

"I began by letting them see that I knew the whole of
their game. 'I know more than you do,' I said, 'I have
second sight, and second hearing, and I know just what you
say when you talk together in whispers in your lodges.
And I've got one tongue, not two '—I meant I wasn't a liar,
see? 'I know very well,' I said, 'that you intend to kill
me—I know that you think you've carried Mr. Mitchell far
enough, that you think he's got too many blankets, and too
much tobacco, and a fine carbine, and that you want to
divide up all his goods among yourselves. Well,' I said,
'that's all right ; I am ready to go, though I know very
well that there are some of you who are not ready.' I said
that to let them see I wasn't afraid of the thing, which
wasn't by any means true. Then I changed my tune a
little bit. 'But though I'm ready to go,' I said, ' I'm sorry
—not for myself, but for you. Yes ; I'm sorry for you.
Do you remember what the old lady said? She said that
you must all take the greatest care of me, and feed me and
take me down to Fort McPherson in the spring. And she
said, too, that if you didn't do right by me you would have
Hell. Well, now, I can tell you more than that,' I said ;
'I know just what will happen and I'm going to tell you.
You all know about Queen Victoria—you know the treaties
she makes with the Indians, and the great silver medals she
gives to chiefs, and the British flag that flies on that pole
down at the Fort? Well, one day Queen Victoria will ask,
"Where is Chief Mitchell?" Nobody will know. Then,
when she can get no answer from her councillors, she will
send out scouts, and the scouts will travel all over the

country asking who has seen Chief Mitchell until at last they meet someone who will say, " I saw him in such and such a month at Fort McPherson ; he is with the Indians on the Wind river." And when that scout returns to Queen Victoria she will send her redcoats, an army of them, more than all your men together, and each as strong as three of your men : they will have long rifles, and swords on the ends of their rifles, and drums—great drums far bigger than your poor little drums—and they will ask you, " Who killed Mr. Mitchell ? " Then what will you do ? You will not know who killed him—one of you will say that he died, another that he fell over a precipice or went into a crevasse, another that he was lost in a blizzard, and another that he never was with you at all. But that sort of talk won't satisfy Queen Victoria's officers. They will never let go of you until they know the truth. You may sink into the ground ; they'll dig you out as a bear digs out gophers. You may dive into the water ; they'll follow you as an otter dives after salmon. You may hide in the woods ; they'll chase you as a fox chases a hare. You may run out on to the open barrens ; they'll ring you round and round like grey wolves ringing caribou. And in the end if nobody knows who killed Chief Mitchell the redcoats will take four of your men from every ten and hang them on trees like dogs—and that won't leave you many hunters. Or they may do more ; they may drive you out of your valley into another country, or even kill you all. Only the wolverines and ravens will be fat and laughing when the redcoats march away.'

" And then I stopped dead. It's a great thing to stop at the right point. It was the strongest speech I ever made by a long way—I tell you one does speak strongly when one's talking for one's life. But I saw I'd won my case. As I was piling it on about the redcoats I could see the Indians' eagerness all dying away and a kind of wooden look coming over their faces which meant that they were hiding some unpleasant personal considerations. When I stopped speaking there was a dead silence for a few moments and then the weakest link cracked. It was Johnny, Amos' own right-hand man, who was the first to come over to my side—a mean kind of skate who'd have been the very one to sell his own pals if the Mounties really had come up to look for me. Anyway, he jumped up and ran across to where I was lying, beaming with smiles, and shook hands with me over and over again, saying, 'I am your friend.' I waved him to one side and waited for more to come, but at first the others hung back, not liking to follow Johnny for fear I might have marked him off for special punishment. But when they saw that it was all over and done with after we'd shaken hands they began to come over in shoals—' I am your friend, I am your friend,' each man smiling and shaking my hand as if it was his own bloody life now that depended on *my* good pleasure ! Only Amos faded away.

" When the handshaking was over I called for the feast to be brought on, and we ate and ate and drank vast quantities of tea—they like to get almost drunk on tea, if it's possible to do that. We finished up all the stored provisions and pretty well walked into what was left of my pipe-tobacco ; and proceedings lasted until well on towards noon of the next day. After the main point had been won and the feast got well under way the Indians began to make speeches themselves ; there must have been twelve or fifteen of them who spoke, all at very great length, and all laying stress on their determination to see me through. Last of all Francis and the councillors spoke, and fairly ripped them all up for a pack of fools. Colin spoke for an hour at least, going carefully into the situation of the tribe from every angle, showing what a fatal mistake it would have been to murder me, and pointing out fifty good reasons why they must carry out the promises they'd made. And Francis came out strongest of all ; he not only damned them in heaps the way Colin and the other councillors had done, but he threatened them, if they ever went back to their idea of harming me, that he would go away and abandon them out and out—and then, he said, they could go to Hell in their own way and would get no caribou. (It's an odd thing, Angus, but do you know, when I heard Francis threaten to abandon the Indians like that, I couldn't help being reminded of the miraculous child that I've told you about, and how he told the Indians that he would be 'recalled' if they went back to their bad old ways?)

"After the whole thing was over I was so terribly exhausted with the strain, and the exertion of making my speech, and the prolonged feast and interminable orations that followed, that I just rolled over on my side in a kind of stupor. I guess I must have slept for the best part of two days!"

CHAPTER XXXIV

THE SKIN BOATS

WINTER is hard to shake off in the Peel river country, and in 1899 the Indians continued their caribou-hunting all through the month of April. But by the beginning of May the sun had begun to defeat the snow—the surface became too soft and sugary for easy snow-shoe running except in the very early mornings, and hollows began to form round the bases of trees and rocks which absorbed and radiated the heat. Even little pieces of bark and fallen twigs began to sink down into pits that had melted out below them. At the same time the earth itself seemed to be getting warmer underneath by some mysterious process, working on the foundations of the snow and causing small streams to run treacherously under a caving cover that would no longer support a man. It was time for the Indians to think about their journey to Fort McPherson, and they accordingly moved down to the banks of the main Wind river to build their boats and make the other necessary preparations.

The boats which the Indians used for their spring migration consisted of a wooden framework covered with skins, and may probably have been copied from the so-called *umiak* of the Eskimo. They were long and narrow in shape, flat-bottomed, and large enough to hold up to fifteen or twenty people with their accompanying children, dogs, and baggage. The bottom framework was made up of two main timbers stayed apart with cross-pieces, and converging to form a pointed bow and stern. Into the main timbers of the bottom upright side-pieces were fixed with an out-wards splay, and these, with a stout stempost and sternpost, carried the gunwales, which formed the upper rim, as it were, of the structure. The gunwales were stayed apart by the rowing-benches, which performed the same function as the cross-pieces of the bottom framework in preventing the boat from closing up. The covering was of raw moose hides, which were thinner than the dressed hides but very much tougher ; these were put on to the framework wet, drawn tight, and laced to each other and to the gunwales with lacing that the Indians somehow managed to render watertight. After the skins had been laced on a pole was fitted lengthwise underneath the bottom to act as a keel and to prevent damage on rocks and sand-bars. The boat, when it was finished, was so strong that nothing could harm it short of a direct crash on a rock or malicious cutting of the hides.

In boat-building as in all their other activities the Indians obtained their results with the slenderest of material equip-ment and remarkable economy of effort. Whereas Mitchell had required a saw-pit and a carpenter's chest before he could rebuild the *Amisk*, the Indians made shift with axes, stone-headed hammers, and their extraordinary crooked knives. These knives, which Mitchell had often mentioned, were peculiar in curving not forwards, like a pruning-knife, nor backwards, like a sabre, but sideways, out of their own proper plane. Blades of such a pattern would turn a civilized cutler giddy, but the Indians made them regularly for themselves, generally out of old file-blades which they heated, shaped, retempered, and fitted into wooden handles. When finished they were something like good-sized pocket-knives, but Mitchell found their crookedness excessively unhandy ; The Indians, however, depended upon them as tools of the highest general utility, so much so that an axe and a crooked knife were all that an Indian needed for making toboggans, snow-shoes, bows, arrows, fish-spears, dead-falls, and the hundred and one wooden and bone objects that are used in a primitive household. In fact, the crooked knife is just one of those straws which show the way the wind blows through an Indian's mind.

The building of the boats was only part of the process of remobilization which the Indians underwent in spring. Ever since the previous autumn they had, of course, been living in the big dome-shaped lodges, moving themselves by toboggan and wearing their warm winter clothing of clipped moose skins. But with the melting of the snow they changed over to a summer scale of equipment, putting on light clothes of caribou skin tanned brown and water-proofed by smoking, and getting ready teepee covers, canoes, paddles, and all the miscellaneous gear that was needed for fishing and summer hunting along the rivers. (Actually when the weather was very hot the Indians used to wear nothing but a pair of light breeches, though the squaws always persevered with a shirt or upper garment of some kind.) All this summer equipment had to be taken from the cache in which it had been laid away at the beginning of winter, while at the same time the winter lodge-poles and lodge-covers, heavy fur clothing, snow-shoes, toboggans, dog-harness, and so forth had to be cached against the return of cold weather. Having no regular homes or permanent base-depôts, the Indians were forced to rely on caches for the storage of their surplus effects, and the woods must have been full of their dumps of equipment, clothing, dried meat, pemmican, and furs—all carefully placed, no doubt, where they could most readily be found at the appropriate time. Mitchell was always astonished at the accuracy with which the Indians remembered these places without the help of maps and notebooks; caches were actually very seldom missed, and indeed it was only this same accurate memory for landmarks and the look of places in general that enabled the Indians to move freely about the country without losing their way.

Before Mitchell could start on his journey a rather ludicrous difficulty had to be overcome. The camp was pitched on the brow of a very steep slope some four or five hundred feet above the river, so high, in fact, that Mitchell could only watch the building of the boats through his glasses ; and nobody could devise any means of conveying him down this slope to the water's edge. Most of the snow had gone, so that a dog-team was out of the question ; and although Mitchell was so far recovered by that time that he could hop about a little on flat ground with the help of his crutch-pole, he could not think of attempting to climb down to the river on foot. The chief and council and all his friends debated the question for days, but no practical suggestion was made except that he should be strapped into a toboggan and lowered on a raw-hide rope, and this he himself vetoed fearing that the rope might chafe through.

"At last one night," he said, " an Indian called Julius came into the lodge and asked if he might speak to the chief, and when permission was given he said he had a scheme to carry me down on his back. He'd already tried it out, as he explained, first with a hundred-pound pack, then with a two-hundred-pound pack, and finally with his squaw ; and he'd done it all right, only he was afraid that my stiff leg might sometimes catch on the ground and upset his balance. However for that he said he'd have his squaw walking just ahead, so that he could support himself on her if he needed steadying. This Julius was a particular friend of mine and I had great confidence in him : he was a giant of a man—not tall so much as immensely broad and strong— with a dour face but such kindly eyes. So I agreed to his plan and in due course he brought it off quite successfully. He had arranged a kind of leather sling for me to sit in which passed over his forehead, and I put my arms over his shoulders and a leg out each side and we got down all right with no mishaps—his squaw went ahead just as he'd said, and once when the leg did catch he only had to lay his hand on her shoulder to recover himself. Meanwhile all the Indians were craning their heads over the top of the bank to see, and those down below were craning up, but they never let a sound out of them till I'd got to the bottom. Then they broke out into a chorus of yells—awfully pleased, you see, that I was down safely, and also very proud of Julius for having worked it. When I got on my feet again I publicly shook hands with Julius and thanked him (he was very shy about it all, by the way), and I also told him publicly before the crowd that I'd give him a credit for twenty skins if he reminded me about it when we got to the Fort. But I didn't have to be reminded, and the Indians appreciate that too, when one remembers."

" How ever did an Indian come to be called Julius, Mr. Mitchell ? " I asked when the story was finished.

" Oh, I guess the missionary who christened him was running short of names when he came along, and had to fall back on that. Of course he had an Indian name too, as we all of us had." Mitchell, I may point out, often vindicates his status as a tribesman by this use of the first person plural.

" I only wish, my dear Angus," he continued, " that I could give you some idea of what our life in the skin boats was like. You must imagine us all stuffed into the boat with dogs and fur packs and all the squaws' paraphernalia— the men working their sweeps in leather loops, Francis in the stern with his long steering-sweep, and an emergency man with a pole standing in the bows. The bottom of the boat was well lined with furs and skins to prevent any damage, and I made myself very comfortable in spite of the children and puppies. I tell you I enjoyed every minute of that trip ! There was a tremendous racket all the time, with the Indians and squaws whooping with delight at the rushing water, dogs howling, and children squealing and fighting. And in stretches of easy water we used to have great boat-races, like Noah's Ark racing, that occasioned the wildest excitement. But in spite of the apparent chaos they really had the thing marvellously organized—you found that a given person, or pack, or basket of puppies, was always in the same place in the boat, day after day, in spite of unpacking and going ashore for the night. The result was that a squaw could always find anything she wanted, and seemed able to produce any damn thing you asked for out of those mysterious packs, from a blanket to a dried caribou's tongue. I tell you that capacity for laying their hands on things and storing them away again was a constant revelation to me !

" It was a treat too to see the way Francis handled his boat, when I thought of the way we'd sweated ourselves with our boats going up the river in the fall. Of course, he knew the channels like the back of his hand, and where they ran through rock they seldom or never changed ; but among the sand-bars he confessed himself that you never could tell where they'd be from one day to the next, and we quite often went aground on bars for all his experience. Then all hands had to get overboard and lift her off just as we used to do with the *Amisk*. And that was where that keel-pole came in so useful, saving her from getting ripped. The river used to rise very violently sometimes just as it had done in the fall—we'd see a regular wall of water two or three feet high coming down the river behind us like a tidal wave, and after that the water would stay high for several hours. I guess it was the effect of torrential rains higher up all rushing down straight into the river—we used to have the most awful sudden storms of rain sometimes where we were, with terrific thunder and lightning. I never shall forget the way the thunder used to echo from those great cliffs and steep mountains alongside the river—first a Hell of a crash, then a pause, and then the crash repeated almost more intensely by the echo before it finally settled down into a long rumble.

" But the greatest thrill of the whole trip was when we

came down through the Ramparts. I told you, I think, about the great cauldron in the cliff on the right bank that we had to pass when we were coming up, with the cavern like a keyhole away up in the face of the rock : well, I guess coming down past that place in the heavy skin boat, all

THE PEEL RIVER CANYON.

loaded down with women and dogs et cetera, was just about the riskiest thing I ever did in my life. You must under-stand, Angus, that the opening into the cauldron is rather narrow, and the water goes raging in and round inside in a most awful whirlpool—particularly when the river's in flood, as it was then. Well, as I told you, the Indians didn't dare try to slip past the entrance going down-stream in case they might get drawn in backwards, out of control, so instead they ran right into the cauldron with the current and then turned out again in the nick of time to carry on down-stream. We didn't go all the way round the cauldron, only just so far, and then made that right-angled turn out to the left.

"You can imagine what an awe-inspiring business it was—the great height of the cliffs, that made the river look only a few yards wide, the rush and clamour of the white water, and then that deadly oily black look of the whirlpool and the eddies that swirled up from God knows what depth so that you felt the boat almost being lifted as she passed over them ! The Indians were wildly excited, but nobody made a sound as we went through—they were just shocked quiet by the tremendous danger. (Though all Hell broke out when they got down into safe water below !) And here's a point you don't want to miss, Angus, that not a damned one of those boats went through that place without the chief himself being at the helm. Yes, sir—he took every one down himself, and walked back over the bloody mountain between each trip. So that you may say he risked his own life time and time again to take care of his people, while no other Indian was in danger more than once. I think you should put that in the book, just to show them what it means to be a chief."

CHAPTER XXXV

SUMMER HUNTING

THE descent of the rivers to Fort McPherson took up the whole of the months of June and July. Mitchell has told me a good deal about his memories of this time, though the journey as a whole seems to have been too leisurely to provide material for a continuous narrative. I have accordingly put my records of his conversation into this chapter very much as they stand, in the hope that they will present some kind of picture of the life which the Indians led in summer.

"Our ordinary practice," he told me in describing their method of travel, " was to run the boats all day and then go ashore in the evening to cook a meal and sleep. There was getting to be practically no darkness, of course, by the month of June, but we had to take our sleeps just the same. The Indians used to move me in and out of the boat as best they could depending on the kind of shore—Julius often carried me when the bank was too steep. If it was raining or blowing they built what I call *wickiups*, sort of lean-to shelters of boughs, and they did it twice as well and twice as quickly as any white man ; but generally if it was fine we slept in the open. (And, my God, didn't the mosquitoes tune up again when it began to get hot ! Though I guess I was pretty well immunized by that time, and am still.) Colin and Jane and the other family that had lived in our lodge through the winter always camped with us when we went ashore even when they were travelling in different boats ; and as we got lower down the river we were constantly being joined by other parties from the different side-streams, who used to come and sit round with us all night comparing notes about good and bad hunting and the various deaths and accidents and adventures of the past winter. Our life was always very irregular—I never knew when the Indians were going to stop or start, though I guess they always had some good reason, and very often the squaws would be packing up the stuff before I had any idea that we were due to strike camp. It was an amazing thing, though, how the dogs always seemed to know when a move was on—as I've told you, they weren't being fed now that they weren't working, so they had to forage for themselves round camp and back in the woods, but I never knew them get lost or miss the boats when the Indians started off.

" Sometimes we might stay two or three days in the same place if the Indians wanted to fish, or hunt beaver, or if it was soaking wet, and then they used to cut poles and put up teepees—or sometimes there might be teepee poles cached ready to hand, as they used the same camping-places from generation to generation. Of course, you know, Graham, what I mean by a teepee—an erection of poles criss-crossing at the top, like stacked rifles, with a cover stretched over them. The poles would be young spruce trees or alder wands, driven into the ground roughly in a circle—they might make it about eight feet in diameter perhaps for four or five people, or larger for more. A narrow teepee would be peaky, and a broader one naturally lower. In old times the teepee cover was generally caribou hide (or moose hide, though this was heavy), but by my time some of the Indians had traded with the miners and got fairly good tents, and many had got hold of spare bits of canvas and jute bagging and odds and ends which they used for covering their teepees. The coverings overlapped so as to be waterproof, and the door was a flap arranged on a swinging pole so that it could be opened or shut ; the lower fly could also be raised for ventilation, which was badly needed in the intense heat. The whole thing was so rough you'd have thought it would fall over at a touch, but teepees used to stand up all the same through the damnedest wind and rain storms, just as beavers' houses stand up although they only look like a heap of sticks. They weren't too bad inside, as they were always set up in dry places and there was a *copious* bedding of spruce boughs on the floor with skins laid over them. The smoke was really the worst thing about a teepee—we had a fire in the centre with two Y-sticks and a cross-bar for slinging the kettle or meat for roasting, and the smoke was supposed to go out through an opening up at the top, but there was generally such a haze of terrible acrid smoke inside that you were better to keep sitting down, as it thinned out a bit at the lower levels. They put the fire outside in very hot weather, and then it was a good deal more comfortable. I've told you before about the Indians' extraordinary skill in making fires, and I never lost my admiration of the way they'd put a few sticks together and get a brilliant hot, *hot* blaze, and have a duck or a muskrat roasting before you had time to turn round. I've seen them do it hundreds of times, and I really think, Graham, that the explanation is that they knew just where to put the fire to get the proper draught. And they'd get their fire going just the same—incredibly quickly—even in heavy lasting rain when everything was soaking ; in that case I think they did it by splitting their logs so as to expose only the dry centre to the flame, and the same with kindling wood.

" I can't tell you all the fun we had on that trip with fishing and duck-hunting and beaver-hunting and every kind of sport. And oh, boy, wasn't it glorious to get berries and fresh ptarmigan eggs and all sorts of game after that eternal diet of nearly raw caribou ! There was a plant that grew on the gravel-bars, I remember, with a big tuberous root that was almost as good as a sweet potato.

Beaver-meat was our great delicacy at this time and we always stopped at any small creek and explored it for beaver. Of course, the Hudson's Bay Company refuse to touch a summer-killed pelt for the very purpose of discouraging summer hunting so as to keep up the stock, so we killed for food only. The meat is like very tender mutton, and what we Indians found best of all was the tail, roasted in the skin, though most white men abominate it as being too greasy—really it's about like the under-belly part of a salmon. Muskrat is another great favourite—skinned, and roasted on two little sticks ! The Indians recognize the muskrat as the younger brother of the beaver, because he builds houses in the same way and stores food ; in fact, the muskrat stores about five times as much food as he can possibly eat and his elder brother often comes and robs his store.

"I think, Angus, you'd have enjoyed that summer beaver-hunting the way the Indians did it. In winter they simply break open the top of the *cabane* and lift the old beavers out through the hole—as you know, the *cabane* is divided into three stories, with the store of food on the first ledge above the plunging-hole, the young beavers on the second, and the old ones at the top, so they're easy to get. But in summer they get them outside, and the way to do it is to climb up the face of one of their dams and chop through one or two logs at the top, so as to cause an overflow, and then run off and hide. Very soon the old chief beaver finds the level of the water falling in the pond and goes out to survey the damage : he sizes up the trouble and whistles for assistance, and if enough of his people come, all right, otherwise he whistles for more according to what he figures he'll want. Then they all set off to collect the materials for making repairs, and when they are all on the job you can select your animal and shoot him. The Indians were very expert at shooting beaver either with a rifle or a bow and arrow, aiming just at the base of the head so as not to damage the skin. It was the damnedest thing how, when I shot a beaver, they always sank, and when the Indians shot them they floated—they seemed to know just when to take them, perhaps when their lungs were full of air. They used to do some wonderfully good shooting too at the swans and geese that were passing down the valley of the Wind to breed in the far north : the geese always flew well above the river, so the Indians used to station themselves at a certain height up on the banks, and as they had no shot-guns they had to make out as well as they could with the bullet. But they often dropped their bird pretty accurately just the same.

" Another great line was the shooting of muskrat and ducks, which was mainly the boys' work—they used a special kind of blob-headed arrow for it, which would stun a rat or a bird and then float head upwards so that it could be retrieved. There were certain places where the boys would lie up and wait for the muskrats to come swimming silently across the calm water, and giving them damn little to aim at except just a V-shaped ripple in the water. But they shot with extraordinary accuracy, taking them right in the head, and they didn't mind waiting either. They got their ducks in the same way, hiding in the high reeds by the waterside and letting the ducks float past, and then loosing on them at very close range. And what they thought was the greatest joke of all was when we got among a flock of young ducks that just couldn't fly—then there'd be a Hell of a hurry and scurry and the boys would make great killings. But the men would never take part in anything like that—it was entirely below their dignity.

" And then I mustn't forget to tell you about our fishing— the Indians were great fishermen, and we all relished the fresh fish as another most welcome change of feed. I didn't like their idea of barbless bone fish-hooks, though, and we caught a lot more fish when I got them to file barbs on the hooks ; but they did good work with their nets—they used to plait up nets out of spruce roots or willow bark on the spot, as required, and then drove the fish into them in some *cul-de-sac* and netted them right out on to the bank. They used a spear, too, just like the *nigogue* that our Frenchmen use here in the East. When we got away down the Peel we came to the regular fishing-stages which I'd passed on my way up the year before, and there the Indians had proper twine nets cached and went about the thing on a large scale—I guess they had a contract to supply the Fort with dog-feed for the winter. The stages were double rows of stakes joined up with stringers running out from the bank into the stream, with cross-pieces and boughs here and there to let you walk along. Damned cranky dangerous-looking structures they were. The Indians used to get out on these things to spear fish, and also used their nets from them ; the plan was to set out the net in a bow down-stream from the stage, and then the boys went out in canoes and raised Hell and drove the fish into the net. Then they unfastened the outer end of the net from its stake, and walked back along the stage pulling the net after them inshore. Sometimes they got large catches—mainly salmon and whitefish. Every now and then somebody would fall into the water, and then there'd be a terrible hurroosh and everyone would rush to his assistance in a canoe. Generally they couldn't swim—certainly I never myself saw one of my Indians swim.

" Finally we reached the last cache above Fort McPherson, where the Indians changed their clothes. All the skin boats were drawn ashore, the beautiful caribou skin clothing was carefully cached away, and the Indians turned up in the God-damnedest outfit of civilization clothes—wrecks and ruins of old jackets, and trousers with the knees out, and I can't tell you what. They'd picked up a lot of cast-off stuff at Wind City too as they came down past it, what the miners had left behind—in fact Wind City had been quite a gold-mine to them, not only for old clothes but for numberless odds and ends like tools and frying-pans and broken axe-handles, and all that. (They're always keen to get a bit of hickory, which of course doesn't grow in the north country.) But though their other clothes were so bad they all wore splendid coloured sashes, and stuck in them long knives, like cooks' knives, with beautifully worked sheaths, and their best smoke-bags with the tassels hanging out. They also put on curious little velvet caps, heavily beaded, that they stuck on the side of their heads like forage-caps, and every squaw fitted out her man with the handsomest moccasins she had made during the winter. Those Loucheux moccasins, I may tell you, were eagerly traded for at the Fort and fetched good prices in Edmonton and even as far as Winnipeg on account of the very heavy moose-skin foot, the beautiful embroidered toe-panel, and the upper part of pure white caribou skin.

" But what really pained me, Angus, was to see the way those Indians changed their demeanour when they changed their clothes. As soon as they'd put on their damned old rags they quite discarded their natural free independent characteristics and assumed that humble and quiet air I'd noticed when I first saw them down at the Fort the previous summer. You'd have thought they were different people altogether—couldn't say ' bo ' to a goose ! "

CHAPTER XXXVI

MITCHELL REMAINS AN INDIAN

WHEN the boats drew near to Fort McPherson they formed into single file and covered the last few miles in an ordered procession, Francis' boat leading. As they turned the last corner and came into view of the Fort Mitchell heard the boom of two small guns and saw the Union Jack and the Company's flag run up to the top of the flagstaff. They made for a landing-place that lay just up-stream from the Fort, in order to avoid the Eskimo who were as usual encamped on the sands, and approached the shore in complete silence to mark the solemnity of the occasion. As the boats touched ground the men and boys leapt ashore accompanied by a wave of dogs, then the younger children climbed out, and the squaws with their babies followed. Francis, Colin, and a few of his other friends immediately surrounded Mitchell and helped him up the path to the Fort buildings.

They found Firth standing at the door of the trading-room—it was his custom to receive his visitors in the Fort itself, and not to meet boats at the landing. He shook hands very formally with the leading Indians, but took Mitchell into the inner office and gave him what Mitchell described as " a royal welcome ". Firth was tremendously pleased with Mitchell's success in dealing with the Indians, and regarded the mere fact that he had stayed alive as a considerable feat in itself. " Well, well, Mitchell," he said, " I never thought to see ye alive again. I heard there was a white man lying wounded with the Indians on the river, but I said, ' By God, they'll kill him—he'll never come doun ! ' " Actually Firth had twice sent a dog-team up the river to bring Mitchell down to the Fort ; but the drivers had failed entirely to obtain any news of him, and Mitchell supposes that Francis had purposely prevented information from reaching them, wishing, out of pure friendliness, to keep Mitchell with him as long as he possibly could. Firth now pressed Mitchell to stay in the Fort while he waited for the Mackenzie river steamer, but Mitchell felt bound to refuse—as he said himself, " It was hardly fair to drop the Indians cold after all they'd done for me, and go and live in luxury as soon as I got the chance." He accordingly returned to Francis' teepee, which had been pitched about fifty yards from Firth's house, and found his couch ready laid out, his mosquito-net set up, and everything perfectly in order, although the squaws had hardly been ashore for more than an hour. All the teepees, in fact, were already up and smoking, and the boys and girls were ranging expectantly round the store—from which, however, they were rigidly debarred until regular trading began. " I tell you, Angus," Mitchell said, " I felt just like a kid in a fifteen-cent store myself when I got inside that place and started to buy candy and pipes and fish-hooks, et cetera, for presents ! "

Next morning Francis asked Mitchell if he would trade on the Indians' behalf. I have described the method of trading in an earlier chapter, and explained how the Company's trader and the chief agreed upon a scale of prices from which the amount that was due to each Indian followed automatically when the skins were counted and graded. But the process was not really quite automatic as an Indian could always put forward some plea for special treatment, supposing, for example, that he had been handicapped by illness or accident, or had had to support a widow, or had lost his traps or furs. Or again he might have taken some particularly valuable skins, for which the trader could allow him a special rate. So now, Francis and Colin having had their conference with Firth and arranged the basic prices for that season's trading, the Indians were anxious that Mitchell should act as their go-between in presenting their special requests. Mitchell, not unnaturally, demurred on the score of his own lack of expert knowledge, but he finally consented to act as he knew that he could safely rely on Firth's absolute integrity and fairness.

Mitchell impressed on me that the Indians knew their business—that they were keen and honest and looked for honesty in the white men who traded with them. He told me the following story, which relates to another tribe, to illustrate this point and also to show how a chief would look after his people's interests. It seems that the band in question once came down, as their custom was, to trade at a certain post on the upper Liard, and found a new trader in charge, a young man who was a stranger to them. The chief held his people back, entered the post alone, without announcing himself as chief, and produced a bundle of very valuable marten skins. The trader, before touching the skins, enquired through the interpreter how many there were in the bundle, and the chief replied, "Twelve." The trader then counted them over, found that there were really thirteen, and told the Indian to trade on the value of thirteen marten skins, whatever that happened to be. The Indian, however, insisted that there were only twelve until at last the trader forced him either to trade on thirteen skins or take the thirteenth back ; and then the Indian, who had by that time found out what he wanted to know, took back the thirteenth skin and showed it to his tribe, assuring them that the trader was an honest man and that they could safely go up and trade.

The Loucheux, at any rate, were evidently fully satisfied that they were being fairly dealt with. Firth and his assistants would run through a pack of skins without appearing to give them any very close attention, sorting them rapidly into classes and rejecting any that had been taken out of the proper season. This classification was nearly always accepted as final, as no Indian ever questioned or complained about the grading of his skins ; the most that any Indian would do if he was displeased with Firth's ruling would be to pack up his furs again and walk out of the store in dignified silence, hoping, no doubt, to meet with better luck another day.

Mitchell was amazed by the numbers and beauty of the skins which passed through Firth's trading-room. The Indians brought in foxes of several kinds,—red, black, silver (which was far the most valuable), and " cross-fox ", which had a black cross on the back and shoulders ; brown and grizzly bear ; beaver and muskrat in hundreds ; very large fine marten, that were exactly like Russian sable ; otter, mink, fisher, wolverine, lynx, and an occasional wolf ; and in addition to the furs a large number of their fine dressed moose hides, which were asked for as far away as Edmonton on account of their exceptional size and the excellence of the tanning. The Eskimo at the same time were trading white arctic fox, musk-ox, the rare sea otter, polar bear, and seal, besides walrus ivory, eider-down, feathers, and carved models and toys. When each man's skins had been graded the clerks made up the total and told him the amount of his credit—so many " skins ". And then, as Mitchell said, the fun began, as his squaw was brought in and they went through the store together choosing their supply of trade-goods for the coming year.

" Those Indians, Graham, when they once got going in the store would ask for, and get, the God-damnedest assort-ment of stuff you could possibly imagine—all of the very highest quality. They took Sheffield knives, file-blades for making their crooked knives, Hudson's Bay blankets (half-point to four-point), genuine copper kettles of various sizes and for various purposes, needles—some bent ones—and awls for perforating skins, ammunition for ·44 rifles, gunpowder well packed in canisters, and caps and balls for the old-fashioned muzzle-loading guns, sheet-lead (probably off tea-chests), brass wire for snares, fish-hooks, flour, fat pork or bacon sides (they keep better than pork), the best beads I ever saw anywhere—both glass and cut steel, sewing-silk, broadcloth for leggings, large quantities of rice in packets and large quantities of sugar and tea—the sugar and tea were generally made to fill up the whole of the credit balance, as an Indian is quite irresponsible in matters of money and will always insist on taking the full value of his credit even though he may have got every damned thing he wants. Of course, there were some Indians who failed through some accident or bad luck to bring down enough fur to pay for their next winter's supplies : Firth didn't favour long credits, but he used to advance these men what they needed for the winter provided that they paid a certain proportion and cleaned up the balance next year. I guess he had a good idea of each man's powers as a hunter, and knew pretty well what the hard-luck stories were worth."

Mitchell passed the next fortnight pleasantly enough, and lived like a fighting-cock on fresh fish, ducks, ptarmigan, and blueberries, besides the civilized rations that he obtained from Firth. He described his ordinary life at the Fort as follows.

" After my morning shave and wash Francis or another of the Indians would generally accompany me on a walk round the buildings and the nearer teepees. I used to have a talk with everyone, getting to know Indians I hadn't met before and hearing endless stories from a number of stranded miners who were hanging about the Fort—men who had failed to get over the Rat Portage and were now waiting for a chance to work their passage home up the Mackenzie. Talking takes the place of books with fellows who were fixed like we were. Then I loved, too, to see the Indian boys at their wrestling matches with the Eskimo —as I've told you before, it's a truly beautiful sight. Then

I often went over to the missionary's house, where I had
a most delightful welcome ; his wife was a friend of friends
of mine in Toronto, and it seemed just like home. And
Firth always made a point of coming to see me every day
in the teepee, just to show his friendship, as an officer in
charge of a fort would never call in at a teepee in the ordinary course. Whenever Firth came over the squaws very
quickly polished up the pannikins, made a fresh brew of
tea, and spread out a white-tanned caribou skin so that he
might drink the official bowl of tea with due ceremony. I
do believe Firth used to slip some little present to the squaws
and children, though I never saw him do it—I only recognized their look of pleasure.

" One day I remember the Eskimo chief came to call on
me—I've told you, I think, that he was a great hulking
devil six feet high, and a real bad man. The Indians
reported his arrival with an air of the utmost repugnance
and dislike, but I wasn't taking any sides and I wasn't
taking any indirect dictation either, so I told them to bring
him in and to bring some tea as they did for Firth. (They
brought the tea, but there weren't any frills about it, and
they damn well didn't produce the tablecloth !) The
Eskimo made quite an oration, which nobody understood,
but the interpreter said he wanted to make great friends
with me, and then at the appropriate moment he ushered
in two magnificent young Eskimo girls dressed in the height
of their fashion and looking as pleased as Punch with themselves. Well, I immediately saw a riot of trouble coming
from the Indians, who jumped to the conclusion that I
should fall for the girls and began to look as black as thunder.
So I ordered them out of the teepee with the utmost dis-
patch, and then turned my attention to the ruffian of a
chief ; and to prevent him from taking offence I presented
him with two or three plaits of tobacco—the blackest of
black-strap—and bought his snow-knife for the ridiculous
price of a Hudson's Bay blanket that cost me twenty-two

dollars. In that way I managed to get rid of the whole gang quickly and without raising bad blood—otherwise the chief might have stayed all day making speeches. And the Indians came right back as friends at once when they saw that no outside women were going to be introduced.

" But I found they were very disgusted with me for buying the snow-knife. They claimed it was poisoned, for one thing, and I guess the filth in those Eskimo tents was quite enough to poison any knife that had been lying around inside them. The squaws insisted on boiling this one at once, and then one of them made me that very nice embroidered moose-hide sheath which you see is on it still. Firth told me afterwards that this particular knife had been made from the broken barrel of a rifle—forged out, the blood-grooves cut with a crooked knife, and then retempered in oil. The handle, as you can see—lift it down, eh ?— is all of one piece with the blade, with that flattened ring forged on and then bound round with willow.

" But there was one thing I found quite un-pleasant during my stay at Fort McPherson, and that was that I was constantly running into two samples of the lowest and vilest type of criminal that it is possible to imagine —certainly the worst men I've ever met in my life. They were Americans off a whaling steamer : they said they'd lost their ship, but I suspect that their ship had damn well lost

MITCHELL'S SNOW-KNIFE.

them, and for some bloody good reason too. They seemed to have fastened themselves on to the Eskimo, and were living with them and had taken a couple of Eskimo girls each, but they were in and out of the Fort all the time behaving like ruffians and bullies and never opening their mouths without producing some filth or blasphemy. I remember particularly seeing one of them come into the store one day with a very handsome Indian girl that he'd taken in addition to his Eskimo—he wanted to buy a mackinaw coat for her, but the way he spoke of her, snarling through his nose, something about ' This squaw's too good to lose, and she's always getting a cough,' just as if he was buying a collar for a new dog, was enough to make one sick. At last Firth forbade them the Fort altogether, everyone was so fed up with them for all the trouble they made. The last straw, as a matter of fact, was when they made some home-brew with yeasty flour and raisins and staged a surreptitious drinking-party—I was invited but left in the very early stages, but the awful concoction they'd made led to a regular riot and some of the men who drank it seemed to go clean crazy. They had to be hit on the head, as a matter of fact, and tied up until they recovered. (Firth always acted splendidly in any such cases, and he was ably supported by the Company's Indian servants and the better element of the tribe.)

" As far as I could see, what those two devils seemed to enjoy more than anything else was bragging about some damnable piece of cruelty. They made no secret at all about having done cold-blooded murder, because I myself heard one of them telling his story right out before a bunch of the stranded miners. When they *lost* their ship, it seems, they had a boat and rifles and some tea and tobacco and a little flour, but no tents or cooking-pots or solid provisions of any kind, and if they were going to spend a winter on the shore of the Arctic Ocean they had to get all those things somehow. Then one day as they were coasting along in their boat they noticed a curl of smoke going up from somewhere along the beach, so they thought this might be their chance and went ashore to investigate. They stalked that smoke as you'd stalk a caribou and found a little tent down on the sands with a fire burning in front of it ; it was a prospector's camp, as a matter of fact—men often worked along the sea-shore to pan the sand as there was a certain amount of gold to be found in it here and there. As they lay up watching a man came to the door of the tent and stood up yawning, and one of the Americans fired and killed him stone-dead. The other miner rushed out with his rifle when he heard the noise, but they killed him too before he could see where the shooting was coming from, and then they took the tent and provisions and went away leaving the bodies lying on the sand.

" Now, Angus, when I heard the fellow telling this terrible story and boasting how he had ' dropped his man ' with the first shot, I just couldn't contain myself, and I burst right out at him. ' God damn you,' I said—I was wild ! ' Damn you both to Hell for a pair of sneaking cowardly murderers ! You may think you're fine fellows going round boasting about your accursed and horrible crimes, but I tell you right now, and it's God's truth, that the police will hear of this one day, and when they're good and ready they'll come and get you, and then you'll be tried and you'll be bloody well hanged, and a bloody good riddance of a couple of damned dirty scoundrels ! There'll be no whining off it and getting sent to Seattle for an American court to let you go—they'll take you up to Edmonton in irons, and they'll hang you right there in the gaol. You mark my words ! '

" And it turned out just like that. Word leaked through somehow to the Mounted Police, and the next year two constables came down the river and arrested the two men who were still living with the same Eskimo band. The Eskimo told the constables the whole story and showed them the very place where the prospectors were killed, and the murderers were hanged in Edmonton just as I said they would be.

"As a matter of fact, I asked the Eskimo chief once why he'd stood them all that time, and why he hadn't had them quietly killed long before. He seemed quite perplexed to give an answer, and I really believe he was such a stupid type of savage that the idea had never even entered his head ! "

CHAPTER XXXVII

THE LAST OF THE INDIANS

" ALL this time," Mitchell went on, " we were just waiting from day to day for the whistle of the steamer, which was due any moment. Lots of the Indian boys made trips down the river in their canoes to meet her, but Captain Mills ended by fooling them all somehow, and suddenly brought the *Wrigley* round the bend just when nobody was looking out for her. She was a fine-looking, well-built paddle steamer, fitted out to burn wood which she picked up at dumps here and there along the river, and she made an inspiriting sight as she came up past the Fort at full speed with both smoke-stacks belching out smoke and her whistle going to beat the band. All the Indians and Eskimo on the shore were yelling and leaping with wild excitement, and as soon as she came to anchor off the sands about two hundred yards up-stream there was a tremendous rush for the canoes and *kayaks*—every native in the place wanted to get on board if possible, but it wasn't possible, because Captain Mills knew just how to handle such people. Bishop Bompas was on board, and Chief Factor Camsell, both making tours of inspection, and very shortly they and the captain and officers crossed the sands and came up to the Fort, where Firth met them at the door according to his regular custom. The Fort was his post, you see, and he didn't leave it ; that's why he never met boats.

" Unloading began at once, and the winter's stores and supplies of trade goods were soon coming ashore—all the blankets, kettles, tea, weapons, broadcloth, beads, et cetera just as I'd seen them in the trading-room. After that the fur-packs had to go on board : the people at the Fort had been very busy sorting and packing the furs that my Indians had traded in, and now they were all waiting ready in the fur-storage warehouse. You may imagine the covetous glances that the Eskimo cast on all that wealth as it was carried across the sands ; but everything was damn carefully convoyed by the Fort servants, so looking and longing was as far as anybody got. Then it was quite a problem how to deal with our crowd of stranded miners, who wanted to get a passage up the Mackenzie. The captain felt practically forced to take them, as if they'd been left in the north the Company would have had to feed them to save their lives ; but just the same they made a Hell of a crush on board, and the grub was short too as she wasn't provisioned for anything like that number. Anyhow the captain told them to find themselves places as best they could, and this they did and were sleeping all over everywhere. There were one or two pretty hard fights before all was settled, but Mills was a leader of men and simply told them clearly and definitely at the start that if the crowd couldn't stop them fighting he'd bloody well put them ashore to walk home. That put an end to all wicked fighting—nobody minded the little scraps—for I tell you, Graham, those fellows had the fear of God and Hell on them after the horrors they'd been through that previous winter ! They were just terrified of Indians and wolves anywhere on shore away from the Fort, and wouldn't dream of losing touch with humanity again. You know, people were afraid of Indian massacres in those days even as far as Edmonton—quite needlessly, of course.

"When they started to ship the furs Firth came and drew me aside looking remarkably square about the jaw and asked for what he called ' a direct straight answer to a direct question '—Had I or had I not got any furs hidden away ? If I had any special gifts he was prepared to pass them, but

trading could not be allowed. I assured him, what was
true, that I had nothing, and with that he was perfectly
satisfied. But I did not tell him how I'd just had a quarrel
with Francis about an extraordinarily valuable pelt—the
only quarrel I ever had had with him. Francis had the
finest black fox pelt that had been taken that season, and
you must remember that this was before the days of fox-
farming, and a pure black like that was valued at the
Fort at a thousand dollars or more. Well, Francis had
begged and prayed me a few nights before to accept this
pelt as a personal gift, but fond as I was of Francis, I
still somehow couldn't get over the idea of accepting
such a valuable present from an Indian. So I refused,
and Francis was absolutely broken-hearted. But I did accept
from him and his wife twelve pairs of beautiful embroidered
moccasins and the costume of white caribou skin that they
were going to have buried me in that time. And the night
before I left I gave him the most valuable article the
Indians had ever seen, that was my field-glasses, made by
Lemaire ; they were just large enough to carry all the time
on one's chest, and their power was wonderful considering they weren't prismatic. It seemed a miracle to the
Indians how one could pick out game with them right
across a valley.

" In these last days I also paid off the sum I'd promised
for my rescue, and other sums I owed different Indians for
one thing and another they'd done for me. (I'd kept a
memorandum list made up from time to time, so as to be
sure not to miss anyone out.) I made my payment by
private deals with each individual Indian, taking each man
and his squaw into the store and letting them choose what
they liked up to the amount of the credit. By the way,
Amos never turned up at all—I never saw him once at the
Fort. I'm inclined to think there were some Indians who
weren't in favour with Firth and who possibly handed over
their furs to their cousins to trade for them ; so Amos may

have been one of those, or he may have been in debt at the Fort.

"I also told the Indians I would come back and live with them if I could, but that I wasn't a ' fork-tongue ' and so I wouldn't promise to come when I wasn't sure. When I found I couldn't go back I sent them, from Quebec, two packing-cases of straight presents, something for each individual man and woman, like bolts of red flannel, a dozen babies' blankets (couldn't I just *see* the squaws' delight over them !), knives, scissors, needles, awls, files, fish-hooks, strong twine for fishing-lines or nets, pipes, and agate beads such as I knew they'd never seen before. I may say the Hudson's Bay Company took over those cases at Edmonton and delivered them to Firth at Fort McPherson without ever charging me one cent for freight down the river. Somewhere I guess I've still got a letter from Firth telling me how much the things were appreciated and thanking me in his own and the Indians' names for not forgetting the North. There are so many people, Angus, who go, and promise everything, and then forget !

" Another thing I did before I left was this—I got Francis and the councillors together and made them hold up their hands and swear that they'd never let their people go through to Dawson City. God knows I'd seen what degenerate Indians came to when they were debauched by the white man, and God knows I knew what miners could be like when they were freed from all restraint. And there was Dawson, as I very well knew, only ten days' travel from the heart of my Indians' country ! I figured that if once they started going through to Dawson the end of those splendid people would come very quickly, and the only chance I could see was for the chief to keep them strictly to their own side of the mountains. So I got the idea of the oath, to bind Francis and his council to remember and follow my advice after I'd gone away.

" Then came my farewell feast. When the day had been

fixed for the steamer to sail I went to Firth and told him I wanted to give a huge feast, but only just a couple of days before sailing because otherwise it might have gone on for a week. In the end I gave it on the second day before we sailed, so as to leave one day for the Indians to give their return party. My spread consisted of ducks, geese, swans, beaver, rice, unlimited sugar served in large bowls, raisins, and any other canned luxuries that Firth would part with. There was absolutely lavish food, tea, and tobacco. Being host I had damn little to say, that being Indian etiquette, though the next night—or day, as there wasn't any night— when I was the guest I had to talk my head off. (I was speaking the language well, of course, by that time.) My feast lasted all night—or day—and we were all so tired by the end of it we just went off to sleep pretty much as we were. It was a damn good thing there was no liquor ! The next night, the night before the ship was due to sail, the Indians put on their feast ; but I'd tipped a wink to Firth beforehand that he was to shut down on credits, and so with that and the short notice they'd had for preparations I prevented them from making it an elaborate affair. That time my job was to make a eulogy of the country, the hunting and the people themselves, particularly their character and their feats as hunters. Above all I urged them to keep up their high standing and traditions. I was really and truly cut up to be going away, and with that and the ten hours' effort that this feast cost me I was quite exhausted when it was over.

" Then a runner arrived to say that the boat was waiting for me, and Firth came over too not to say good-bye but to walk down to the boat with me. I asked Francis as a personal favour to keep all the Indians at the top of the bluff, so as not to crowd me on the steep path, and to give me one good volley ; but said that he himself and the councillors were of course to come down to the boat, with Firth, if they wished. I also asked old Julius to walk on my left-hand side, and Francis on my right, and explained to Firth to walk ahead of us so as to let my friends have the honours while he himself still kept the first place. (I may say Julius and Francis practically carried me down, and without them I could hardly have got down except head-first.) There was perfect silence on the top of the bluff while we were going down, but as soon as we reached the level sands there were two or three rapid volleys from above —a very pretty picture. I turned and waved, but didn't fire in return—I wished to express that I was too sorry to fire, and I guess the Indians probably caught on to this.

" I had an awful job getting my stiff leg across the soft sands, but I hurried as much as I could for I knew that Captain Mills was eager to get off. As soon as we reached the deck Julius turned to me, bowed, and left in silence ; then Firth shook hands and left, but Francis sat down on a bench and showed no signs of going back on shore. Mills stood it for five minutes, and then for another five minutes, and then came up to me and whispered to me to ' get that bloody Indian off the boat'. (He said it so low that I'm certain Francis couldn't have understood.) So I stood up and said, ' My friend, it's time to say good-bye,' but Francis never winked an eye—he just asked me, ' Why ? ' I explained that the captain said he'd got to leave right off, but all Francis did was to look round calmly and say, ' Tell him to leave when he wants to.' That rather took me aback, but I called the captain and explained very courte-ously and with dignity, so that Francis shouldn't be offended, that it would be best to pull right out, as I knew Francis would ask me to have the boat stopped when he wanted to go ashore. The captain's reply was not printable, but he agreed, and gave up worrying, thinking that after all it was the Indian's business.

" I'm sure we must have gone quite ten miles down the river like that, and then Francis said :

" ' Please tell him to put his big canoe ashore.'

" The captain immediately turned her in towards the shore, and out of the goodness of his heart made the crew run out the wide gang-plank, to do the chief honour. Francis shook hands with me quietly and firmly, with a straight look into the eyes, and said :

" ' Come back—we wait for you.'

" I replied, ' I will, if it's possible,' making the same proviso, you see, as before. Then without looking at anyone, and without a trace of emotion showing on his face, Francis walked slowly along the deck and down the gang-plank, and stood perfectly still like a statue while the steamer drew out into the current. Just as the engine-room telegraph rang for full speed he raised his right arm above his head with the palm turned outwards, and then without any further motion or sign turned on his heel and vanished into the forest."